READING
the
SERMON
on the
MOUNT

READING *the* SERMON *on the* MOUNT

Character Formation and
Decision Making in Matthew 5–7

CHARLES H. TALBERT

Baker Academic

a division of Baker Publishing Group
Grand Rapids, Michigan

© 2004 by University of South Carolina

Paperback edition published in 2006 by Baker Academic
a division of Baker Publishing Group
P.O. Box 6287, Grand Rapids, MI 49516-6287
www.bakeracademic.com

Cloth edition published in 2004 in Columbia, South Carolina, by the University of South Carolina Press

Printed in the United States of America

Library of Congress Cataloging-in-Publication Data
Talbert, Charles H.
    Reading the Sermon on the mount : character formation and decision making in Matthew 5–7 / Charles H. Talbert.
        p.   cm.
    Originally published: Columbia, S.C.: University of South Carolina Press, c2004.
    Includes bibliographical references and indexes.
    ISBN 10: 0-8010-3163-X (pbk.)
    ISBN 978-0-8010-3163-2 (pbk.)
    1. Sermon on the mount—Criticism, interpretation, etc. I. Title.
BT380.3.T35 2006
226.9'06—dc22   2006042874

The author thanks *Biblica* for permission to use material from the article "Indicative and Imperative in Matthean Soteriology," *Biblica* 82, no. 4 (2001): 515–38.

For Palmer Joe Whitt in friendship

CONTENTS

PREFACE

This small volume has grown out of a class on the New Testament and ethics done for undergraduates at Wake Forest University and for a mixture of undergraduate and graduate students at Baylor University over approximately a fifteen-year period. As usual, my students have been my teachers and colleagues in the venture of re-thinking issues, which to them and me have been without satisfactory resolution to date.

Impetus was given to the development of the project by four gracious recent opportunities: an invitation to serve as the Catholic Biblical Association's Visiting Professor at the Pontifical Biblical Institute in Rome during spring 2001, where I taught a course on the Sermon on the Mount to a class of thirty international students and produced an article, "Indicative and Imperative in Matthean Soteriology," published in *Biblica* (82, no. 4 [2001]: 515–38); the invitation to do the prestigious Nadine Beacham and Charlton F. Hall Sr. Lectureship in New Testament Studies and Early Christianity in spring 2002 at the University of South Carolina; the generous invitation to deliver the A. O. Collins Theology Lectures at Houston Baptist University in spring 2003; and the invitation to contribute an article ("Is It with Ethics That the Sermon on the Mount Is Concerned?") to the Robert Tannehill Festschrift, to be published by T. and T. Clark. It is my hope that with all the advantages I have had in developing this fresh reading of Matthew 5–7, the result will reflect lucid brevity and will prove helpful to its readers, both generalists and specialists.

Abbreviations throughout conform to those set forth in *The SBL Handbook of Style,* edited by Patrick H. Alexander et al. (Peabody, Mass.: Hendrickson, 1999).

Once again, I owe special thanks to my graduate assistant, Michael W. Martin, whose editorial contributions were invaluable. As always, my debt to my wife, Dr. Betty W. Talbert, for her unwavering support and stimulating companionship is beyond repayment.

Easter 2004

PART ONE

Getting Ready to Read
the Sermon on the Mount

ONE

The Setting of the Sermon
What Is Matthew's Relation to Judaism?

Matthew's Gospel is clearly set in the context of ancient Judaism. It is usually recognized as the most Jewish of all the four canonical Gospels. The question is what is Matthew's relation to the Jewish milieu?

In the secondary literature this issue is normally phrased in terms of Matthew's separation from the synagogue. Most New Testament scholars have come down in favor of Matthew's being outside of Judaism.[1] The break with the synagogue has already taken place, and Matthew represents a Christian, as opposed to a Jewish, identity. One can, however, also find in earlier research scholars who claim Matthew comes before the break with the synagogue and so remains within Judaism.[2] It is also possible to find a scholar who argues that Matthew comes from a time when his community is at the point of departure from Judaism, on the verge of becoming a new religion.[3] All of these positions assume that a break with the synagogue means a break with Judaism. Leaving the synagogue implies the beginning of a new religion.[4]

A new understanding of ancient Judaism has gained a foothold in the past generation.[5] It is one that requires the reorientation of old assumptions and answers to the question of Matthew's relation to the synagogue and to Judaism. A representative

1. So Carter, *What Are They Saying,* 64. Among those so disposed are Davies, *The Setting,* 296–97; Hare, *The Theme;* Stanton, "The Gospel of Matthew," 264–84, and *A Gospel;* Luz, *Matthew 1–7,* 88, 214–17.
2. The early Bornkamm—"End-Expectation and Church," 39; Barth, "Matthew's Understanding," 58–164; Hummel, *Die Auseinandersetzung.*
3. Douglas, "On the Way Out," 151–76.
4. Would that mean that Qumran represented a new religion? Hardly.
5. It is not without its earlier advocates: e.g., Smith, "Palestinian Judaism," 67–81, highlights the great variety in first-century Judaism, denying Pharisaism a normative role, and explains the traditions that make them such as due to the bias of the Rabbinic material; Parkes, *The Foundations,* sees Second Temple Judaism as the common foundation of both Rabbinism and Christianity; Tombs, *The Threshold of Christianity,* speaks of Rabbinic Judaism and Christianity as the two legitimate successors of the Old Testament tradition.

of this new stance is Gabriele Boccaccini. In a brief methodological chapter, he contends that Christianity and Rabbinism became normative systems only in the second century C.E. after the end of the second Jewish revolt (135 C.E.).[6] Prior to that time they were only two of the many forms of Judaism of their time. The blood tie between Christianity and Rabbinism is not to be conceived as parent (Rabbinism) and child (Christianity). The two are rather to be viewed as fraternal twins born of the same womb. Both are coherent developments of ancient Judaism. To say that Rabbinism is a development from ancient Judaism while Christianity is a new religion is to rely unjustifiably on Rabbinism's revision of the common history.

At least three models of the relationship of Christianity and Judaism have found advocates in the modern world. In one, Judaism is the religion of the Old Testament. By the time of Christ it had become a decadent religion (late Judaism) that was replaced by the Christian revelation. Rabbinic Judaism was an attempt at the codification of the ancient religion, late Judaism. This was the view of Weber and Bousset,[7] a view popularized by Rudolf Bultmann.[8] In a second model, Judaism is a developing and pluralistic religion that at the beginning of the Christian era split into a number of different groups. This creative age (early Judaism) produced both a new stage of the inner evolution of Judaism (Rabbinic or normative Judaism) and a different religion (Christianity). This is the view of G. F. Moore,[9] and until Boccaccini's time seems to have been critical orthodoxy. It is within this frame of reference that the questions about Matthew's relation to Judaism have traditionally been asked and answered. That is, when did Matthew stop being Jewish and become Christian (i.e., when did Matthew's community break with the synagogues of formative Judaism)? In a third model, Judaism is the genus, denoting the whole range of monotheistic systems that sprang forth from the same Middle Eastern roots. Middle Judaism is the creative period between third century B.C.E. and second century C.E. It encompasses numerous species of Judaism: for example, Samaritanism, Pharisaism, early Christianity, Essenism, apocalyptic Judaism, and others. This has become the view of Judaism that is now on the cutting edge in New Testament studies. Reading the New Testament texts through these spectacles alters the frame of reference for Matthew's relation to Judaism.

Plurality of Judaisms

---

6. Boccaccini, *Middle Judaism,* 7–25. Cf. A. Segal, *Rebecca's Children,* and Boyarin, *Dying for God.*

7. Weber, *System,* sees legalism as the essence of the Jewish religion, which relegated God to be the inaccessible Lord of Torah. Bousset, *Die Religion des Judentums,* coined the term "late Judaism."

8. Bultmann, *Primitive Christianity,* 59–71.

9. Moore, *Judaism,* portrays Rabbinism as the normative Judaism in the first century C.E. Does not E. P. Sanders, who sees Palestinian Judaism as a homogeneous covenantal nomism, also fit into this category?

Three New Testament scholars may be taken as representative of this new way of seeing Matthew's relation to Judaism.[10] J. Andrew Overman is the first. He says: "So varied was Jewish society in the land of Israel in this period, and so varied were the Jewish groups, that scholars no longer speak of Judaism in the singular when discussing this formative and fertile period in Jewish history. Instead, we speak about Judaisms. In this time and place, there existed a number of competing, even rival Judaisms."[11] Matthew's Gospel is also a Judaism. Christianity as an identifiable entity distinct from Judaism had not emerged by the time of the writing of Matthew's Gospel. So Matthew is not a book that describes the split between Christians and Jews, rather it reflects the tensions between different forms of Judaism at the close of the first century C.E. in Palestine. It shows Matthean Jews contending with another group of Jews (Pharisees and scribes, the representatives of formative Judaism[12]) for influence. In this post-70 C.E. period formative Judaism did not speak for Judaism as a whole. For example, between 70 and 135 C.E. apocalyptic Judaism was alive, revolutionary Judaism thrived through the second revolt, Christian Jews were a growing group, mystical Jews existed, and the Samaritans continued. These various groups struggled against formative Judaism and one another for control. Matthew's self-understanding was not that of a Christian but a Jew. His type of Judaism he regarded as the true Israel.[13] John Riches is a second scholar reflecting the new view of Judaism as it relates to Matthew. What is going on in this Gospel, he says, is a struggle within Judaism for legitimacy. These developments are within Judaism, not outside of it. The break from the establishment synagogues does not mean a break from Judaism into a new religion. Rather, the parting of the ways with formative Judaism was analogous to that of Qumran—within Judaism but distinct from establishment synagogue practice.[14] Anthony J. Saldarini is a third representative scholar in this camp. He contends that Matthew's group is within Judaism and directs its polemics against those closest to it. "Matthew is not denying the whole

---

10. Cf. A. Segal, "Matthew's Jewish Voice," 3–37; Sim, *The Gospel of Matthew.*

11. Overman, *Church and Community,* 9. Cf. Overman, *Matthew's Gospel.*

12. Saldarini, "Johanan ben Zakkai's Escape," 189–204, explores the tradition of Jamnia's origins; Cohen, "The Significance of Yavneh," 27–53, makes several relevant points related to its function: (1) Prior to the destruction of the Temple in 70 C.E. there were twenty-four Jewish sects (*j. Sanh* 10.6 [29c]) due to the variety of interpretations of the Law and the prophets (Origen, *Cels.* 3.12); (2) The major contribution of Jamnia to Jewish history was the creation of a society that tolerated disputes without producing sects; (3) The Tannaim never explicitly call themselves Pharisees, avoiding appealing to sectarian origins even though there must have been some close connection between the post-70 rabbis and the pre-70 Pharisees. Rabbinic Judaism, then, is not to be regarded as the triumph of a sect (the Pharisees) but as a grand coalition. By common convention, this emerging coalition between 70 and 135 is called formative Judaism. Only after 200 C.E. could it be called normative Judaism.

13. Overman, *Matthew's Gospel,* 5.

14. Riches, *Matthew,* 61, 64.

Jewish symbolic universe and system . . . but proposing an alternative understanding of it and its actualization in life."[15] Specifically, this involves a different symbolic center (Jesus instead of the Torah); a modified understanding of God's will (the kingdom of God instead of a nation sanctified by temple purity, tithing, Sabbath, and festivals); and a delegitimation of Jewish leaders by accusing them of bad faith. But in all of this Matthew remains within middle Judaism. Matthew's group is still functionally Jewish, even after it has been expelled from the public assembly.[16]

Donald Hagner's contention that Matthew represents Jewish Christianity rather than Christian Judaism does not negate the new understanding of ancient Judaism and Matthew's relation to it being advocated here.[17] One should note his distinctions. He acknowledges that Matthew's community thought of itself as Judaism—the true Judaism. He agrees that the First Evangelist would never have thought of his as a new religion. It was rather the perfection and fulfillment of Judaism. He grants that non-Christian Jews would have perceived of Matthew's group as apostates from Judaism. There is, then, no question about how the Evangelist, his community, and their opponents viewed the Matthean group. Hagner grants that all of them saw the Matthean group as part of Judaism. What Hagner suggests is that we, from our vantage point, can understand the Evangelist and his community better than they understood themselves. Our modern understanding is that Matthew and his group were Christians, not Jews. In the argument being put forth in this chapter, however, the concern is with how the First Evangelist and his group saw themselves. About that there is no question: they saw themselves as a part of Judaism.

Given this new perspective on ancient Judaism, earlier ways of asking and answering the question about Matthew's relation to Judaism are, for the most part, outdated and incorrect. A correct reading involves two levels of questions and answers. On the first level, Matthew's Gospel must be considered one more form of middle Judaism. On the second level, Matthew's group must be seen as distinct from the establishment synagogues of formative Judaism (e.g., their synagogues—4:23; 9:35; 10:17; 12:9; 13:54; your synagogues—23:34; their scribes—7:29; their cities—11:1; scribes and Pharisees as a deficient form of Judaism—5:20; chap 23; the church has its own entrance rite—28:19–20; the presence of Jesus with the church [18:20; 28:20] supercedes the presence of God in the Temple; the kingdom is transferred to another people—8:5–13; 15:13; 21:41, 43; a rival Jewish group has an account of

15. Saldarini, "Delegitimation of Leaders," 668. Cf. Saldarini, *Matthew's Christian-Jewish Community*.

16. Ibid., 679. Sim, *The Gospel of Matthew*, is yet another scholar who falls within this camp.

17. Hagner, "Matthew: Apostate, Reformer, Revolutionary?" 193–209. Becker and Reed (eds.), *The Ways*, argue for an even more nuanced understanding of the relations between Judaism and Christianity from the Bar Kokhba Revolt to the rise of Islam than one finds among the scholars Hagner opposes.

the resurrection different from that of the church—28:15). Like Qumran, however, Matthew's separation is separation *within* Judaism, not *from* it. Matthew's community, "in seeking to give clearer definition to its organization and world view, is engaged in the same task as other forms of post-70 Judaism."[18]

An Implication

Can rabbinic materials that are known to us from late sources be used in New Testament interpretation? Only with great care. How does one know what can and cannot be used? In the past, a number of ways of arguing for the relevance of rabbinic materials have been tried. Some scholars use sayings that in the late rabbinic writings are attributed to rabbis from the earliest period. For example, W. D. Davies cites sayings associated with the name of Rabbi Eleazar (80–120 C.E.) and Rabbi Simeon b. Eleazar (165–200 C.E.) because he thinks it is probable that these men's names attached to logia give the sayings a likely dating.[19] Challenges to this practice have become common among scholars so that it is a precarious argument. Other scholars claim that if two rabbis take opposite sides in the interpretation of an anonymous tradition, then the anonymous tradition is earlier than the debate about it. If, then, the two dueling rabbis are early, the tradition is earlier still.[20] Logically this is a good argument. The difficulty is the same as that used against the first method: one cannot be sure about the attribution of sayings to specific rabbis. Still others claim that if a saying is part of the teaching of both great schools of the second century (Ishmael and Akiba), then it represents part of the common earlier tradition upon which they drew.[21] This follows the same logic as the second argument but has the virtue of not being tied to attributions to specific individuals. The safest test runs thus: a position described in later rabbinic sources can be used in the interpretation of the New Testament only if an independent Jewish witness from the New Testament period confirms that such a position existed at that time. For example, if a position stated in later rabbinic writings is found independently in the Dead Sea Scrolls, or Philo, or Josephus, or in appropriately dated Pseudepigraphical writings, then it may be assumed to have been a part of middle Judaism at that time. An example or two will clarify the matter. *Sifre* Deuteronomy 18.19 states that if a prophet who starts to prophesy gives evidence by signs and miracles, he is to be heeded; if not, he is not to be followed. This anonymous saying is allegedly early because a discussion between Jose ha-Gelili and Akiba presupposes the existence of such a statement (*b. Sanh.* 90a; *Sifre* Deut 13.3). This argument is supported by the

---

18. Riches, *Matthew,* 61.
19. E.g., Davies, *The Setting,* 162, 169, passim.
20. E.g., Sanders, "Defending the Indefensible," 466–67, uses an anonymous saying that is debated by R. Eleazar and R. Joshua, leading rabbis of the period 70–90 (*t. Sanh* 13.2).
21. E.g., Moore, *Judaism,* 1:277.

fact that Josephus (*Ant.* 2.280) reports that God gave Moses three signs and said: "Make use of these signs, in order to obtain belief among all men, that you are sent by me and do all these things according to my commands." An independent tradition confirms that there was something like the rabbinic tradition at the end of the first century C.E. *Genesis Rabbah* 11:10 has R. Phinehas quote R. Hoshaiah (early third century) as saying: "When you say that God rested on this day from all his works, it means that he rested from work on his world, but he did not rest from work on the unrighteous and the righteous." Both Philo (*Cher.* 86–89; *Alleg. Interp.* 1.5–6) and the *Epistle of Aristeas* 210 know a tradition of God's working on the Sabbath. This confirms the antiquity of something like the rabbinic tradition preserved in late sources.

Since Christian Messianic Judaism was a part of first-century middle Judaism, if a New Testament reference either states or implies such a tradition as is found in later rabbinic sources, then something like the rabbinic tradition may be presumed to have existed in some early form independent of Christian Messianic Judaism. Again, several examples will clarify the issue. John 9 opens with Jesus' seeing a man blind from birth, a sight that provoked a question from his disciples: "Rabbi, who sinned, this man or his parents, that he was born blind?" If sin causes suffering as the Deuteronomic theology claimed, then what sin caused the man to be born blind? Either the iniquity of the fathers was being visited upon the child (Exod 20:5; 2 Kings 5:27) or a prenatal sin had been committed by the fetus in the womb, as a tradition in *Genesis Rabbah* 63 argues is possible. Although the rabbinic tradition is late, the Johannine question implies that some such view existed in the milieu of the Fourth Gospel. Only on such an assumption is one able to make sense of the New Testament text. In John 1:51 Jesus makes a prophecy about himself: "You will see the heaven standing open and the angels of God ascending and descending upon the Son of Man." This is almost certainly an echo of Genesis 28:12. The preposition phrase *bō* in Hebrew can mean either "upon it" (the ladder) or "upon him" (Jacob), since both nouns are masculine in Hebrew. The Septuagint (hereafter LXX) favors "upon the ladder" and translates *ep' autē* (upon it). *Genesis Rabbah* 68:12:6 records a debate between R. Hiyya the Elder and R. Yannai (third century). One of them said, "They were ascending and descending on the ladder"; the other said, "They were ascending and descending on Jacob." The option "on Jacob" verbalized in this late rabbinic source is implied to have been in existence in some form at the time of the Fourth Gospel. Only thereby can one make sense of the Johannine text. 2 Corinthians 12 demonstrates that traditions like the third-century story of the four rabbis being caught up to Paradise (*b. Hag.* 13a–15b) existed as early as the first century. This is also confirmed by the Angelic Liturgy from Qumran (4QShirShab).[22]

22. A. Segal, *Paul the Convert*, 36, 40, 48.

If Matthew is considered a representative of another religion (Christianity), then the question becomes is Matthew, the Christian, borrowing from rabbinic Judaism? Of course not. The rabbinic sources are too late for such borrowing. If Matthew is deemed yet another sect within middle Judaism, then the question is, is Matthew able to assist in the task of determining how many of the rabbinic traditions had first-century Jewish roots? Of course.

In the commentary on the Sermon on the Mount, it is this last perspective that is assumed in its use of rabbinic and other Jewish materials.

TWO

The Context of the Sermon

Who Speaks and to Whom?

In this volume, the Sermon on the Mount is to be read in the context of Matthew's distinctive portrait of Jesus. Who is this one who speaks in Matthew 5–7? To whom does he speak? The answers to these two questions involve reading from the beginning and from the end of the First Gospel. Reading from the beginning is obviously the way to start. Three types of data from this reading can contribute to our answers.

First, a sequential reading of Matthew 1:1–5:2 yields its contribution. The material prior to the Sermon falls into three sections: chapters 1–2, 3:1–4:17, and 4:18–5:2. Each should be addressed in order.

Matthew 1–2 consists of a genealogy followed by five scenes dealing with Jesus' origins. Each of the five scenes contains the same components.

The genealogy (v. 1—*geneseōs*), 1:1–17, is held together by an inclusion (v. 1—Christ . . . David . . . Abraham; v. 17—Abraham . . . David . . . Christ). To begin such a narrative with a genealogy is a convention. The biblical account of Noah (Gen 5–9) begins with a genealogy (Gen 5:1–31); Abraham's story (Gen 11–25) does so as well (Gen 11:10–32). Hellenistic biographies often open with genealogies or accounts of a hero's ancestors (e.g., Plutarch, *Alex.* 2; *Brut.* 1; Suetonius, *Jul.* 6; Tacitus, *Agr.* 4; Josephus, *Life* 1–6). Although women are usually not named in Jewish genealogies, there are exceptions (e.g., Gen 11:29; 22:20–24; 35:22–26; 1 Chron 2:18–21, 24, 34, 46–49; 7:24). The four women in Matthew 1:1–17 could be regarded either as sinners or foreigners,[1] people who though irregular were the means of God's providence. Jesus, the son of Abraham and David, came from a lineage that was inclusive.

The five scenes, 1:18–2:23 (v. 18—*genesis*), each contain the same components.

---

1. Gal 2:15—Gentile sinners—shows that from an establishment Jewish perspective there would have been little difference.

1:18–25—dream—command
    fulfillment of the Scriptures
    obedience to the command
2:1–12—fulfillment of the Scriptures
    dream—command
    obedience to the command
2:13–15—dream—command
    obedience to the command
    fulfillment of the Scriptures
2:16–21—fulfillment of the Scriptures
    dream—command
    obedience to the command
2:22–23—dream—command
    obedience to the command
    fulfillment of the Scriptures

These five scenes present Jesus as one conceived by the Spirit (1:18), Savior (1:21), Immanuel (1:23), King of the Jews (2:2), God's Son (2:15), and a Nazorean (2:23).

Matthew 3:1–4:17 ends with a refrain similar to that ending the previous unit (1:18–2:23): 2:22–23—when he heard, he withdrew to Galilee, he went in and dwelt in, that what was spoken by the prophets might be fulfilled; 4:12–16—when he heard, he withdrew into Galilee, he went and dwelt in, that what was spoken by the prophet might be fulfilled. The material in 3:1–4:17 falls into a chiastic pattern.

A 3:1–2—John preaches, Repent for the kingdom of heaven is at hand.
  B 3:3—John fulfills the Scriptures (Isa 40:3).
    C 3:4—John is Elijah (cf. 2 Kings 1:8).
      D 3:5–10—Various responses to John's baptism and John's responses to them.
        E 3:11–12—John compares himself with the Mightier One. (Some Jewish sources regarded the work of judgment as delegated by God to another figure: e.g., *1 En.* 69:27–29; 11 QMelch 2; *2 Bar.* 72–74; *4 Ezra* 12:31–34; *Pss. Sol* 17:21–23.)
      D' 3:13–17—Jesus' response to John's baptism and John's responses to him.
    C' 4:1–11—Jesus is the Son of God (who reverses Israel's failures in the wilderness: hunger [Exod 16]; testing God [Exod 17]; idolatry [Exod 32]).[2]

2. Gerhardsson, *The Testing.*

B' 4:12–16—Jesus fulfills the Scriptures (Isa 9:1–2).

A' 4:17—Jesus preaches, Repent for the kingdom of heaven is at hand.

In this segment Jesus is depicted as the Lord (3:3), the Mightier One (3:11), the one who will baptize with the Holy Spirit and fire at the Last Judgment (3:11), the one who fulfills all righteousness (3:15), the beloved Son (3:17), the victorious Son of God (4:3, 6), the light of the Gentiles (4:15–16), and a preacher of repentance (4:17). "It is a general rule in ancient texts: the more titles, the more honor—and the more understanding, because each title makes its own unique contribution."[3]

Matthew 4:18–5:2 consists of two types of stories about gathering disciples (4:18–22—summons; 4:23–25—attraction) followed by Jesus' preparation for teaching them (5:1–2). On the one hand, some circles understood the gathering of disciples in terms of a summons and a response. Diogenes Laertius, for example, tells of Socrates' call of Xenophon (*Lives* 2.48). The story goes that Socrates met Xenophon in a narrow passage and that he stretched out his stick to bar the way, while he inquired where every kind of food was sold. Upon receiving a reply, he put another question. "And where do men become good and honorable?" Xenophon was puzzled. "Then follow me," said Socrates, "and learn." From that time on he was a pupil of Socrates. The reader of the canonical Gospels will recognize this type of call story in Mark 1:16–20 (Matt 4:18–22); 2:14; Luke 5:1–11; 19:5; John 1:43. In Matthew 4:18–22, therefore, the ancient auditor would have recognized Jesus' summons of Peter, Andrew, James, and John and their following him.

On the other hand, other circles viewed the gathering of disciples in terms of attraction by magnetism. Epictetus (*Diss.* 3.23.27), for example, asks: "Does a philosopher invite people to a lecture?—Is it not rather the case that, as the sun draws its own sustenance to itself, so he also draws to himself those to whom he is to do good? What physician ever invites a patient to come and be healed by him?" Philostratus (*Life of Apollonius* 1.19) has Damis come to the philosopher, exhorting him to follow God as he (Damis) will follow Apollonius. When Eliezer desires to study with Yohanan ben Zakkai, it is because of the fame of the rabbi (*Avot R. Nat.* [B] 13). Indeed, the characteristic of the rabbinic tradition is to locate the initiative with the person wanting to study with the rabbi. The reader of the Gospels will recognize the attraction type of story in John 1:36–39, 40–42, 45–49, and also here in Matthew 4:23–25.[4]

There is admittedly some debate about whether the crowds in Matthew 4:23–25 are to be regarded as Jesus' disciples even if they follow him (v. 25).[5] Two strands of evidence seem decisive. On the one hand, the context demands it. In 5:1–2 we

---

3. Allison, *The New Moses,* 319.

4. Droge, "Call Stories," 245–57; Robbins, *Jesus the Teacher,* 103, 105.

5. Cousland, *The Crowds.*

are told that Jesus' disciples came to him and that he taught them. In 7:28 we are told that when Jesus finished his teachings the crowds were astonished. These two framing texts for the Sermon make it sound as though it is directed to disciples. On the other hand, the larger Gospel context makes this reading possible. The contrary argument runs like this. There have been basically three views of the identity of the crowds in Matthew: they are basically neutral, not attached to Jesus in any serious way; they are representatives of believers, although a mixed group; they represent the ordinary believer, lay Christians.[6] The verb *akolouthein* in Matthew is used both in a strictly literal sense of "coming or going after a person" and in a theological/metaphorical sense of discipleship. Based on 4:20, 22; 8:22–23; 9:9; 10:38; 16:24; 19:21; 19:27–29, where the theological/metaphorical sense is clear, "following" is seen to involve both commitment and sacrifice. This rules out passages like 4:25; 8:1, 10; 8:19–20; 9:27; 12:15; 14:13–14; 20:29; 20:34; 21:9; 26:58; and 27:55. The crowds in 4:23–25, then, are not disciples. They are representative of those who literally follow Jesus (without commitment and sacrifice).[7] Other interpreters, however, see the verb *akolouthein* in Matthew used consistently with a metaphorical meaning.[8] Even if the verb is used in Matthew with the two meanings, literal and metaphorical, the elimination of many of the passages listed above from the theological group is incorrect. In 27:55–56 the women who followed Jesus from Galilee manifest a continuing commitment (so metaphorical); in 21:9–11, the crowds confess Jesus as Son of David and Second Moses (so metaphorical); in 20:29–34 the two blind men who address Jesus as Son of David and are healed are probably part of the crowd (if so, then metaphorical); in 14:13 the crowds manifest a commitment that involves sacrifice (so metaphorical); in 9:27–29 the blind men manifest faith (so metaphorical); in 8:19–20 following involves a cost (so metaphorical). Given this data, it is obvious that in Matthew the crowds can be understood as disciples of Jesus; not always, but sometimes. This fits with the fact that Matthew sometimes speaks of disciples other than the Twelve (8:19, 21); that he knows a wider circle of disciples (10:24, 25, 42); and that he names Joseph of Arimathea a disciple (27:57). In Matthew 4:23–25, the crowd that follows Jesus is best understood as part of the wider circle of Jesus' disciples. They have been attracted to Jesus by the magnetism of his proclamation and healing. It is these disciples, as well as those representative of the circle of the Twelve, that are the audience to whom the Sermon is given.[9] The one who speaks is, therefore, one who has the authority and attractiveness to gather disciples.

6. Wilkins, *The Concept of Disciple*, 170. Wilkins opts for the first option: the crowds are the object of Jesus' ministry.

7. Kingsbury, "The Verb *akolouthein*," 56–73.

8. Strecker, *Der Weg der Gerichtigkeit*, 230–31; Betz, *Nachfolge und Nachahmung*, 7.

9. As Gundry, *Matthew*, 65, rightly sees. Cf. Patte, *The Gospel*, 62.

By reading Matthew 1:1–5:2 consecutively the auditors have a sense of who is speaking in the Sermon. He is son of Abraham, son of David (1:1–17), one conceived by the Spirit (1:18, 20), Savior (1:21), Immanuel (1:23), King of the Jews (2:2), Messiah (2:4), fulfiller of all righteousness (3:15), God's beloved Son (3:17), God's victorious Son (4:1–11), a preacher of repentance (4:17), a gatherer of disciples (4:18–22, 23–25), a healer (4:23–24), and a teacher of disciples (5:1–2). This mountain of praise would prepare the auditors to hear the Sermon as the words of a dominant authority figure.

Second, a typological reading of the early chapters of Matthew would also prepare the auditors' perceptions of the one who speaks in Matthew 5–7. Early Christians often wrote using typological writing, describing a person, event, or thing in the present in terms of a person, event, or thing in Scripture so as to make a claim about the nature of the present person, event, or thing. For example, John the Baptist is described in Matthew 3:4 in terms of Elijah in 2 Kings 1:8 in order to make the point that the Baptist is Elijah who was to come (Mal 4:5–6; Matt 11:14); the Christian pilgrimage is described in Hebrews in terms of the Exodus, wilderness wanderings, and possession of the land of promise in order to issue a warning about the need for Christian faithfulness between conversion and the heavenly rest (Heb 3–4). In the Gospel of Matthew typological writing is used throughout to depict Jesus as the Prophet like Moses, in fulfillment of the prophecy of Deuteronomy 18:15–19.[10]

The birth narratives are the proper place to begin. Consider some of the similarities between the traditions about Moses and those about Jesus in Matthew 1–2. There is a dream (of Miriam) in which an angel prophesies of Moses that he will save the people (L.A.B. 9:10). In Matthew 1:21, Joseph is told by an angel in a dream that Jesus will save his people. At the time of Moses' birth, Pharaoh gave orders to do away with every male Hebrew child (Exod 1:15–22). The birth of Jesus was accompanied by Herod's slaughter of the infants (2:16–18). Josephus (Ant. 2.205–09) says the reason for the Pharaoh's decision to kill the male Hebrew babies was because he had learned of the birth of the future liberator of Israel. Matthew 2:2–18 tells that Herod killed the infants because knowledge came to him of the birth of the king of the Jews. Just as Herod learned of the coming savior from the chief priests and scribes (Matt 2:4–6), so Pharaoh, says Josephus (Ant. 2.205, 234), learned of the future deliverer from the sacred scribes. In Matthew 2:13–14 Jesus is providentially taken from the land of his birth because Herod wants to kill him. When Moses was a young man, he was similarly forced to leave his homeland because Pharaoh sought his life (Exod 2:15). After the death of Herod, Joseph was

---

10. Allison, *The New Moses*. Acts 3:22–23 shows that at least by the time the First Gospel was written Christians were seeing Jesus as the fulfillment of the prophecy of Deuteronomy 18.

commanded by the angel to return to Israel (Matt 2:19–20). Likewise, after the death of Pharaoh, Moses was commanded by God to return to Egypt (Exod 4:19). According to Exodus 4:20, Moses took his wife and his sons and returned to Egypt. Similarly, Matthew 2:21 says Joseph took his wife and son and went back to Israel. Without spending more time on the Matthean typology, let us say that an auditor who had been conditioned to think of Jesus in Mosaic terms in chapters 1–2 would approach Matthew 4–5 a certain way, looking for more parallels. Deuteronomy 9:9 has Moses speak thus: "When I went up the mountain to receive the tables of stone, the tables of the covenant which the Lord made with you, I 'sat' on the mountain forty days and forty nights; I neither ate bread nor drank water."[11] The combination of fasting for both forty days and forty nights and sitting on the mountain as teacher find echoes in Matthew 4:2 and 5:1.[12] It is as a new Moses that Jesus will speak in 5:3–7:27.[13] Lest one think the typology ceases with the Sermon, consider the words of the Ps-Clementine *Recognitions* 1.57: "As Moses did signs and miracles, so also did Jesus. And there is no doubt but that the likeness of signs proves him [Jesus] to be that prophet of whom he [Moses] said that he should come 'like myself'" (cf. Matt 8–9, etc.). The typology continues beyond Matthew 5–7. The function seems clear. God said in Deuteronomy, "I will put my words in the mouth of the prophet, who shall speak to them everything that I shall command. Anyone who does not heed the words that the prophet shall speak in my name, I myself will hold accountable." Anyone aware of this typology would consider the Sermon as God's words and one's response to them as something for which God would hold him or her accountable.

Third, the overall structure of Matthew has its contribution to make. Consensus about what that arrangement is, is elusive. Five different structural plans have been proposed: a five-book arrangement (chaps 3–7; 8–10; 11–13; 14–18; 19–25), with each book containing both what Jesus did (3–4; 8–9; 11–12; 14–17; 19–22 [23?]) and what he said (5–7; 10; 13; 18; [23?] 24–25), followed by a formula of conclusion (7:28–29; 11:1; 13:53; 19:1; 26:1), with birth narratives (chaps 1–2) and passion narrative (chaps 26–28) serving as prologue and epilogue;[14] a three-section

---

11. Cf. the rabbinic tradition about Moses "sitting" when on the mountain (*b. Meg.* 21a) and the second century B.C.E. tradition in the *Exagōgē* of Ezekiel, cited by Alexander Polyhistor (in Eusebius, *Praep. ev.* 9.29.4–6).

12. Cf. Allison, *The New Moses,* 172–80.

13. The sequence of events in Exodus 1–20 and in Matthew 1–7 is remarkably similar: the slaughter of infants (Exod 1:22; Matt 2:16); return of the hero (Exod 3–4; Matt 2:19–23); passage through the water (Exod 14; Matt 3:13–17); temptation in the wilderness (Exod 15:22–16:36; Matt 4:1–11); mountain of lawgiving (Exod 19–20; Matt 5–7). So Farrer, *St. Matthew,* 182–83.

14. Bacon, "The 'Five Books,'" 56–66; in *Studies in Matthew* he holds Matthew was a new Pentateuch and the Sermon on the Mount a new law; Stendahl, "Matthew," 673, who contends there is nothing to suggest that the fivefold structure was meant as a new Pentateuch.

arrangement (1:1–4:16, the person of Jesus; 4:17–16:20, the proclamation of Jesus; 16:21–28:20, the suffering, death, and resurrection of Jesus) signaled by the formula "from that time" in 4:17 and 16:21;[15] a chiastic outline (A—1–4, B—5–7, C—8–9, D—10, E—11–12, F—13, E'—14–17, D'—18, C'—19–22, B'—23–25, A'—26–28) with alternating narrative and discourse;[16] a lectionary hypothesis that sees the First Gospel composed in accordance with an annual weekly Jewish lectionary cycle;[17] and a reading that recognizes no grand scheme or fixed arrangement.[18] Davies and Allison contend that there are three important conclusions that have been reached in scholarly discussions about Matthew's overall structure: there are five major discourses; the discourses and the narrative material are alternated; and whenever the Evangelist is on his own, he uses triads. The first two seem beyond dispute; the third, while sometimes true, is not always so.[19] The first two conclusions bring the reader back to Bacon's scheme for Matthew, minus his claims about the First Gospel being an imitation of the Pentateuch and the Sermon on the Mount a new Law.[20]

The number five was widely used as a principle of organization in antiquity. Ancient Jewish materials use it: for example, the Pentateuch; the five books of Psalms (1–41; 42–72; 73–89; 90–106; 107–150); the five megilloth (Esther, Ruth, Song of Songs, Lamentations, Ecclesiastes); the five divisions of Proverbs (1–9; 10–24; 25–29; 30; 31); 1 Enoch (1–36; 37–71; 72–82; 83–90; 91–108); Jason of Cyrene's five books (mentioned by 2 Macc 2:23).[21] Greco-Roman tradition uses it: for example, Diogenes Laertius says that Aristophanes of Byzantium, the renowned grammarian, literary critic, and lexicographer at Alexandria, was the first scholar to organize the *Corpus Platonicum,* doing so by arranging the Platonic dialogues into five trilogies (*Lives* 3.61–62); Xenophon's novel, *An Ephesian Tale,* is also organized in five books. Early Christian authors also used the number five as an organizing

---

15. Krentz, "The Extent," 409–15. Kingsbury, *Matthew;* Bauer, *The Structure.* For a critique, see Goulder, review of J. D. Kingsbury, 145; Matera, "The Plot," 233–53, and Neirynck, "*Apo Tote Erxsato*," 21–59.

16. E.g., Lohr, "Oral Techniques," 403–35; Combrink, "The Structure," 61–90; Fenton, "Inclusio and Chiasmus," 174–79.

17. Goulder, *Midrash and Lection.*

18. Gundry, *Matthew,* 10–11; Hagner, *Matthew 1–13,* l–li, liii. Ingelaere, "Structure de matthieu," 10–33, critiques Bacon's five-book plan, Trilling's geographical plan, Kingsbury's plan based around the three phases of Jesus' life, and Leon-Dufour's literary critical structure.

19. Davies and Allison, *Matthew 1–7,* 71–72. Gaechter, *Das Matthäus Evangelium,* shows the use of fives and sevens also in the material where the Evangelist is on his own.

20. Barr, "The Drama," 349–59, contends Bacon's five blocks are hard to ignore, even if there is no reason to believe the five blocks are imitating the Pentateuch. Via, "Structure, Christology, and Ethics," 199–215, contends that despite the objections, "the five-fold division is too obvious and unmistakable . . . for this structure not to be an—if not the—organizing principle" (200).

21. Note that the five "books" in most cases are not of the same length.

principle: for example, Papias's *Expositions of the Dominical Oracles* consisted of five books; Irenaeus's *Against Heresies* is in five books; Tertullian's *Against Marcion* is also in five books. That Matthew is organized around five big discourse sections does not, in and of itself, prove the First Gospel is intending a new Pentateuch. Given the Mosaic typology in Matthew, the fivefold arrangement may merely be a piece of this larger pattern.

One aspect of the five-discourse scheme remains undiscussed to this point. The narratives are subservient to the discourses, in the sense that they prepare the auditors for the discourses.[22] There are two aspects to this contention. First, each narrative concludes with material that provides a well-planned transition to the discourse that follows; for example, 4:23–5:2 sets the stage for chapters 5–7; 9:32–10:1 prepares for chapter 10; 13:1–3, 36–37 offer double introductory formulae for chapter 13; 18:1–3a prepares for chapter 18; and 24:1–3 sets the stage for chapters 24–25.[23] Second, the often-unnoticed fact is the Matthean tendency to link each big teaching section loosely with the narrative material immediately preceding it by means of linguistic and thematic connections.[24] For example, the discourse in chapters 24–25 is organized around the theme of the Last Judgment, and throughout chapters 19–23 the theme of judgment also crops up (19:28; 20:1–16, 20–28; 21:12–13, 18–22, 33–41; 22:1–10; 23). The discourse in chapter 18 is concerned that Jesus' followers not be an offense to others, causing them to sin, and that they be compassionate, forgiving as they have been forgiven. In Matthew 15 Jesus is depicted as compassionate and in 17:24–27 as concerned not to give offense to others. The collection of parables in Matthew 13 speaks, in part, of the mixed responses to the Gospel, and the same motif is met in the preceding narrative section (e.g., 11:2–6, 16–19, 20–24, 25–27; 12:24–32). Again, the discourse in Matthew 10 begins with the statement that Jesus gave the Twelve "authority over unclean spirits, to cast them out, and to heal every disease and every infirmity" (v. 1). In verse 8 the charge is given to the Twelve: "Heal the sick, raise the dead, cleanse lepers, cast out demons." This teaching section follows a narrative section in which Jesus performs ten miracles, including the healing of a leper (8:2–4), the healing of all who were sick (8:16), the casting out of demons (8:28–34), and the raising of the dead (9:18–19, 23–25). Also as Jesus preached the gospel of the Kingdom (9:35), so the disciples are charged to do (10:7). It would seem, then, that the First Evangelist not only organized his Gospel around five discourses, each of which is preceded by a

---

22. Ellis, *Matthew,* 17.

23. Keegan, "Introductory Formulae," 415–30. Ellis, *Matthew,* 18, has a slightly different list.

24. The weight of such evidence shows that 4:23 and 9:35 are parallel introductions to their respective discourses (5–7; 10) and not an inclusion that holds 5–7 (teaching) and 8–9 (healing) together. Contra Kingsbury, "Observations," 556–67.

narrative section, but also linked the two types of material together in a thematic way.[25]

This second aspect of the Matthean organizational tactic is important for a proper reading of the context of the Sermon on the Mount. In the Sermon there is a strong emphasis on righteousness: for example, 5:6, "Blessed are those who hunger and thirst for righteousness"; 5:10, "Blessed are those who are persecuted for righteousness' sake"; 5:20, "I tell you, unless your righteousness exceeds that of the scribes and Pharisees, you will never enter the kingdom of heaven"; 6:1, "Beware of practicing your righteousness before others in order to be seen by them"; 6:33, "Seek first his kingdom and his righteousness, and all these things will be yours as well." Given the linguistic and thematic links between preceding narratives and subsequent discourses in Matthew, it cannot be a coincidence that the First Evangelist's recounting of Jesus' baptism by John contains the distinctively Matthean 3:14–15: "John would have prevented him, saying, 'I need to be baptized by you, and do you come to me?' But Jesus answered, 'Let it be so now; for it is proper for us in this way to fulfill all righteousness.' Then he consented." The Matthean narrative depicts Jesus as fulfilling all righteousness before he teaches his disciples about righteousness.

How would ancient auditors have heard this point? In Mediterranean antiquity there was a strong emphasis on the ideal of a unity of life and teaching. In Greco-Roman paganism examples abound. The conviction is rooted in Aristotle's *Rhetoric* 1.2. He says: "Persuasion is achieved by the speaker's personal character. . . . We believe good men more fully and readily than others. . . . It is not true, as some writers assume in their treatises on rhetoric, that the personal goodness revealed by the speaker contributes nothing to his power of persuasion. On the contrary, his character may almost be called the most effective means of persuasion that he possesses." Xenophon, *Memorabilia* 1.2.17, says that "all teachers themselves show their disciples how they themselves do what they teach, and lead them on by speech." Quintilian, *Istitutio Oratoria* 12.1.3, argues: "I do not merely assert that the ideal orator should be a good man, but I affirm that no man can be an orator unless he is a good man." Musonius Rufus, *What Means of Livelihood Is Appropriate for a Philosopher* 11, says that pupils are benefited not so much by meeting with their teacher in the city and listening to formal lectures and discussions as by seeing him at work in the fields, demonstrating by his own labor the lessons that philosophy inculcates. In Fragment 32, he says: "Do not expect to enjoin right-doing upon men who are conscious of your own wrong-doing." Seneca, *Epistle* 52.8, says that one's teacher should be someone who will teach by his life, someone who will tell us what we ought to do and then prove it by practice, who shows us what we should avoid, and then is never

---

25. Talbert and McKnight, "Griesbach Hypothesis," 346–47.

caught doing that which he has ordered us to avoid. In *Epistle* 20.2 he says that the highest duty and highest proof of wisdom is "that deed and word should be in accord." Dio Chrysostom, *Discourse* 70.6, says that the word alone, when unaccompanied by the act, is both "invalid and untrustworthy," but that the act alone is "both trustworthy and true, even if no word precedes it." The anonymous *Life of Secundus the Silent Philosopher* tells of a sage who had taken a vow of silence. The emperor Hadrian summoned him and commanded him to speak. Secundus refused. Hadrian sent for the executioner. Privately he told him if Secundus spoke to save his life, he was to be killed. But if he refused to speak even at the cost of his life, his life should be spared and he should be returned to the emperor. When Secundus refused to speak even in the face of death, he was returned to Hadrian, who then acclaimed him a true philosopher. He allowed Secundus to write his answers to the emperor's questions. His answers were then deposited in the sacred library under the name of Secundus the Philosopher. Porphyry, *Letter to Marcella* 8, contends: "It is a man's actions that naturally afford demonstrations of his opinions, and whoever holds a belief must live in accordance with it, in order that he may be a faithful witness to the hearers of his words."

Ancient Judaism provides numerous examples of the same belief. Philo assumes the same mind-set and says: "I know, indeed, that he who is to obtain excellence as a legislator should possess all the virtues fully and completely" (*Moses* 2.2). He regards Moses as the very embodiment of law, "a model for those who are willing to copy it" (1.28). This was because Moses "exemplified his philosophical creed by his daily actions. His words expressed his feelings and his actions accorded with his words, so that speech and life were in harmony" (1.29). In *Joseph* Philo says that Joseph's companions in prison "were rebuked by his wise words and doctrines of philosophy, while the conduct of their teacher effected more than any words" (16.86). Joseph "by setting before them his life of temperance and every virtue, like an original picture of skilled workmanship . . . converted even those who seemed quite incurable" (16.87). In *Every Good Man Is Free* 14.92–96, Philo tells of the Indian philosopher Calanus, who was threatened by Alexander the Great. The philosopher responded: "There is no king, no ruler, who will compel us to do what we do not freely wish to do. We are not like those philosophers of the Greeks who practice words for a festal assembly. With us deeds accord with words and words with deeds." The Pharisaic-Rabbinic stream of Judaism believed that a pupil learned from his teacher's deeds as well as his words. A rabbi taught by what he did as well as by what he said. A disciple could say that he learned by what he "saw" his teacher do (e.g., *b. Ber.* 24a, b; 38b; 39b) as well as by what he "heard" him teach (e.g., *m. Erub* 2:6; *m. Or.* 2:5). It was assumed that there would be a unity of life and teaching.

Early Christian writings outside the New Testament echo the same sentiment. The *Didache* 11:8 says: "not everyone who speaks in the Spirit is a prophet, but only if he has the ways of the Lord. So the false prophet and the prophet will be known by their ways." In 11:10 we read: "Every prophet who teaches the truth, if he does not do what he teaches, is a false prophet." Ignatius of Antioch, *Ephesians* 15:1, says: "It is better to be silent and be, than to talk and not be. Teaching is good, if the teacher does what he says." Eusebius, *Church History* 6.3.7, says that Origen's conduct revealed "the right actions of a most genuine philosophy" and that the maxim "as was his speech, so was the manner of his life" could be fittingly applied to him. In 7.30.6ff, Eusebius relates that Paul of Samosata is said not only to have taught heresy but also to have used his position to acquire wealth, a fact that invalidated his teaching.

The cultural repertoire of the ancient Mediterranean world included the conviction that a teacher's words were only to be believed if and when he lived them out in his daily existence. When Matthew's auditors heard that Jesus fulfilled all righteousness before he spoke to his disciples about seeking a righteousness that surpassed other models, they would have inferred the legitimacy of Jesus' teachings and would have accorded the authority due a true teacher. When the auditors of Matthew approached the Sermon on the Mount, they would have been conditioned by the preceding narrative to accept what is said therein as the authoritative utterances of one who practiced what he preached.

From the three strands of argument derived from a reading from the beginning of the Gospel, the answers to the two questions proposed at the start of this section can be answered. Who is it that speaks in Matthew 5–7? He is an authority figure for sure. In many and various ways the point has been made. Listen to him! He represents God! To whom does this one speak in the Sermon? The answer is clear. The Matthean Jesus addresses disciples in Matthew 5–7.

If a sequential reading yields these answers, what about a reading from the end of the First Gospel? Matthew 28:18–20 provides clear answers. Who is it that speaks in the Sermon? "All authority in heaven and on earth has been given to me. Go . . . teaching them to obey everything that I have commanded you." If this one is not an authority figure, who is? God has given to him all authority (not the devil— 4:9–10). To whom does this one speak? The answer is clear. "Go therefore and make disciples of all nations, baptizing them in the name of the Father and of the Son and of the Holy Spirit, and teaching them to obey everything that I have commanded you." It is to disciples that the teaching is addressed.[26] The end of the First Gospel stands in agreement with the beginning of Matthew. The Sermon on the Mount is spoken by one to whom God has given authority and is spoken to Jesus' disciples.

26. Allison, *The Sermon*, 5, says: "Neither Jesus nor Matthew was interested in addressing secular authorities or in laying down legislation for them."

Ch. 1 and Ch. 28 may not be same-same...

THREE

The Structure of the Sermon

In What Order Does Jesus Speak?

The "problems of the composition and structure of the Sermon on the Mount . . . , while a continuing concern, have remained unsolved."[1] It is instructive to survey selected attempts to discern the arrangement of the Sermon as both an illustration of the previous judgment and as a preparation for yet one more effort in that direction.

Augustine and M. D. Goulder are among those who see the Beatitudes as the key to the arrangement of the Sermon, although in quite different ways.[2] Compare the following:

Augustine	Goulder
Matt 5:3 developed in 5:21–24	Matt 5:3 developed in 7:7–12
Matt 5:5.........5:25–26	Matt 5:4.........7:1–6
Matt 5:4.........5:27–28	Matt 5:5.........6:19–34
Matt 5:6.........5:29–37	Matt 5:6.........6:5–18
Matt 5:7.........5:38–48	Matt 5:7.........5:38–6:4
Matt 5:8.........6:1–7:12	Matt 5:8.........5:27–37
Matt 5:9.........7:13–23	Matt 5:9.........5:21–26
	Matt 5:10.......5:11–16

These schemata have been regarded as arbitrary and have had little influence among interpreters, ancient and modern.   *well!*

Grundmann and Bornkamm are representative of those who see the Lord's Prayer (6:9–13) as the clue to the arrangement of the Sermon.[3] Grundmann sees the Prayer as the center of the Sermon. There are thematic connections between it and

---

1. Betz, *The Sermon*, 49.
2. Augustine, *The Lord's Sermon*. Goulder, *Midrash and Lection*, 269. Grawert, *Die Bergpredigt nach Matthäus,* had earlier made a similar proposal regarding a chiastic unfolding of the Beatitudes in Matthew's Sermon.
3. Grundmann, *Das Evangelium nach Matthäus,* 204–5; Bornkamm, "Der Aufbau der Bergpredigt," 419–32.

the two halves of the Sermon. For example, "thy kingdom come" is linked with 5:3b, 10b; "hallowed be thy name" with 5:13–16; "thy will be done" with 5:17–48; "our daily bread" with 6:19–34; "forgive us our debts" with 7:1–5; and "deliver us from evil" with 7:13–27. While recognizing the shared verbal links in some of these connections, scholars have not concluded that they represent a structural principle of arrangement.[4] Bornkamm attempted to explain the most difficult passage in the Sermon, 6:19–7:12, as directly arranged in accordance with the petitions of the Prayer. So 6:9–10, the first three petitions, are expounded in 6:19–24; 6:11, the fourth petition, in 6:25–34; 6:12, the fifth petition, in 7:1–5, and 6:13, the sixth and seventh petitions, in 7:6. In spite of approval given by Guelich and Stanton, most scholars find the links neither obvious nor compelling.[5]

Ulrich Luz and Daniel Patte see Matthew's Sermon organized in terms of a chiastic structure.[6] Consider the following charts.

Luz	*Patte*
5:1–2 Situation	A—5:3–10 Who the disciples are
5:3–16 Introduction	B—5:11–16 Disciples' vocation
5:17–20 Introit	C—5:17–19 Implementing the vocation
5:21–48 Antitheses	D—5:20 Framing material
6:1–6 Righteousness before God	E—5:21–47 Overabundant righteousness
6:7–15 Lord's Prayer	D'— 5:47–48 Framing material
6:16–18 Righteousness before God	D"—6:1 Framing material
6:19–7:11 Possessions, judging, prayer	E'—6:12–18 Overabundant righteousness
7:12 Conclusion	D'"—6:19–21 Framing material
7:13–27 Conclusion	C'—6:22–7:12 Implementing the vocation
7:28–8:1a Reaction of hearers	B'— 7:13–20 Disciples' vocation
	A'— 7:21–27 Who the disciples are

Because of the difficulty seeing the proposed sections as really corresponding to one another and because the patterns often break up the natural thought units, the chiastic proposals have not been successful in gaining adherents.[7]

4. Syreeni, *The Making*, 170–71.

5. Guelich, *The Sermon*, 324–25; Stanton, *A Gospel*, 298. Cf. Syreeni, *The Making*, 171–72; Carter, *What Are They Saying*, 44–45.

6. Luz, *Matthew 1–7*, 212; Patte, *The Gospel*, 65.

7. Carter, *What Are They Saying*, 41–42, 43–44, for a summary of criticisms.

George A. Kennedy has brought his expertise in ancient rhetoric to bear on Matthew's Sermon.[8] He sees 5:3–16 as the proem, 5:17–20 as the thesis, 5:21–7:20 as the headings, and 7:21–27 as the epilogue. Matthew 5:17–20 is the proposition of the Sermon. It enunciates but does not explicate the two principles that are the basis of much that follows: the Law is authoritative, and the hearers' actions must exceed that of the scribes and Pharisees. In 5:21–48 Jesus explains his view of the Law. In 6:1–18 and 6:19–7:20, he explains the higher righteousness. The epilogue, 7:21–27, has two functions: to recapitulate the major points and to seek to stir the audience to action. While reflecting the scholarly consensus on the boundaries of various subunits, this proposal fails in several major ways. Can 5:17–20 really be reduced to Kennedy's twofold thesis? It is likely that 5:21–48, just like 6:1–18 and 6:19–7:12, explains the higher righteousness. It seems that 7:13–20 belongs with 7:21–27 as a conclusion that serves mainly to stir the audience to action. It is, moreover, not at all clear that 5:3–16 should be conceived of as a proem.

Dale Allison may be used as a representative of those who see numerical patterns (triads) controlling the Sermon and who also see the Sermon as in some way linked to the response of the Gospel to contemporary Judaism at Jamnia.[9] He sees

Nine Beatitudes (5:3–12)—3 x 3
    The task of the people of God in the world (5:13–7:12)—
        The three pillars
            Jesus and Torah (5:17–48)—2 x 3
            The Christian Cult (6:1–18)—3
            Social Issues (6:19–7:12)—includes two triads
    Concluding statements and warnings (7:13–27).

The three pillars are understood as Matthew's attempt to reinterpret Simeon the Just's dictum: "By three things is the world sustained: by the Law, by the [Temple] service, and by deeds of loving kindness."[10] The preoccupation with triads seems forced, however. Why see 3 x 3 Beatitudes instead of 4 + 4 + 1? The number 2 is used widely as well (e.g., two images—5:13–16; two groups of antitheses—5:21–48; 6:19–7:12 subdivides into two units; the two ways—7:13–14; two houses—7:24–27). The comparison of 5:21–7:12 with the three pillars of the rabbis may loosely fit the first two, but 6:19–7:12 is not about deeds of loving-kindness. Once again, the proposed arrangement leaves something lacking.

8. Kennedy, *New Testament Interpretation,* 49–62. Kennedy's reading is foreshadowed in Neil J. McEleney, "The Principles," 552–70.
9. Allison, "The Structure," 423–45; Davies and Allison, *Matthew 1–7,* 63–64. The source of the idea that the structure of the SM reflects a confrontation with Jamnia is Davies, *The Setting,* 315.
10. *m. Aboth* 1.2 (Herbert Danby, *The Mishnah,* 446).

Robert Guelich, Jack D. Kingsbury, and Hans Dieter Betz[11] are typical of those who see the coherence of the Sermon in some theological theme: for example, righteousness or way of life. Guelich's outline reflects his views.

The Blessings of the Kingdom (5:3–16)
> 1) The Beatitudes (3–12)
> 2) Discipleship (13–16)

The Greater Righteousness (5:17–7:12)
> 1) Jesus and the Law (5:17–20)
> 2) Righteousness with reference to others (5:21–48)
> 3) Righteousness with reference to God (6:1–7:11)
> 4) Conclusion (7:12)

The Alternatives (7:13–27)
> 1) The two ways (7:13–14)
> 2) False prophets (7:15–23)
> 3) The two builders (7:24–27)

The Sermon is set between an introduction (4:23–5:2) and a conclusion (7:28–29). Kingsbury thinks the sections of the Sermon all explicate the greater righteousness. His outline is revealing.

1) Introduction: On those who practice the greater righteousness (5:3–16)
2) On practicing the greater righteousness toward the neighbor (5:17–48)
3) On practicing the greater righteousness before God (6:1–18)
4) On practicing the greater righteousness in other areas of life (6:19–7:12)
5) Conclusion: Injunctions on practicing the greater righteousness (7:13–27)

Betz's outline reflects a similar tack.

5:3–16 Exordium
5:17–7:12 The Way of Life
> 5:17–48 The interpretation of Torah
> 6:1–18 The practice of cult
> 6:19–7:12 The conduct of daily life

7:13–23 Eschatological Warnings
7:24–27 Peroration

In all three of these proposals, the theme of righteousness or way of life dominates the organization of the Sermon. Various scholars think other themes are the organizing principle around which the Sermon is organized.[12] Perhaps the most interesting thing

---

11. Guelich, *The Sermon*, 39; Kingsbury, "The Place, Structure, and Meaning," 131–43; Betz, *The Sermon*, 50–58.

12. E.g., the double commandment of love (so Olav Hanssen, "Zum Verständnis des Bergpredigt," 94–111) or the will of God (so Christoph Burchard, "The Theme," 57–91).

to observe about all of these surveyed attempts is their broad agreement about the major units that make up the Sermon.

Other proposed arrangements for Matthew's Sermon are legion. In spite of the diversity of opinion, about certain things there is a remarkable agreement, if not unanimity. Usually there is a recognition that 5:3–12 and 5:13–16 are subunits; sometimes they are regarded as subunits of a larger unit, 5:3–16. Matthew 5:17–20 is recognized as a subunit, even if there is not agreement about whether it is the introduction to 5:21–7:12, 5:21–7:27, or only 5:21–48. Most scholars agree that 5:21–48 and 6:1–18 are distinct units. There is disagreement about 6:19–7:12: should it be taken as a whole; should 6:19–34 be separated from 7:1–12; should 6:19–24, 6:25–34, and 7:1–12 be taken as three separate units? There is widespread agreement that 7:13 begins the final segment of the Sermon. Recognizing that unanimity does not exist, the following proposal about the structure of the Sermon reflects the views of what I consider the majority reading of its arrangement. Only the reading of the individual segments of the Sermon reflects my own perspective.

The Setting: 4:18–5:2 (the premise of the Sermon: it is directed to disciples)
    Unit One: 5:3–16
        1) Portrait of and promises to disciples given in eight third-person Beatitudes and one second-person Beatitude (5:3–12)
        2) Portrait of and expectation of disciples given in two second-person descriptions and one second-person exhortation (5:13–16)
The Higher Righteousness: 5:17–7:12 (a large unit held together by an inclusion, 5:17 and 7:12—law and prophets)
    Unit Two: 5:17–48
        1) The fact and implications of the continuing validity of the Law (5:17–20)
        2) Illustrations both of how Jesus fulfills the Law and the prophets and of the higher righteousness (5:21–48)
    Unit Three: 6:1–18
        1) The principle for a proper practice of piety (6:1)
        2) Examples of the proper practice of piety (6:2–4, 5–6, 7–15, 16–18)
    Unit Four: 6:19–34
        1) Getting one's priorities straight about possessions (6:19–24)
        2) Trusting God to provide for one's necessities (6:25–34)
    Unit Five: 7:1–12
        1) Against judging (condemnation of another) by one who has not judged her/himself (7:1–5)
        2) In support of judging (discernment) by one who has been given wisdom by God and who follows the Golden Rule (7:6–12)

Unit Six: 7:13–27

    1) Exhortations about living in line with God's will/Jesus' words (7:13–14, 24–27)

    2) Warnings about false prophets (7:15–20, 21–23)

The Ending: 7:28–8:1 (the effects of Jesus' teaching on the crowds)

The thought units in the Sermon are generally agreed upon. Where the differences lie is in the relation of the sections to one another and the reading of the individual units. This outline reflects the general consensus of what the units of thought are; it is less reflective of consensus in its view of relations of the sections to one another, though it stands with a large group of interpreters in its views. Where innovations might be expected is in the reading of the contents of the various thought units. This, of course, will come clear in the reading of the Sermon that follows in part 2 of this volume.

FOUR

The Functions of the Sermon

Character Formation and Decision Making ← ⟵

More about this than this? (handwritten annotation)

It is necessary first to clarify certain categories that are normally used in ethical discussion.

Ethicists draw a distinction between character formation and decision making.[1] Character formation concerns who we are. Character includes our perceptions (how we see things), dispositions, and intentions and motivations. Decision making and the resultant action concern what we do. Making a decision involves an analysis of the situation, a method for arriving at the right choice, and the character of the decision maker. Hence, who we are conditions what we do. Nevertheless, most ethical thought tends to focus on decision making instead of on the moral agent who makes the decision.

The focus on decision making involves several levels of thought. In the first place, there are three dominant types of criteria employed in making moral judgments: consequentialist, deontological, and perfectionist.[2] A consequentialist argument determines the morality of an action by the likely results of one's actions, whether they be good or bad for human life. Consider the consequences of your actions. A deontological argument is concerned with the regulative principles that establish the ground rules for action. These may be negative (do not do this) or positive (do this). Acting morally involves doing one's duty. A perfectionist argument is concerned with the self-actualization of virtue by persons. Morality consists of being who you are and what you can be. These three criteria are not mutually exclusive but rather should be seen as complementary components of an overall method of decision making.

Two observations should be made about these three criteria. On the one hand, all three are used in the Bible: consequentialist (cf. Deut 28:1–2, 15; Matt 6:2–4, 5–6, 14–15, 16–18; and Rom 13:4–5); deontological (cf. Exod 20:13, 14, 15, 16,

---

1. Birch and Rasmussen, *Bible and Ethics,* 79–123.
2. Ogletree, *The Use,* 15–46.

17; Lev 19:18; Matt 5:27–28; 5:38–42; Rom 13:8–10); and perfectionist (cf. Lev 21:7; Deut 14:1–2, 21; Matt 5:14–16a; Rom 6:11–13). The same author may use first the one and then the other (e.g., Eph 5:3—perfectionist; 5:4—perfectionist; 5:5—consequentialist; 5:6—consequentialist; 5:7–9—perfectionist; 5:10—deontological). In the modern world, however, when someone appeals to Scripture as the authority for moral action (e.g., "The Bible says . . ."), that is a deontological argument. When someone in our culture says "It is the law" or "That is what the Constitution says," that is a deontological argument.

On the other hand, in the deontological appeal to what the Bible teaches, the Bible can function in multiple ways: for example, in fundamentalism, old liberalism, neo-orthodoxy,[3] narrative theology, and natural-law thinking, Scripture functions differently. Fundamentalism considers the Bible as a book of revealed morality in the form of particularized commands that are viewed as timeless truth (e.g., "Do not commit adultery"; "Do not covet your neighbor's wife"). Liberalism regards the Bible as a book of revealed morality in the form of overarching norms, values, and ideals that, often because of their culturally conditioned character, must be applied or translated in the present (e.g., "Love your neighbor as yourself"). Neo-orthodoxy understands the Bible as a book of revealed reality in the form of a picture of God to whom one responds that functions as the primary "story" for the moral life. (E.g., "What the Creator has joined together, let no one put asunder." If one does, the Judge will hold that one accountable. The Redeemer who said, "If one lusts, he has already committed adultery," did what was necessary that "the just requirement of the law might be fulfilled in us, who walk not according to the flesh but according to the Spirit" [Rom 8:4].) Narrative theology sees the Bible as a book of revealed reality in the form of a story with a clear-cut plot in terms of which human life is to be interpreted: i.e., creation, corruption, covenant, Christ, church, consummation (so, for example, if one says of oneself, "That is just the way I am; I just cannot resist the opposite sex; it is just the way God made me," one answers, "God did not make you an adulterer; that is due to the Fall"). Natural-law thinking regards the Bible as either corroboration of a morality that can be discerned by rational reflection apart from revelation or as a book that sometimes completes such a natural morality.[4] (E.g., sexual differentiation exists to guarantee the perpetuation of the species. The human offspring matures slowly and needs care all that time. Continual sexual desire in humans keeps the couple together year-round, and the bonding produced by continued sexual activity keeps the pair together over a long period of time. All

3. The categories used in the first three are those of Birch and Rasmussen, *Bible and Ethics,* 22–23.

4. Spohn, *What Are They Saying,* 38–55, offers a helpful summary of the variations in Roman Catholic natural-law reasoning as it applies to ethics.

of this provides for the nurture of the human offspring: the pair's willingness to raise the offspring at all is tied to the acknowledgment of the offspring as theirs, and if the partners cannot be sure the offspring is theirs, they are less inclined to provide nurture for it. Hence, adultery is morally wrong because it undermines the continuation of the couple who have responsibility for the care of the human young; this is against the purpose of sexual differentiation in nature. This product of human reasoning is corroborated by the prohibition in the Bible against adultery, a prohibition that also motivates Jesus' disciples.)

Given these categories, it is possible to state the twofold thesis of this reading of the Sermon on the Mount. The primary thesis of this study is that the Sermon on the Mount functions primarily as a catalyst for the formation of character. The secondary thesis is that the Sermon can also contribute to decision making when it is taken together with the whole of the Gospel of Matthew,[5] the whole of the New Testament,[6] and the Old Testament.[7] This twofold thesis demands that each section of comment on the pericopes making up the Sermon deal with both levels: catalyst for character formation and contribution, in content, to decision making. This will be done throughout, although the emphasis will be on the primary thesis. In so doing, this study flies in the face of a long and venerable tradition of interpretation of the Sermon that sees the function of Matthew 5–7 exclusively as providing norms for ethical decision making.

For example, Harvey K. McArthur surveys twelve types of interpretation of the Sermon on the Mount that deserve attention, of which he says six are of secondary value, six are of primary value.[8] The six of secondary value are the modification view (modifying phrases are introduced into the text of the Sermon without appeal to specific historical or theological principles: e.g., the textual variant in Matt 5:22, "without a cause"); the double standard view (Jesus' ethical teaching is divided into

---

5. Allison, *The Sermon*, 9, says: "The Sermon on the Mount belongs to a book apart from which it was never intended to be read. This matters because so often interpretation has gone astray by ignoring the Sermon's context." Stanton, "The Origin and Purpose," 181–94, argues against Betz that the Sermon on the Mount is part and parcel of Matthew's Gospel. The Mennonite theologian Joseph Kotva, in *The Christian Case for Virtue Ethics*, contends that an interpersonal tutoring from a practically wise person is a constitutive component of virtue ethics. The person of Jesus shapes the distinctive virtue ethics in Matthew's Gospel. Jesus is himself the lesson we seek to know.

6. Hagner, "Ethics and the Sermon," 55, contends that an adequate hermeneutic for reading the Sermon must take into consideration the whole of the New Testament with the love command as its guide.

7. McArthur, *Understanding the Sermon*, 120–22, critiques the "analogy of scripture view" because it reduces all of Scripture to the same level and undermines the radical character of Jesus' demands. Appeal to the biblical plot avoids this criticism because within the overall plot of the Bible there are different levels of authority.

8. Ibid., 105–48.

"precepts" and "counsels." Obedience to the former is necessary for salvation; obedience to the latter is necessary for perfection); the two realms view (in the spiritual sphere the Christian is obligated to obey all the commands of the Sermon; in the secular sphere Christians follow a somewhat different standard); the analogy of Scripture view (assuming there is a single ethical level throughout Scripture, the Sermon should be interpreted in light of other parts of Scripture: e.g., Matt 5:22, "You fool," must be interpreted in light of Gal 3:1, "O foolish Galatians"); the interim ethic view (Jesus' ethical teachings were given for the brief interim before the End. Since the End did not come and since we do not live in such an interim, the ethical teachings do not have relevance for us); and the modern dispensationalist view (the ethic in the Sermon was intended for the Kingdom dispensation and so has only a secondary application to Christians who live in the dispensation of grace).

The six readings that are of primary value are the absolutist view (the commands of the Sermon on the Mount should be interpreted literally and applied universally and absolutely); the hyperbole view (since Jesus resorted to hyperbole, his demands need to be toned down before application: e.g., Matt 5:29ff—"If your right eye causes you to sin, pluck it out"); the general principles view (Jesus intended to teach general principles through specific illustrations: e.g., Matt 5:39b—"Turn the other cheek"); the "attitudes-not-acts" view (Jesus' concern was not for acts but rather with the spirit lying behind the acts); the repentance view (the demands of the Sermon have as their primary goal the bringing of people to a knowledge of their own sinfulness and, thereby, to repentance); the unconditioned divine will view (in the Sermon Jesus proclaims the unconditioned divine will apart from any historical conditioning factors—as such it is not to be taken as law that tells Christians what to do but rather demands that we be something—and it creates a new type of person; in light of one's historical circumstances, then, one accepts responsibility for compromises and detours in what is done).[9]

Whatever one thinks of this collection and evaluation of the different approaches to the interpretation of the Sermon on the Mount, one thing comes clear. All of the interpretative options see the Sermon as an ethical text. All, with the exception of the unconditioned divine will view (to which this book is heir), see it as directed to ethical decision making.[10] This has been the thrust of the history of interpretation since the time of the early church,[11] with rare exception.[12]

9. Dibelius, *The Sermon*, 136–37.

10. Deidun, "The Bible," 33, says, "nearly all of them regard the 'Sermon' as a source of law (binding on some or all)." Note the surveys in Fascher, "Bergpredigt II: Auslegungsgeschichte," 1050–53; Kissinger, *The Sermon;* Bauman, *The Sermon;* Berner, *Die Bergpredigt;* Dumais, *Le Sermon.* Perusal of these surveys confirms the generalization.

11. Grant, "The Sermon," 215–31.

12. Alternate ways of reading are occasionally suggested. Keck, "Ethics in the Gospel," 51, says: "The entire SM is to be understood not as Jesus' legislation for morality, but as a series of

This reduction of the Sermon on the Mount to ethics also makes it necessary to clarify that "there is not just ethical instruction in the Sermon on the Mount but instruction in worship and prayer" as well.[13] Matthew 5–7 is concerned with the vertical (5:3, 4, 5, 6; 5:33; 6:1–18; 6:24; 6:33; 7:7–11) as well as the horizontal (5:21–26; 5:27–30; 5:38–42; etc.) relations of life. The Sermon contains material focused on piety as well as that concerned about ethics. This concern for right relations in both horizontal and vertical dimensions of life is characteristic of Old Testament Law (vertical—Exod 20:3, 4–6, 7; horizontal—Exod 20:13–17), prophecy (vertical—Jer 4:1–2; Hos 14:1–8; horizontal—Hos 4:1–3; Amos 6:4–7), and wisdom (vertical—Prov 3:11–12; 3:9–10; horizontal—Prov 15:1; 16:32). This dual focus in the Old Testament is understood in terms of covenant faithfulness. Faithfulness to the covenant with Yahweh involved both a right relationship with God in prayer and worship on the one hand and a right relationship with other humans in ethical action on the other. In this book, therefore, the reading of the Sermon will not be reductionist in the sense of reducing it to its ethics (the horizontal dimension) any more than in the sense of reducing it to a discourse on decision making. The Sermon on the Mount is about covenant faithfulness, involving both vertical and horizontal relations. It aims in the first instance to function as a catalyst to shape the character of its auditors in the direction of covenant faithfulness. Recognition of this fact will be reflected throughout in the subsequent reading of Matthew 5–7.

---

concretions of what a proper response to the news of the Kingdom entails." That is, the SM tells what repentance looks like. Ligon, *The Psychology,* reads the SM as psychological advice. Lischer, "The Sermon on the Mount," 157–69, takes the SM as pastoral care. Thornton, *English Spirituality,* ch. 3, and Warren, "Focuses on Spirituality," 115–24, advocate a reading of the SM as spirituality. Tannehill, *The Sword,* 60–88, offers a reading of three pericopes from the SM that treat them as shaping the character of the auditors in both vertical and horizontal ways. My work is a development of Tannehill's pioneering efforts. Harrington and Keenan, *Jesus and Virtue Ethics,* 61–62, contend that the Sermon "is best taken as proposing an ethics of Christian character or a Christian virtue ethics." They say: "Being a student in Jesus' wisdom school involves formation in character. . . . Rather than providing a complete code of conduct, the Sermon on the Mount shapes Christians to discern wisely and to act accordingly" (66). My work moves in the same direction but sees character being formed not only in ethics but also in piety, that is, as the shaping of a character of covenant faithfulness.

13. Riches, *Matthew,* 68.

FIVE

Is Matthew a Legalist?

Enablement of Obedience in Response to the Sermon

Most New Testament scholars regard Matthew as a theological problem for Christians. Although most New Testament writers "shared a more or less explicit awareness that the Christian 'ought' now flowed from a specifically Christian indicative"[1] (i.e., the new action of God in Christ and the continuing action of the Holy Spirit), the linkage between the indicative (God's gift) and the imperative (the divine demand) is less apparent in Matthew. Selected scholarly opinion helps clarify the issue.

The State of the Question

Willi Marxsen contends that Matthew is legalistic.[2] Marxsen contrasts two types of ethics. In the first, God is conceived as one who sets requirements and makes his relationship with people dependent on their fulfilling these demands. In this case, ethical practice promises the realization of the relationship. It is assumed that humans are capable of meeting the admission requirements. In the second type, God is conceived as one who has already come to humans with love—without any precondition. In this case, the relationship already exists, and humans act ethically out of gratitude. It is assumed that humans can act rightly only if they are enabled by God's prior act. The first type, Marxsen thinks, is a Pharisaic ethic; the second, a Christian ethic. Marxsen, moreover, believes that Matthew represents the first ethic. If so, then Matthew's imperative consists of admission requirements for entering the kingdom of heaven. Jesus' ethical teachings in the First Gospel, on this reading, constitute God's requirement of humans if they are to attain a relationship with him. There is no prior indicative, gift, or grace that bestows a relationship, unconditionally, quite apart from human performance and to which human performance can respond.

---

1. Deidun, "The Bible," 36.
2. Marxsen, *New Testament Foundations,* 231–48.

Marxsen's position is problematic on two counts. First, Matthew clearly sees getting in Jesus' community as due to divine initiative. The disciples are called (4:18–22) *before* Jesus gives the Sermon on the Mount. Matthew 28:19–20 specifies that the nations are to be made disciples and baptized *before* they are taught to observe all that Jesus commanded. That the kingdom has been inaugurated in Jesus' ministry (12:28) means that repentance (4:17) is a response to a prior act of God. Matthew is clearly not legalism. A divine initiative enables one's entry into the community of Jesus' disciples. Second, Marxsen represents a perspective on Pharisaic Judaism that is prior to E. P. Sanders, or for that matter, G. F. Moore.[3] Most modern scholars regard a Pharisaic ethic not as legalism (in which one gets into the covenant people by works of law) but as covenantal nomism (in which one gets in the covenant by grace and obeys the Law thereafter out of gratitude). To such scholars, Marxsen's description of the second ethic (his Christian one) sounds very much like the covenantal nomism modern scholars associate with Pharisaic Judaism.

The issue of Matthew's ethic is better focused by asking whether it represents a legalistic covenantal nomism (in which one gets in the covenant relation by grace, then stays in it and gets into the age to come by works of law)[4] or a new covenant piety (in which one gets in the relation by grace, stays in it by grace, and gets into the age to come by grace). Most scholars today believe that entry into Jesus' community is by grace for the reasons cited above. The current debate is over what follows in the disciple's life. Is there in Matthew a divine indicative that underlies and enables fulfillment of the imperative in disciples' lives *after* their entry into the community of Jesus?

Roger Mohrlang's concern is precisely how grace enters into Matthew's understanding of ethics. Is there divine enablement of disciples' obedience to God's imperatives after their entry into Jesus' community by grace? Three summary statements clarify his reading of Matthew. "Matthew does not exploit this assumed structure of grace, and does not build his ethics explicitly upon it (rarely is ethical behavior motivated by considerations of grace); for the most part, it remains in the background, simply taken for granted—the largely unspoken context in which the Gospel is set."[5] "The concept of Jesus's continuing presence with the community is as little explicitly integrated with the evangelist's ethics as his view of the Spirit."[6] Matthew's Gospel, with its emphasis on demand and obedience, results in a Gospel "almost totally devoid of explicit reference to God's aid in the moral-ethical realm."[7] For

3. Sanders, *Paul and Palestinian Judaism* and *Paul, the Law;* Moore, *Judaism.*
4. The issue has been framed thus by Eskola, "Paul, Predestination and Covenantal Nomism," 390–412, and *Theodicy and Predestination;* and Laato, *Paul and Judaism.*
5. Mohrlang, *Matthew and Paul,* 80.
6. Ibid., 112.
7. Ibid., 114.

Mohrlang, the explicit divine demand dominates Matthew; any grace that might undergird Jesus' disciples' obedience to that demand is at best implicit, assumed perhaps, but never explicitly related to their ethical behavior. This sounds very much as though Matthew belongs within legalistic covenantal nomism (where one enters the community by grace but continues within it and enters into the age to come by works of law, motivated, of course, by gratitude for past grace).

This state of affairs has motivated two other scholars to attempt to see both indicative and imperative as present in Matthew and to attempt to explain how the indicative has priority. Hubert Frankemölle and David Kupp[8] both affirm that Jesus' "presence with" the disciples, rooted in the Old Testament view of God's compassionate and caring presence among his people, is Matthew's leading idea. Out of the God-with-us theme Matthew's plot is constituted.

The definitive work on the formula itself was done by W. C. van Unnik in 1959.[9] He found that the expressions "with us/you" and "in your midst" are synonyms. More than one hundred occurrences of this formula are found in the Old Testament, mostly in the historical books. The formula signals empowerment of God's people, individual and corporate. One of the most interesting observations made in this essay by van Unnik concerns the connection between this formula and the Spirit. The relation between God's "being with" someone and the Spirit's involvement is too frequent to be accidental. Consider these examples: Joseph (Gen 39:23—God was with Joseph; 41:38—God's Spirit was in Joseph); Moses (Exod 3:12—God will be with Moses; Num 11:17—the Spirit is upon Moses); Joshua (Josh 3:7—God will be with Joshua; Deut 34:9—Joshua was full of the Spirit); Gideon (Judg 6:12—God is with Gideon; Judg 6:34—the Spirit of the Lord took possession of Gideon); Saul (1 Sam 10:7—God is with you; 1 Sam 10:6—the Spirit came upon you); David (1 Sam 18:12, 14—the Lord was with David; 1 Sam 16:13—the Spirit came upon David); Israel (Hag 2:4—I am with you; Hag 2:5—my Spirit abides among you). Van Unnik concludes that the expression "with you" or "in your midst" refers to the dynamic activity of God's Spirit enabling people to do God's work by protecting, assisting, and blessing them. Although it drops out of usage in most streams of post-biblical Judaism, the formula, applied to Jesus (1:23; 18:20; 28:19–20), is part of Matthew's christology that makes possible his soteriology. This is a significant advance toward understanding the relation of indicative and imperative in Matthew. It enables one to see how God is present in Jesus (1:23); how Jesus is present with the disciples or in their midst; how this presence enables both church discipline (18:20) and mission (28:20). On at least these two

---

8. Frankemölle, *Yahwebund und Kirche Christi* and *Matthäus,* 552–60; Kupp, *Matthew's Emmanuel.*

9. Unnik, "Dominus Vobiscum," 270–305.

fronts the indicative is clearly prior to the imperative and God's grace explicitly enables his people's obedient response in the period subsequent to their entry into Jesus' community. In the form in which it is presented, however, the proposed quilt is too small to cover the whole Matthean bed. Where, for example, is the indicative that covers the ethical activity of disciples? There is a hint of such in Matthew 9:15, but no more: "Can the wedding guests mourn as long as the bridegroom is with them?" More work needs to be done in the direction these scholars are pointing.

It is usually thought, then, that Matthew emphasizes the imperative at the expense of the indicative, demand over gift, either at the point of entry into Jesus' community or after that entry and prior to entry into the age to come. The recent attempt to identify the Matthean indicative with the formula "with you" / "in your midst" is a first constructive step beyond the traditional stereotype. Are there other steps that can be made? I think so.

Additional Constructive Steps

How would one recognize Matthew's indicative, if there is one? It seems obvious that Matthew does not operate in the Pauline conceptual world (e.g., divine indwelling). Could it be that there are other conceptual worlds beside those used by Paul for speaking about divine enablement of human activity, in particular ethical activity? It is my contention that Matthew has a strong indicative if one knows where to look. In attempting to clarify Matthew's conceptual world we will need to indicate both (A) the type of narrative approach he uses and (B) at least two techniques employed in such a type of approach. We begin with the former: the type of narrative approach used.

Matthew's Narrative Approach

Matthew begins and ends his Gospel with narratives that attest repeated divine inbreaks into human affairs. Here God very much has the initiative and humans respond. For example, the birth narratives begin with the miraculous conception of Jesus (1:18), about which Joseph is reassured by an angel (1:20–21). The wise men are directed by a miraculous star (2:2) and are sent on their way by a warning in a dream (2:12). Joseph is warned by an angel to flee to Egypt (2:13). After Herod's death an angel tells Joseph it is safe to return to Israel (2:19–20). At the end of the Gospel, when Jesus dies, the earth shakes, rocks are split, and many bodies of saints are raised and appear to many in Jerusalem (27:51–53). In connection with the stories of Jesus' resurrection, there is a great earthquake and an angel descends from heaven, rolls back the stone from before the tomb (28:2), frightens the soldiers nearly to death (28:4), and tells the women that Jesus has been raised (28:6). The beginning and ending of the Gospel are full of explicit divine interventions into human affairs. The main body of the Gospel that contains the five big teaching sections (chaps 5–25) is narrated in a different way. Especially when the text concerns disciples' obedience to the teachings of Jesus, divine intervention appears to be either absent or well hidden in the background. Hence the problem about the indicative and imperative in the First Gospel.

Meir Sternberg notes that in the Hebrew Bible the books mix overt and implicit guidance by God. The difference in style, he contends, is due to a "compositional alternative of treatment, in the interests of plotting and variety." In Genesis, for example, one starts out with: God said, and it was so. This has a long-range effect on one's perceptual set. "It develops a first impression of a world controlled by a prime mover and coherent to the exclusion of accident. Reinforced at strategic junctures by later paradigms and variants, it also enables the narrative to dispense with the continual enactment of divine intervention that would hamper suspense and overschematize the whole plot."[10] This way of dealing with the divine activity (indicative) he calls "omnipotence behind the scenes."[11] It is seen at work, for example, in the stories about Joseph and about David's accession to the throne. Other scholars have seen the same technique at work in the New Testament, for example, in the activities of Paul in Acts 23–28.[12] I would suggest, then, that what is to be looked for are techniques that are appropriate to a narrative style that often deals in "omnipotence behind the scenes." It is this type of narrative that one encounters in Matthew 5–25, insofar as the disciples' obedience is concerned. It is, therefore, for techniques that allow the evangelist to speak in terms of "omnipotence behind the scenes" that one is to search.

Techniques Employed in Matthew's Narrative

I know of two techniques in addition to Jesus' being with the disciples that fit such a method of narration, that are found in Matthew, and that relate to the Sermon on the Mount. They are "invocation of the name" and "being with Jesus." We may examine them in order.

One technique that the First Evangelist employs to speak about divine enablement of disciples is associated with "the name." In the Scriptures of Israel the name was considered part of the personality.[13] So the name is used interchangeably with the person (Ps 7:17; 9:10; 18:49; 68:4; 74:18; 86:12; 92:1; Isa 25:1; 26:8; 30:27–28; 56:6; Mal 3:16; also in the New Testament—Acts 1:15; 5:41; 18:15; Rev 3:4; 11:13; 3 John 7; Matt 6:9).[14] The Old Testament used the name as a way to speak about the presence of God involved with humans. For example, when one swears (1 Sam 20:42; Lev 19:12), curses (2 Kings 2:24), or blesses (2 Sam 6:18) invoking the

10. Sternberg, *The Poetics*, 105–6.
11. Sternberg, *The Poetics*, 106.
12. Tannehill, *The Narrative Unity*, 2:294; Talbert and Hayes, "A Theology," 333.
13. Bietenhard, "*onoma*," *TDNT* 5.243.
14. Ibid., 5.257.

name of Yahweh, the name thus pronounced evokes Yahweh's presence, attention, and active intervention.[15] Or again, the name of Yahweh is said to assist humans: Psalm 54:1 (in response to prayer, where name is used in synonymous parallelism with might or power); Psalm 89:24 (where the presence of God's steadfast love with him is used in synonymous parallelism with "in my name shall his horn be exalted"); Psalm 20:1 (in response to prayer, where God's name is used together with God's protection). The same motif of divine assistance is used in the New Testament related to the name of Jesus: 1 Corinthians 6:11 (where the name of Jesus is used in parallelism with the Spirit of God and the two are credited with the converts' being washed, sanctified, and justified); Acts 4:12 (where we are saved only through the name of Jesus); Acts 10:43 (where forgiveness comes in his name); 1 John 5:13 (where eternal life comes through his name); Mark 9:39 (where mighty works are in his name); Acts 3:6 (where the lame man is told to walk "in the name of Jesus"); Acts 4:7 (where Peter is asked "by what name or power do you do this?"); Romans 10:13 (where those who "call on the name of the Lord" will be saved).

In the New Testament one meets the phrase "to be baptized in the name of." Generally speaking, "in the name of" conveys the meaning "under the authority of" or "with the invocation of." Given its background and roots, however, it can also carry the connotations of "in the presence of" (name and presence are interchangeable— Ps 89:24; 1 Cor 6:11) or "in the power of" (name and power are parallel concepts— Ps 54:1; Acts 4:7).[16] Since name and person are interchangeable (cf. Acts 3:6 with 9:34), moreover, there does not seem to be any significant difference between being baptized in the name of Christ and being baptized into Christ.

Matthew 28:19–20 indicates that evangelization involves new disciples being baptized into the name of the Father, the Son, and the Holy Spirit. At least three inferences may be drawn. First, certainly implied is that such a one is in a relation of belonging to and being under the authority of the Father, Son, and Holy Spirit. This bonding is reflected in Matthew 10:40 (whoever receives you receives me, and whoever receives me receives Him who sent me); in Matthew 18:5 (whoever receives one such child in my name receives me); and in Matthew 25:31–46 (as you did it to one of the least of these [Christians], you did it to me). This cannot be all that is implied, however. Second, Matthew 18:20 shows that the invocation of Jesus' name evokes his presence among the disciples. By extension, whenever the disciples pray the "Our Father" (6:9–13), the invocation of the name of the Father would evoke His presence in and provision for the disciples' lives (including leading not into temptation and delivering from the Evil One). To invoke the name of God unleashes the power that makes intelligible the words "with God nothing is impossible"

15. Ibid., 5.255.
16. Ibid., 5.271.

(19:26). Third, there is at least the possibility and perhaps the probability that the First Evangelist understood Christian baptism in terms of Matthew 3:11 (He will baptize you with the Holy Spirit).[17] If so, then the Spirit's presence is presumed by Matthew to be a part of the disciples' lives to enable them. To be baptized into the Triune Name, therefore, is to enter into a bonded relationship that will provide one with the divine resources to enable following the guidance of what comes next (all that I have commanded you). This is a key technique used by the First Evangelist to indicate the indicative in disciples' lives after their entry into the community of Jesus.

The second technique by which the author of the Gospel of Matthew speaks of divine enablement of disciples between entry into the community of Jesus' followers and entry into the New Age beyond the resurrection is "being with Jesus." Let us to look at this technique in terms of two major images of Jesus found in the First Gospel: teacher and king.

Writings of this period speak of four types of teachers with adult followers: philosophers (e.g., Socrates); sages (e.g., Sirach); interpreters of Jewish Law (e.g., scribes, Pharisees, Essenes); and prophets or seers (e.g., John the Baptist; the Egyptian Jew mentioned by Josephus, *J. W.* 2.261–73, and *Ant.* 20.169–72; Acts 21:38).[18] When auditors of Matthew's Gospel heard the story of Jesus and his followers, into which of these categories would they have unconsciously slotted the teacher Jesus and his disciples?

The overall picture of Jesus and his disciples in Matthew can be sketched with about four strokes of a brush. In the First Gospel Jesus gathers followers, either through a summons (4:18–22; 9:9) or attraction (4:23–25). They follow him (4:20, 22; 4:25; 9:9). They are "with him" (the Twelve—17:1; 26:51; 26:69; 26:71, this man was with Jesus; the crowds—15:32, they had been with Jesus three days). They derive benefit from his company (crowds—4:25, healings; 8:1–4; 9:10, acceptance; 14:13–20, food; 19:2; the Twelve—8:23, safety; 19:27–29, eschatological benefits; 17:1–8, vision of Jesus and message from heaven).

For a Mediterranean auditor of this Gospel, the closest analogy to the teacher Jesus and his disciples would have been a philosopher and his disciples. The four strokes with which the Gospel paints Jesus and his followers would have seemed familiar from depictions of philosophers in antiquity.[19] Philosophers gathered disciples either by summons (e.g., Aristophanes, *Clouds,* has Socrates tell Strepsiades to "follow me"; Diogenes Laertius, *Lives of Eminent Philosophers* 2.48, tells of Socrates

17. Hartman, *Into the Name,* 153, thinks this is how Matthew understood Christian baptism. So also Overman, *Church and Community,* 409, says that baptism in the name of the Spirit, John the Baptist's prophecy of 3:11, is fulfilled.

18. Perkins, *Jesus as Teacher,* 1–22.

19. Robbins, *Jesus the Teacher,* 89–105, offers further data.

meeting Xenophon and saying "follow me" and learn) or by attraction (Philostratus, *Life of Apollonius* 1.19, says Damis was drawn to Apollonius).

A philosopher's disciples followed him. (E.g., *Life of Apollonius* 1.19 has Damis say to Apollonius: "Let us depart . . . you following God, and I you"; 4.25 has Demetrius of Corinth follow Apollonius as a disciple. Josephus, influenced by the philosophical schools, depicts the Elijah-Elisha relation as that of a philosopher-teacher and disciple: in *Antiquities* 8.354, Elisha follows Elijah as his disciple.)

The disciples are with him (e.g., *Life of Apollonius* 1.19 has Damis stay with the philosopher and commit to memory whatever he learned; *Antiquities* 8.354 says that Elisha was Elijah's disciple and attendant as long as Elijah was alive).

The disciples receive benefit from being in the company of the philosopher. Several examples suffice. Xenophon, *Memorabilia* 4.1.1, says of Socrates: "Socrates was so useful in all circumstances and in all ways, that any observer gifted with ordinary perception can see that nothing was more useful than the companionship (*suneinai*) of Socrates, and time spent with him (*met' ekeinou*) in any place and in any circumstances." In *Memorabilia* 1.2.24–28, Xenophon says: "So long as they were with (*sunesten*) Socrates, they found him an ally who gave them strength (*edunasthen*) to conquer their evil passions." Seneca, *Epistle* 6.5–6, says in the same vein: "Cleanthes could not have been the express image of Zeno, if he had merely heard his lectures; he also shared his life, saw into his hidden purposes, and watched him to see whether he lived according to his own rules. Plato, Aristotle, and the whole throng of sages who were destined to go each his different way, derived more benefit from the character than from the words of Socrates. It was not the classroom of Epicurus, but living together under the same roof, that made great men of Metrodorus, Hermarchus, and Polyaenus." In his *Epistle* 94.40–42, Seneca says association with good men is an aid to virtue. "We are indeed uplifted by meeting wise men; and one can be helped by a great man even when he is silent." In the *Cynic Epistles,* "The Epistles of Crates," 12, Crates says: "It is not the country that makes good men, nor the city bad ones, but rather time spent with good men and bad. Consequently, if you want your sons to become good men and not bad, send them . . . to a philosopher's school." It was being with the teacher that gave the disciples their benefits and made them better people.

These statements about the benefits disciples received from "being with" a philosopher do not refer to the disciples' imitation of their teacher but rather to their being enabled by their association with him. This is a philosophic variation on the general Mediterranean belief that one's being in the presence of a deity causes transformation of the self. Pythagoras, for example, declared that "our souls experience a change when we enter a temple and behold the images of the gods face to face" (Seneca, *Epistle* 94.42). This conviction was widespread in antiquity: e.g., *Corpus Hermeticum* 10.6—the vision of the gods changes one's whole person; 13.3—

the vision of deity transforms; it is being born again; Philo, *Embassy* 1.5—seeing God yields virtue and nobility of conduct; *Contemplative Life* 2.11—the Therapeutae desire a vision of God, which vision results in changes for the better in their behavior (e.g., 2.13, 2.18, 4.34); *Life of Moses* 2.69—Moses preferred the better food of contemplation, through whose inspiration he grew in grace; *On Rewards and Punishments* 114—to gaze continuously upon noble models imprints their likeness in souls that are not entirely hardened; *On the Preliminary Studies* 56—in the mind that has the vision of God, God enables the acquisition of virtue; 2 Corinthians 3:18—Christians who behold the face of the Lord are being changed from one degree of glory to another; 1 John 3:6—no one who sins has seen him who has no sin (cf. 3 John 11); *Diognetus* 2:5—Are these what you worship and in the end become like them? In all such cases, it is a matter of human transformation by vision. In the case of the philosopher, the vision is not of a god but of a godlike man. The effects are the same, however: human transformation.

The benefits, it was believed, were not limited to being with the philosopher in person. Recollection had its impact. Xenophon, *Memorabilia* 4.1.1, speaks about the recollection of Socrates by his disciples, when they were separated from him, as an aid to virtue: "The constant recollection of him in absence brought no small good to his constant companions and followers." Further, books and the use of the imagination also played a part. Seneca, *Epistles* 52.7 and 11.8–10, advocates looking to the ancients for models with whom to associate. In *Epistle* 25.6, he says that if one cannot be in a philosopher's presence, one should come to know him through books, acting as if he were constantly at one's side. *Epistles* 25.5, 11.10, and 11.8 advocate using the imagination to picture one's teacher as before him and himself as ever in the teacher's presence. The point of all this is that disciples' being with their teacher was viewed as an aid to personal transformation. Being with him conveyed benefits in their moral progress. Being with him enabled them to do better and to be better people. Plutarch captured part of why that is so. He says that one's being in the presence of a good and perfect man has the effect: "great is his craving all but to merge his own identity in that of the good man" (*Virt. prof.* 84D).

Matthew's auditors would have sensed that the disciples' being with their teacher conveyed part of the indicative of the Gospel. During Jesus' earthly career his disciples were with him. They heard him teach and saw him act. They saw the correspondence between his life and teaching. They could ask him questions and hear his answers. Their common life would have been assumed by ancient auditors to have provided enablement for the disciples' progress in their formation by Jesus. For example, in the Sermon on the Mount Jesus says to his disciples that they are salt and light (5:13–14) and are sound trees that bear good fruit (7:17–18). That is, Jesus assumes some transformation of the disciples' characters has taken place. From the plot of the Gospel, the only thing that has occurred so far that could explain the transformation is the fact that, having been called, they followed Jesus (4:20, 22).

That is, they were with him, and this association had a transforming quality to it. If being in a philosopher's presence was regarded as transforming by the ancients in a way that was more than disciples' imitation of their master, so likewise the disciples' being with Jesus speaks of more than their imitation of him.

If the Jesus of the First Gospel is a teacher, he is also depicted as a king (1:1; 2:2). It was likewise believed in Mediterranean antiquity that through being exposed to a virtuous ruler one may be transformed ethically and personally, just as when one viewed a deity. Two examples suffice.

Plutarch, in his *Lives,* "Numa," 20.3, says of the effect the second king of Rome had on subjects and neighbors alike: "For not only were the Roman people softened and charmed by the righteousness and mildness of their king, but also the cities round about, as if by some cooling breeze or salubrious wind wafted upon them from Rome, began to experience a change of temper, and all of them were filled with a longing desire to have a good government, to be at peace, to till the earth, to rear their children in quiet, and to worship the gods." Indeed, in 20.7–8, Plutarch says "he is most a king who can inculcate such a life and such a disposition in his subjects."

This being with a righteous king was sometimes spoken of in terms of vision. In the Pythagorean Diotegenes' *On Kingship,* fragment two, one hears that as the king has righteousness in himself, he is able to infuse it into the entire state when they see him live. Of the king he says: "so will he succeed in putting into order those who look upon him. . . . For to look upon the good king ought to affect the souls of those who see him no less than a flute or harmony." E. R. Goodenough says that the point of this text is that "One needs only to gaze at a king . . . to be affected as by music, to be softened, and to have the discordant element of his life brought into the perfect harmony of *dikaiosune* (righteousness)."[20] The vision of a king, like that of a philosopher or a deity, effected change in the personhood of the one who gazed upon him. This is transformation by vision. In Matthew, a disciple's being with or having a vision of the one who fulfilled all righteousness (3:15) enables the disciple to live with a righteousness that exceeds that of the scribes and Pharisees (5:20).

Transformation by vision is, moreover, heightened in the First Gospel by the fact that Jesus is here depicted as divine. In Matthew, God is present in Jesus (1:23). The Evangelist, as a consequence, speaks of the worship of Jesus before his resurrection (e.g., 2:11; 8:2; 9:18; 14:33; 15:25; 20:20—all unique to Matthew) as well as after (28:9, 17—also unique to Matthew).[21] Since in 4:10 Jesus says that worship belongs to God alone and since Jesus does not reject the worship, he must be viewed as Emmanuel, the one in whom and through whom God is present (1:23). By presenting Jesus as an appropriate object of worship, the Evangelist "does, for all

---

20. Goodenough, "The Political Philosophy," 91.
21. Powell, *God with Us,* 28–61.

practical purposes, portray Jesus as divine."[22] Hence the disciples' being "with him" has not only the philosophic frame of reference but also the overtones of being changed by beholding deity. In Matthew, then, for the disciples to be "with Jesus" is for them to be transformed by their vision of God-with-us.

After Jesus' departure, they could have been with him early on, in part, through their memory and recollection of him. Later it would have been through their reading of the First Gospel. They were "with Jesus" as they moved through the narrative plot with him. The being with him made possible by the story powered their transformation. Being with him and experiencing the vision of God-with-us—in person, by means of recollection, or by means of the book (the First Gospel)—was a powerful assistance in their life of obedience.

Implications   *Philosopher, king, deity*

To this point we have noted three key techniques that function in a narrative with "omnipotence behind the scenes" to provide an indicative of divine enablement for the disciples' obedience to the divine demand *after* they have entered Jesus' community by grace: they are linked to the divine name, Jesus is "with them" or "in their midst," and they are "with Jesus." These three techniques underlie the imperative of the First Gospel in an ongoing way.

That Jesus is "with the disciples" is clearly linked with the indicative undergirding their mission (28:19–20), their congregational discipline (18:20), and perhaps their general lifestyle (9:15).

That the disciples are linked with and invoke the name of the Father, the Son, and the Holy Spirit provides divine enablement in key situations: to be gathered in Jesus' name invokes his presence (18:20); to invoke the Father's name in prayer involves His activity in supplying one's needs, whether physical or spiritual (6:9–13).

When the disciples are "with Jesus," their character is shaped for the better. The First Gospel assumes one's actions arise out of one's character (12:35—"Good people out of their good treasure bring forth good, and evil people out of their evil treasure bring forth evil"; 15:18–19—"What comes out of the mouth proceeds from the heart, and this defiles a person. For out of the heart come evil thoughts, murder, adultery, fornication, theft, false witness, slander"). The Sermon on the Mount assumes Jesus' disciples have been transformed (5:13, 16—"You are the salt of the earth"; "You are the light of the world"; 6:22; 7:17–18).[23] How is this possible (in the plot of the First Gospel)? All that has gone before is their call and their following Jesus, that is, their being with him (4:18–22). Being with him, it is implied, has changed their character. As one moves along through the Gospel, it is not difficult to see how this took place. When Jesus teaches with a "focal instance" (e.g., 5:38–42),

---

22. Ibid., 58.
23. Meyer, *Five Speeches*, 47.

it requires the reorientation of the hearer's values;[24] when he teaches in certain parables that shatter one's old world (e.g., 20:1–15) and offer help for a new one, it necessitates a reorientation of life.[25] When Jesus' proverbs jolt their hearers out of the project of making a continuity of their lives (e.g., Matt 5:44; 16:25; 19:24), it demands a reorientation.[26] When Jesus behaves in certain provocative ways before them (e.g., 8:2–3; 9:10–13; 12:1–14), it forces a disciple to a reorientation of life. When the disciples encounter Jesus' healing as visual teaching (e.g., 15:29–30), they join the crowds in glorifying the God of Israel (15:31).[27]

Being with Jesus is a constant aid to transcending one's old ways, to being transformed by the renewing of their minds (Rom 12:2). How so? Achilles Tatius 5.13 puts it this way: "The pleasure which comes from vision enters by the eyes and makes its home in the breast; bearing with it ever the image . . . it impresses it upon the mirror of the soul and leaves there its image." Remember also Philo, *On Rewards and Punishments* 114: "to gaze continuously upon noble models imprints their likeness in souls which are not entirely hardened and stony." What was left untouched, therefore, by the technique of "Jesus's being with his disciples" is, for the most part, covered by the techniques of the disciples' "being linked with the divine name" and their "being with Jesus." These three techniques indicate that the First Evangelist leaves no area of a disciple's life and no stage of discipleship untouched by the divine indicative. "The words of the Sermon on the Mount do not say: this is what with your own resources you have to realize. Thus understood the Sermon on the Mount would be experienced as a crushing mountain."[28] But no, Matthew's three techniques for speaking of omnipotence behind the scenes say that divine enablement covers the disciples' lives from start to finish.

Granted all of this is unobtrusive, almost invisible to the eye that is focused on the surface of the plot of the Gospel. That is as it should be, however, given that in chapters 5–25, as far as disciples' obedience is concerned, the Evangelist is telling his story in terms of "omnipotence behind the scenes." This is not the way Paul or the Fourth Evangelist would tell the story, but it is Matthew's way. Matthew's way, moreover, involves him neither in soteriological legalism nor in legalistic covenantal nomism.[29] Like Paul and the Fourth Evangelist, his soteriology is by grace from start to finish. He just uses a different conceptual repertoire. Surely he cannot be faulted for that.

---

24. Tannehill, *The Sword*, 67–77.
25. Beardslee, "Parable Interpretation," 123–39.
26. Beardslee, "Uses of the Proverb," 61–73.
27. Byrskog, *Jesus the Only Teacher*, 274–75.
28. Hendrickx, *Sermon on the Mount*, 196.
29. Bruner, *Matthew 1–12*, 165, says: "It is a narrow reading of Matthew, not the Gospel itself, that is responsible for legalistic misreadings. . . . 'Moral Matthew' must not be misconstrued as moralistic Matthew."

PART TWO

A Reading of the
Sermon on the Mount

SIX

A Portrait of Disciples
with Promises and Expectations
Matthew 5:3–16

The first major thought unit in the Sermon on the Mount is 5:3–16. Two basic questions must be confronted before it is possible to proceed further with the task of its interpretation.

First, are the Beatitudes entrance requirements or promises of eschatological blessings? On the one hand, some regard the Beatitudes as ethical demands that people must actualize in their lives if they are to be admitted to the yet-future kingdom of heaven.[1] On the other hand, others see the Beatitudes as promises of eschatological blessings on those who have responded positively to God's saving initiative in Jesus. They function to give assurance of participation in the future consummation.[2] Given the fact that the Matthean Jesus has already called and attracted disciples and is now addressing the Sermon to his disciples, and given the fact that in Matthew's Gospel grace underlies every human achievement, the Beatitudes cannot be regarded as entrance requirements but rather as promises of eschatological blessings. They will be so regarded in the commentary that follows.

Second, are the Beatitudes to be understood in terms of a Marxist social analysis (political language) or in terms of the formation of character (virtue ethics)? On the one hand, there is a reading of Matthew 5:3–10 that contends verses 3–6 are a description of economically and politically dispossessed and abandoned people of the world generally who are oppressed, miserable, and humiliated and who hunger for God to put things right, while verses 7–10 are a description of those who are exercised on behalf of the oppressed and who help to bring to reality the blessings of the promises in 5:3–6, being persecuted for their efforts.[3] On the other hand,

---

1. Strecker, "Die Makarismen der Bergpredigt," 255–75, esp. 259–63; Windisch, *The Meaning*, 26–27, 37–38, 87–88 n. 31.

2. Guelich, "The Matthean Beatitudes," 415–34; Allison, *The Sermon*, 42, 44.

3. Powell, *God with Us*, 119–48.

there is a reading of 5:3–10 that sees in the text a portrait of disciples' ideal relation to God (5:3–6) and to others (5:7–10), sometimes spoken of in terms of virtuous behavior.[4] The fact that the Matthean text resists the first reading inclines most interpreters to read in light of the second option. Matthew is a theological, not a political, document.[5] It will be so read in this volume.

Having clarified the slant from which Matthew 5:3–12, 13–16 will be read, it is time to ask the key question. How would this text have been heard by Matthew's auditors?[6] We begin with an overview.

An Overview of 5:3–16

This section is composed of two subunits, verses 3–12 and verses 13–16. The former gives a portrait of and promises to disciples in eight third-person Beatitudes and one second-person Beatitude; the latter gives a portrait of and the mission of disciples in two second-person metaphors, one with a warning, the other with an admonition.

Unit One. Matthew 5:3–12 is composed of nine Beatitudes. The first four deal with the disciples' vertical relationship. The last five focus on horizontal relationships: three with relationships in which disciples have the initiative, followed by two with relationships in which disciples are acted upon. The Beatitudes give a portrait of and promises to disciples.

Portrait	*Promises*
Blessed . . . poor in spirit	theirs is the kingdom of heaven
Blessed . . . those who mourn	they shall be comforted
Blessed . . . the meek	they shall inherit the earth
Blessed . . . those who hunger and thirst for righteousness	they shall be satisfied
Blessed . . . the merciful	they shall receive mercy
Blessed . . . the pure in heart	they shall see God
Blessed . . . the peacemakers	they . . . called children of God
Blessed . . . those persecuted for righteousness's sake	theirs is the kingdom of heaven
Blessed are you when reviled, persecuted, defamed	your heavenly reward is great

4. Most scholars. Cf. Stott, *The Message*, 54, says the Beatitudes show us the disciple "first alone . . . before God," then "with others."

5. Hamm, *The Beatitudes in Context*, 114, puts it well: "Recovering the biblical roots of the beatitudes helps us to see that what is at stake is something much larger than the affirmation of one economic class over another, or a naïve promise of real estate to the nonviolent, or a source of maxims for contemporary peace and justice movements."

6. On reading with the authorial audience, see Rabinowitz, *Before Reading* and "Truth in Fiction," 121–41.

Unit Two. Matthew 5:13–16 consists of two metaphors, one with a warning and one with an exhortation, giving a portrait of the disciples and their mission in the world.

Portrait	*Mission*
You are the salt of the earth	Warning: Be what you are or be discarded.
You are the light of the world	Admonition: Be what you are for God's glory.

In the case of both 5:3–12 and 5:13–16, it is necessary to look first at the form of the text, then at its content.

The Form of Matthew 5:3–12

Matthew 5:3–12 consists of nine Beatitudes. For a series of Beatitudes, compare Sirach 25:7–10, Tobit 13:14–16, *2 Enoch* 41:2–42:14. The first eight are in third person (cf. Pss 1; 40:4; Prov 8:34; Sir 14:1–2; Tob 14:14; *2 Bar.* 10:6; *1 En.* 99:10; *2 En.* 42:7,11), the ninth in second person (cf. *1 En.* 58:2; Isa 33:20, 29; Ps 127:2; *As. Mos.* 10:8). For a move from third person to second person in the same series, compare Sirach 47:12–22 and 48:1–11. The first eight are held together by a variety of rhetorical devices.

(1) "for theirs is the kingdom of heaven"—vv. 3 and 10 = an inclusion
(2) the subjects of the first four all begin with *p* (*ptōchoi*, v. 3; *penthountes*, v. 4; *praeis*, v. 5; *peinōntes*, v. 6)
(3) the verbal forms used in the eight Beatitudes follow an ABCDD'C'B'A' pattern

> v. 3—verb *to be*
> > v. 4—divine passive
> > > v. 5—future active with object
> > > > v. 6—divine passive
> > > > v. 7—divine passive
> > > v. 8—future middle with object
> > v. 9—divine passive
> v. 10—verb *to be*

(4) the first eight break into two sets of four each: vv. 3–6 = thirty-six words, ending with *righteousness;* vv. 7–10 = thirty-six words, ending with *righteousness.*

The ninth Beatitude is linked to the eighth by the catchword *diōkō* (persecute). It functions in three ways. First, it is the climax of the series. A series with the last member extended is frequent in ancient literature, both Jewish and pagan.[7] Second, by

---

7. Daube, *The New Testament,* 196–201; Blass, Debrunner, and Funk, *A Greek Grammar,* 260.

political and theological intertwined

its shift to second person it draws the disciples into an identification with the portrait given. Third, it serves as a transition to 5:13–16, which is also in second person.

The Content of Matthew 5:3–12

The Beatitudes may be taken one by one in their Matthean order.

Verse 3. "Blessed are the poor in spirit, for theirs is the kingdom of heaven." What is meant by "poor in spirit"? Examples of its usage elsewhere give the clue. In Isaiah 61:1, "to bring good tidings to the poor" (i.e., the exiles), the poor are synonymous with the brokenhearted, the captives, those bound, those who mourn (v. 2). In Isaiah 11:4, the poor are synonymous with the meek, as also in Isaiah 29:19. In Isaiah 66:2 the poor are the contrite in spirit. In Amos 2:6–7, the poor are paralleled with the righteous, the needy, and the afflicted, while Zephaniah 2:3 uses the poor in parallelism with those who do the Lord's commandments. In the Psalms of Solomon 10:6 the poor are the devout ("And the devout shall give thanks . . . and God will be merciful to the poor"). In 1QM 14:7, the poor in spirit (the exact phrase) stand in contrast to those with a "hardened heart" (so the humble); in 4Q427 7i&ii the poor are the opposite of those with a haughty heart. A fragmentary text, a Messianic vision 6, equates the poor and the faithful.[8] In Revelation 3:17, the poor are the opposite of those who need nothing. The parallels show that "poor in spirit" is a religious designation. They are those who "embrace the poverty of their condition by trusting in God."[9] They are the humble before God.[10] Matthew is not talking about people who live in material destitution but about those who live with the right disposition.[11] *yes +no*

How should one understand kingdom of heaven? In Matthew, *kingdom of heaven* is synonymous with *kingdom of God* (Matt 19:23–24) and is used with two connotations and in two tenses.

1) a passive connotation and future tense—
   a future hope / the New Age beyond the resurrection (8:11; 26:29)
   whose coming is near at hand (3:2; 4:17; 10:7)
   for which Jesus' disciples are to pray (6:10)
   into which only some will enter (5:20; 7:21; 18:3; 19:23–4; 21:31)
   within which there are degrees of status (5:19; 11:11; 18:1, 4)
2) an active connotation and present tense—
   the present kingly activity of God in Jesus (12:28)

---

8. *Biblical Archaeology Review* 17/6 (1991): 65 translates: "And over the Poor will His Spirit hover and the Faithful will He support with his strength."

9. Keener, *A Commentary,* 169.

10. Hamm, *The Beatitudes in Context,* 78.

11. Hendrickx, *Sermon on the Mount,* 22.

So *kingdom of heaven* stands both for the ultimate blessing and for the activity of God that causes that blessing to come.[12]

Verse 4. "Blessed are those who mourn, for they shall be comforted." What is meant by those who mourn? Again comparison of the use of this language elsewhere is helpful. Isaiah 61:2–3 uses "to comfort all who mourn" to refer to the returned exiles who are facing abundant troubles that grieve them greatly. Joel 2:12–13, "return to me with all your heart, with fasting, with weeping, and with mourning, and rend your hearts, not your garments," associates mourning with repentance. Jeremiah 31:13 (LXX 38:13), "I will turn their mourning into joy; I will comfort them," speaks about the grief connected with the exile. *Testament of Reuben* 1:10 has its hero say that "for seven years I repented before the Lord. I did not. . . . Rather I was mourning over my sin," again associating mourning with repentance. Revelation 21:4 associates mourning, crying, and pain with the experience of the former things of this present evil age. Two religious connotations emerge from this survey: those who are brokenhearted over their situation and those who are repenting from their situation. The link with Isaiah 61 supports a preference for the former. This Beatitude, then, is a variation of the first. The reference is to those who need God's help,[13] who lament that the kingdom has not come and God's will is not yet done.[14] "Until the eschatological reversal takes place, it is not possible to be content with the status quo."[15]

How shall one understand "they shall be comforted"? Isaiah 61:2 equates comfort and salvation. Isaiah 57:18 associates comfort with healing. Jeremiah 31:13 equates comfort and redemption. The comfort in Isaiah 40:1–2 is the announcement of pardon for iniquity; in 49:13 it is freedom for the exiles; in 51:12 it is return from exile; in 66:13 it is nourishment of the people. To be comforted, then, is to experience God's salvation and sustenance.

Verse 5. "Blessed are the meek, for they shall inherit the earth." The order of the first three Beatitudes is that of Isaiah 61: poor, mourners, meek. What is meant by the meek? The Beatitude is a virtual replica of Psalm 37:11 (LXX 36:11)—"The meek shall inherit the earth." The idea is echoed in *2 Enoch* 50:2: "Live in meekness for the number of your days, so that you may inherit the endless age that is coming." How is meekness to be understood? Zephaniah 3:12–13 speaks of "a people meek and lowly," those who seek refuge in the name of the Lord (cf. Matt 11:29—"meek and lowly"). *Praus,* meek, in the LXX is used for three Hebrew terms, one of which is *'ani. Ptochos,* poor, in the LXX is used for three Hebrew terms, one of which is *'ani.* Hence, *poor* and *meek* are virtual synonyms (cf. Isa 11:4 and 29:19;

12. Patte, *The Gospel,* 66.
13. Hamm, *The Beatitudes in Context,* 84.
14. Boring, "Matthew," 8.179; Gundry, *Matthew,* 68.
15. Davies and Allison, *Matthew 1–7,* 448.

they were also so used at Qumran [cf. 4QpPs37]). The first and third Beatitudes, then, are synonyms.[16]

How should "inherit the earth" be viewed? The original intent of Psalm 37:11 may have been to refer to the land of Canaan, but *2 Enoch* 50:2 makes it clear that by the New Testament period the land had taken on an eschatological connotation. Qumran interprets Psalm 37 as referring to the End Time vindication (4QpPs37 [a]). In Romans 4, the Apostle Paul shares this eschatological view of the land and world.

Verse 6. "Blessed are those who hunger and thirst for righteousness, for they shall be satisfied." How should one regard "those who hunger for righteousness"? The term *righteousness* has been taken by scholars in two very different ways. On the one hand, some have understood righteousness in all Matthean passages as the conduct expected by God: as e.g., in Proverbs 21:21 MT ("The one who pursues righteousness will find life and righteousness") and *Testament of Levi* 13:5 ("Do righteousness on earth, in order that you might find it in heaven").[17] On the other hand, others have taken righteousness, at least in some passages, as the activity of God that establishes justice: as e.g., in Isaiah 51:6 ("my salvation will be forever and my righteousness will never be ended") and Isaiah 51:5 ("my righteousness draws near speedily, my salvation has gone forth").[18] Scholarly opinion is divided about its use in Matthew. It seems entirely possible, however, that Matthew 5:6 may echo the second connotation. The hunger and thirst is for the future kingdom and God's vindication of the right.[19]

What is meant by "shall be satisfied"? Psalm 107:9 ("The Lord satisfies the one who is thirsty, and the hungry he fills with good things") and Isaiah 61:11 ("The Lord will cause righteousness to spring forth before all the nations") together with *Testament of Levi* 13:5 and Proverbs 21:21 show that the hunger is satisfied by that for which one is hungry. Those who long for God's saving activity will find their hunger and thirst satisfied by that very saving activity.

Verse 7. "Blessed are the merciful, for they shall obtain mercy." How should one understand "the merciful"? Consider the following examples. The MT of Psalm 18:25–26 reads: "with the merciful you show yourself merciful." In *b. Baba Qamma* 9:30 there is a nearly identical statement ("So long as you are merciful, He will have mercy on you"). Similar sayings are also found in *Sifre* Deuteronomy 13.18 and *b. Shabbat* 151b. Early Christian comments that are similar are found in *1 Clement* 13:2 ("Be merciful in order that you might receive mercy") and James 2:13 ("judgment is without mercy to one who has shown no mercy"). Similar sentiments are echoed in Matthew 18:33; 9:13; 12:7; 15:22; 17:15; and 20:30–31.

16. Hamm, *The Beatitudes in Context*, 89n. 23; Gundry, *Matthew*, 69.
17. E.g., Prsybylski, *Righteousness in Matthew*; Strecker, *Der Weg der Gerechtigkeit*, 154–58.
18. E.g., Reumann, *Righteousness*, 128, 130–31, 134; Meier, *Law and History*, 76–79.
19. Hamm, *The Beatitudes in Context*, 95; Boring, "Matthew," 8.179.

How should "shall obtain mercy" be taken? The sayings in *b. Baba Qamma* 9:30, *1 Clement* 13:2, James 2:13, and Matthew 18:33 indicate that obtaining mercy may be taken either in worldly or eschatological terms. Here in this context it is eschatological.

Verse 8. "Blessed are the pure in heart, for they shall see God." Who are the pure in heart? Consider Psalm 24:3–4: "Who shall ascend to the hill of the Lord and who shall stand in his holy place? He who has clean hands and a pure heart"; Psalm 73:1: "the upright, those who are pure in heart"; *Testament of Joseph* 4:6: "I kept telling her that the Lord would be pleased with those who were pure in heart"; James 4:8: "Cleanse your hands, you sinners, and purify your hearts, you men of double mind." Clean hands and a pure heart are the outer and inner ethical stance of the person. The concern, then, is with horizontal relationships.

What is meant by "shall see God"? A number of texts offer clues. Two are noteworthy: *4 Ezra* 7:98 ("The righteous will one day see the face of Him whom they served in life") and *Jubilees* 1:28 ("in the last time God will appear to all eyes"). Similar sentiments may be found in Hebrews 12:14, 1 John 3:2, and Revelation 22:4. It is the eschatological vision of God about which the Beatitude speaks.

Verse 9. "Blessed are the peacemakers, for they shall be called the children of God." How should one understand "the peacemakers"? The following texts offer assistance. Proverbs 10:10 LXX ("The one who reproves boldly is a peacemaker"); *2 Enoch* 52:11 ("Blessed is the one who cultivates the love of peace"); *m. Abot* 1:12 (Hillel said: "Be of the disciples of Aaron, loving peace and pursuing peace"); and *m. Peah* 1:1 ("These are things whose fruits one enjoys in this world while the capital is laid up for him in the world to come: . . . making peace between a man and his fellow") express sentiments that are similar to those found in Romans 12:18, 1 Corinthians 7:15, and Hebrews 12:14.

How shall "called the children of God" be understood? The statements in Deuteronomy 14:1 ("you are the children of the Lord your God"); Wisdom 12:19 ("the righteous are God's children") and 5:5 ("after death the righteous one is numbered among the children of God, the saints"); Philo (*Spec. Laws* 1.318—"Not every Israelite is God's child, but only the doer of good"); *Jubilees* 1:24 ("They will do according to my commandments and I will be their father and they shall be my children. And they shall be called children of the living God"); Romans 8:19 ("the revealing of the children of God"); Revelation 21:7 ("the overcomer will be God's child"); and Matthew 5:48 point the way. God's children are those who act like God. Who calls them "children"? It is God.

Verse 10. "Blessed are those persecuted for righteousness's sake, for theirs is the kingdom of heaven." Who are "those persecuted for righteousness's sake"? Other texts supply leads for our understanding. Wisdom of Solomon 2:12 ("The wicked say, Let us lie in wait for the righteous person"); 1 Peter 3:14 ("But even if you do suffer for righteousness's sake, you will be blessed"); and Polycarp, *Philippians* 2:3 ("Remember what the Lord said: Blessed are those persecuted for their righteousness"), are especially apt. Persecution comes not because the disciples have done wrong but because they have done right.

One should doubtless read "theirs is the kingdom of heaven" here as in verse 3. It is the eschatological blessing seen here as present in foretaste, at least.

Verses 11–12. "Blessed are you when people revile you and persecute you and utter all kinds of evil against you falsely on my account (cf. Isa 66:5 MT). Rejoice and be glad, for your reward is great in heaven, for so they persecuted the prophets who were before you" (Moses—Exod 16:2; 17:2; Samuel—1 Sam 8:5; Elijah—1 Kings 18:17; 19:2; Micaiah—2 Chr 18:17; Nehemiah—Neh 4). To what does "revile you and persecute you on my account" refer? The references to persecution of Jesus' followers in Galatians 4:29; Revelation 2:9; Acts 4:3; 5:17–18; 6:12; 13:45, 50; 17:5; 18:12; 20:3; 21:30; 23:12–15; 1 Peter 2:12; Matthew 10:24–25; and elsewhere make the reference clear. Being Jesus' disciples is the cause of the reviling.

The words "so they persecuted the prophets before you" reflect a long tradition of belief that the prophet's vocation involved suffering: 1 Thessalonians 2:14–16; Matthew 23:29–35; Acts 7:51–52; Hebrews 11:35–38; *Lives of the Prophets* (Isaiah, Jeremiah, Micah, Amos, Zechariah); Exodus 5:11; 14:11; 16:2; 17:2; 1 Samuel 8:5; 1 Kings 18:17; 19:2; 2 Chronicles 18:17; Nehemiah 4; *Ascension of Isaiah* 5.

The content of the Beatitudes is twofold: promises of eschatological blessings and a portrait of the recipients of these blessings. The first four Beatitudes deal with the vertical relationship; the final four plus one focus on horizontal relationships.

In the Matthean plot Jesus has been depicted as one who knows about the kingdom of heaven (4:17—its imminence and its demand for repentance). Matthew 5:3–12 assumes that Jesus not only knows the character of the kingdom and the criteria of the Last Judgment but also has the authority to pronounce that judgment (cf. Matt 7:21–23 for similar assumptions). Consequently, Jesus can issue congratulations to those who will benefit from its coming. The poem (5:3–12) is in effect *eschatological judgment proleptically given, on the basis of Jesus' assumed knowledge of the End Times and authority at the Last Judgment.*[20] What is said is applicable to disciples (cf. the "you" and "for my sake" in v. 11). It assumes that Jesus' disciples are "attached to him" (5:11—remember 4:18–22) and that they "resemble the portrait" given in 5:3–12 (this is implied in 5:13–16—"You are salt" and "You are light"). At this point we are ready to proceed to an examination of the second subunit in 5:3–16, namely 5:13–16. We begin with its form.

---

20. Betz, *Essays on the Sermon*, 26, 30, who calls attention to similar pronouncements in the Greek world (e.g., Homeric Hymn to Demeter, 480–83, and the so-called Orphic gold plate) as well as the Jewish milieu (*2 En.* 42:6ff; 52:1ff; *4 Ezra* 8:46–54); and Betz, *The Sermon*, 94.

The Form of Matthew 5:13–16

There are two metaphors used for disciples in this subunit: salt and light. The images involve "considerations less of what one does than of what one is."[21] These metaphors control the overall form of the verses.

1. Description: You are the salt of the earth. (v. 13a)
   Question: If the salt has lost its taste, how shall its saltiness be restored? (v. 13b)
   Answer: It is no longer good for anything except to be thrown out and trodden under people's feet. (v. 13c)
2. Description: You are the light of the world. (v. 14a)
   First illustration: A city set on a hill cannot be hid. (v. 14b)
   Second illustration: Nor do men light a lamp and put it under a bushel, but on a stand, and it gives light to all in the house. (v. 15)
   Concluding exhortation: So let your light shine before men, that they may see your good works and give glory to your Father who is in heaven. (v. 16)

Verses 13–16 are linked to verses 11–12 by the repetition of the same *you* (vv. 11, 13, 14) and by the same focus of theme (the disciples in the world).

The Content of 5:13–16

Verses 13–16 describe the status of disciples on earth before people, that is, their commission. These verses function to establish the identity of the auditors through the use of the two metaphors.

Verse 13. Salt is the first metaphor. What connotations does it evoke? The associations of salt in antiquity are so various that no one can be specified for verse 13a.[22] Salt is for the benefit of the earth, whatever that benefit may be. Rabbi Joshua ben Hananiah (c. 90 C.E.) uses salt losing its savor as an example of something that is impossible (*b. Bek* 8b). However, in actual fact, that salt can be so mixed with impurities that it becomes useless was known to Pliny (*Nat.* 31.82). Salt that has become savorless has become useless. It is no longer being what it is. Note that the disciples "are not challenged to *become* salty—their saltiness is a gift of Jesus . . . they are challenged to *stay* salty."[23]

Verse 14. Light is the second metaphor. The Old Testament speaks of God's people as lights to the nations (Isa 42:6; 49:6; Sir 17:19). *Testament of Levi* 14:3 ("You should be the lights of Israel as the sun and moon. For what will all the nations do

21. Keener, *A Commentary,* 172.
22. Davies and Allison, *Matthew 1–7,* 472–73.
23. Bruner, *Matthew 1–12,* 160.

if you become darkened with impiety? You will . . . destroy the light of the Law which was granted to you for the enlightenment of every man") reflects the Jewish concern that God's people be light in the world. The Matthean Jesus reflects this common assumption about God's people.

Verse 16. "That they may see your good works (Matt 7:16–20, 21–23) and glorify your Father in heaven" is a concern echoed in *Testament of Naphtali* 8:4 ("God shall be glorified among the Gentiles through you, but through him that does not that which is good, God shall be dishonored"), 1 Peter 2:12b ("may see your good deeds and glorify God"), and *m. Abot* 1:11; 2:2, 12 (good works honor God's name).

The role of disciples in verses 13–16 is seen in terms of mission: both of *being* (you are salt, light) and of *doing* (good works). Disciples are to act in line with their nature. Jesus is saying, "I have made you into something, now be it."[24] The scope of their mission is universal (of the earth or world). Its goal is to glorify God.

Matthew 5:3–12, 13–16 offers two things and aims at another. There is first an explicit portrait of disciples:

> 1) in terms of their basic relationships (5:3–12)
>> their posture toward God (vertical relations)
>> their posture toward others (horizontal relations)
> 2) in terms of their role in the world (5:13–16)
>> Like salt and light, disciples have the potential to make where they are better. Be who you are—so God will be glorified.

There is second an implicit picture of Jesus in 5:3–16. Who is this one? He is the one who pronounces the judgment of the Last Day within history and who defines the criteria by which judgment is pronounced:

> attachment to him (for my sake)
> submission to God, sorrow for sins, desire to do God's will
> a merciful, ethical, peacemaking orientation to others
> a willingness to suffer for Jesus and for what is right.

At what does the unit 5:3–16 aim? The Beatitudes bestow a blessing and make a promise.[25] What is the significance of blessing and promise? Let us consider first the matter of the promise. J. L. Austin, in *How to Do Things with Words,* has pointed to a type of language/utterance that is not so much description as it is, or is in part, an action. This he called "performative language." The classic example is "the promise." Something occurs in the utterance itself. The issuing of the promise is not just saying something; it is the performing of an action. It obliges the one who utters it;

---

24. Ibid., 161.
25. Davies and Allison, *Matthew 1–7,* 466.

it puts on record one's assumption of a spiritual shackle. Of course, if the proper person does not do it, then the action is void. If the proper circumstances do not exist, then the action is void. Also, in many cases it is possible to perform an act of the same kind not by uttering the words but in some other way.

What is Matthew 5:3–12 doing? The unit is shaping character. Matthew 5:3–12 consists of a poem composed of nine Beatitudes that gives a portrait of and promises to disciples. Of the nine Beatitudes, the first four deal with the disciples' vertical relationships, the last five with horizontal relations. Among the final five, the first three focus on relationships in which the disciples have the initiative, the last two on relations in which the disciples are acted upon in negative ways.

The first eight Beatitudes are in third person. They sketch the outlines of a good person, a person of piety toward God and right behavior toward other humans. Such a portrait would affect the auditors. Plutarch (*Virt. prof.* 84D) tells how. He says that one's being in the presence of a good person has the effect: "great is his craving all but to merge his own identity in that of the good man." In *Pericles* 1–2, Plutarch expounds:

> Since, then, our souls are by nature possessed of a great fondness for learning and fondness for seeing, it is surely reasonable to chide those who abuse this fondness on objects all unworthy either of their eyes or ears, to the neglect of those which are good and serviceable. . . . [O]ur intellectual vision must be applied to such objects as, by their very charm, invite it onward to its own proper good. Such objects are to be found in virtuous deeds; *these implant in those who search them out a great and zealous eagerness which leads to imitation.* . . . the spectator is not advantaged by those things at the sight of which no ardor for imitation arises in the breast, nor any uplift of the soul arousing zealous impulses to do the like. But virtuous action straightway so disposes a man that he no sooner admires the works of virtue than he strives to emulate those who wrought them. . . . The Good *creates a stir of activity towards itself, and implants at once in the spectator an active impulse; it does not form his character by ideal representation alone; but through the investigation of its work it furnishes him with a dominant purpose.* For such reasons I have decided to persevere in my writing of Lives. (emphasis mine)

The ninth Beatitude shifts to second person, thereby drawing the auditors into an identification with the portrait given. This is who we are. A new way of *seeing* themselves occurs with the shift from third to second person. Participation in the dispositions and intentions reflected in the portrait is effected. This really is who we are! Jesus sees us this way. The poem, then, in its portrait of disciples functions to form the character of the auditors in their vertical and horizontal relations.

What about the promises? They constitute eschatological judgment proleptically given, on the basis of Jesus' assumed knowledge of the End Times and authority at the Last Judgment. They promise fullness of eschatological blessing to those who

nature of participation?

participate in the portrait sketched. It is assumed that Jesus' disciples are "attached to him" (4:18–22) and that they resemble the portrait given in 5:3–12 (this is implied in 5:13–16—"You are salt" and "You are light"). Like any promise, these promises are performative language that is not just saying something but is an action. These promises oblige their speaker; they put him on record as assuming a responsibility for the disciples' ultimate destiny. The disciples now see their destiny differently. This is the way Jesus sees us. There is one who by his promises has now undertaken responsibility to enable the fulfillment of the Beatitudes. The disposition that flows from this insight is to trust him. Character is being formed. From the very first thought unit, 5:3–12, the Sermon on the Mount functions in the interests of character formation.

From the first unit, the Sermon also makes clear that divine enablement is involved. This has been recognized in the performative function of the promises. It is also present in the pronunciation of the blessings. As Genesis 27 indicates, the word of blessing, once pronounced, cannot be taken back. The word itself is believed to be effective in accomplishing its content. As Isaac exclaims when he realizes that Jacob has tricked him into blessing the wrong son: "I have blessed him . . . yes, and blessed he shall be." God's word works the same way. Isaiah 55:11 reads: "so shall my word be that goes out from my mouth; it shall not return to me empty, but it shall accomplish that which I purpose, and succeed in the thing for which I sent it." So when the Matthean Jesus pronounces his disciples "blessed," he is granting them divine enablement. In the Old Testament for God to bless someone is a synonym for God's "being with" someone.[26] For Yahweh to be with someone is for God to enable that one to succeed. The blessings, therefore, like the promises, are performative language. They involve the speaker in the sustenance and success of the disciples. The disciples are *being* formed.

---

26. Pedersen, *Israel*, 194. Vetter, *Jahwes Mit-Sein*, starts with Pedersen's assertion of the equivalence of Yahweh's "being with" one and Yahweh's blessing one and devotes a monograph to proving, successfully, this to be the case.

SEVEN

The Antitheses with Their Heading

Matthew 5:17–48

Matthew 5:17–20

Matthew 5:17–20 is a thought unit composed of four sayings: verse 17 (cf. 9:13 and 10:34–35 for other "I came not . . . I came" sayings); verse 18 (cf. 16:28, 24:34, and 26:29 for other "Truly, I say to you" logia); verse 19 (cf. 1 Cor 3:17, Gal 1:9, and Rev 22:18–19 for other conditional judgment words); and verse 20 (cf. 7:21, 18:3, and 19:23–24 for other sayings about entering the kingdom of heaven). It functions as a control on the way 5:21–48 is to be read. It aims to protect against any interpretation of what follows that depicts Jesus as doing away with the observance of the Law or the prophets (cf. Acts 6:13–14 and Epiphanius, *Pan.* 30.16.5, for such charges made against Jesus).[1] In outline form, the unit looks like this.

Verse 17—Jesus' intent is *not* to cause observance of the Scriptures to cease (cf. 1 Macc 1:44–49; 2 Macc 2:22; 4 Macc 5:33; 17:9)
> *but* to realize the intent of God's will in the Scriptures (cf. Rom 8:4; 13:8; Gal 5:14; Matt 3:15).

Verse 18—The ground of Jesus's intent is that the Scriptures endure to the Eschaton (cf. Bar 4:1; 2 Esd 9:37; Jub 3:14; *Exod. Rab.* 1:6; Philo, *Moses* 2.3.14; John 10:35; *j. Sanh* 20c).

Verses 19–20—Two consequences of Jesus' intent and its basis, one for teachers and one for all auditors:
> 1) for teachers (v. 19)—implications for a teacher's status in the kingdom of heaven (cf. 28:18—"all authority in heaven and on earth has been given to me"—i.e., Jesus' status indicates he has not relaxed even the least of the commandments; cf. 23:23–24);
> 2) for all auditors (v. 20)—implications for a person's entry into the kingdom of heaven (righteousness, or covenant faithfulness demanded of humans).

---

1. Davies and Allison, *Matthew 1–7*, 481.

An examination of the details of these sayings is now required.

Verse 17. In form, this verse contradicts a false saying with a correct one. The false saying, attributed by someone to Jesus, runs: "I have come to abolish the law and the prophets" (for similar sayings, cf. the Gospel of the Ebionites, frag 5: "I have come to abolish sacrifices"; cf. also the Gospel of the Egyptians, frag 3: "I have come to abolish the works of femaleness"). Matthew corrects the error with a true saying: "I have come not to abolish but to fulfill."[2]

The meaning of the logion is tied to the understanding of *abolish* and *fulfill*. The term *abolish* (*katalusai*) refers not to the abolition of a single commandment but the rescinding of the whole web of traditional observance (cf. 2 Macc 2:22—Judas Maccabeus restored the laws that were about to be abolished [*kataluon*]; 4:11—Jason destroyed [*kataluon*] the lawful ways of living and introduced new customs contrary to the Law; 1 Macc 1:44–49; 4 Macc 5:33—Eleazar says he will not be responsible for breaking [*katalusai*] the Law of his fathers; 7:9—Eleazar is eulogized: he through his deed has not annulled [*katalusas*] but rather ratified the Law; 17:9—a tyrant was bent on abolishing [*katalusai*] the Law of the Hebrews; Philo, *Gaius* 17.119—Gaius practiced lawlessness: "For considering that he himself was a law, he abrogated [*eluen*] those laid down by legislators in the several states, treating them as empty talk"; Josephus, *Ant.* 16.35—an analogous situation applies to pagans who would not want a dissolution of the customs of their forefathers; 20.81—pagans hated their king for abrogating the laws of their forefathers and embracing foreign [Jewish] customs).[3] The Matthean Jesus denies that he wants to act like a foreign king and abolish the web of observance of the Scriptures.

He rather wants to "fulfill" (*plerōsai*) them. Several ways of understanding this assertion are found in secondary literature. Some see Jesus' fulfilling the Law and the prophets as his doing and obeying the requirements of the Law in his own life,[4] as in 1 Maccabees 2:55 (in the context of a speech by Matthathias to his sons that focuses on being zealous for the Law, he says: "Joshua for fulfilling the word [*plerōsai logon*] was made a judge in Israel"); Philo, *Rewards and Punishments* 83 (speaks of persons who have the sense not to leave the divine commands destitute of corresponding actions but take care to fulfill the words with praiseworthy actions); or Romans 8:4 ("the righteous demand of the law fulfilled [*plerōthē*] in us"). Others take *fulfill* in the sense of building a fence around the Torah in order to protect the individual commands.[5] Still others regard *fulfill* as referring to the fulfillment of the prophecies of the Scriptures (as in Matt 1:22; 2:15; 2:17; 2:23; 4:14; 8:17; 12:17;

---

2. Marcion wanted to eliminate this verse (Tertullian, *Adv. Marc.* 5.14.14), a position opposed by Irenaeus (*Adv. Haer.* 4.13.1).

3. Hendrickx, *Sermon on the Mount*, 49.

4. E.g., Luz, *Matthew 1–7*, 264–72; Harrington, *Gospel of Matthew*, 83–84.

5. Prsybylski, *Righteousness in Matthew*. For the principle of building a fence about the Torah, cf. *m. Aboth* 1:1; for an example of the principle, cf. *m. Ber.* 1:1.

13:14; 13:35; 21:4; 26:54, 56; 27:9, 35).[6] A final group takes *fulfill* in the sense of interpretation of the Law and prophets in light of the correct hermeneutical key.[7] The context seems to favor the last option. In 5:21–48 Jesus is defining righteousness by expounding the true meaning of the Law as opposed to the wrong or shallow understandings of it. L. E. Keck summarizes: "Matthew does not regard Jesus's ethic . . . as a new ethic at all, but the recovery of what has been God's will all along, and which should have been recognized as such. Jesus's ethic is neither a strange import nor a novelty but the recovered original. As Matthew portrays it, Jesus's teaching is so radically different because the distortion of God's will has been so pervasive."[8] Of course, the Matthean Jesus also both practices what he preaches and fulfills the prophecies, and in so doing gives the correct reading of them. It is this combination of readings that is followed in this volume.

Verse 18. Formally, this is a logion following an ABA' pattern:

A—Till heaven and earth pass away;
   B—not an iota (the Greek equivalent of the Semitic *yod*, the smallest letter in the alphabet), nor a dot (literally "horn," that is, a projection or hook of a letter), will pass from the Law;
A'—until all is accomplished.

The form is an assistance in interpreting the saying correctly. Both non-Christian and Christian Judaism spoke of the enduring nature of the Law (Bar 4:1; 2 Esd 9:37; *Jub.* 3:14; *Exod. Rab.* 1:6; Philo, *Moses* 2.3.14; *j. Sanh* 20c; *2 Bar.* 77:15; Luke 16:17; John 10:35). This enduring character was thought to apply to even the smallest part of the Law. For example, Jewish teachers said that the *yod* would not pass from the Law.[9] In *b. Sanhedrin* 107ab we hear that when Sarai's name was changed to Sarah, the *yod* removed from her name repeatedly complained against its removal until finally Moses changed Oshea's name to Joshua, returning the *yod* to Scripture. In *j. Sanhedrin* 2.6 § 2 we hear that when Solomon threatened to remove a *yod* from the Law, God said that he would remove Solomon and a thousand like him rather than a word from his Law. So even the smallest details of God's Law are essential. This is the basis for Jesus' statement in verse 17. The question of interpretation is when the Law will pass away. Interpretations differ. Some say it will never pass away;[10] others say, not until the end of this Age (cf. Matt 24:34–35; Rev

---

6. E.g., Meier, *The Vision of Matthew,* 222–39; Guelich, *The Sermon,* 134–74.
7. E.g., Snodgrass, "Matthew and the Law," 99–127 (the key is the love command and mercy); Hagner, *Matthew 1–13,* 106; Strecker, *The Sermon,* 53; Garland, *Reading Matthew,* 61–62; Lambrecht, *The Sermon,* 84.
8. Keck, "Ethics in the Gospel," 51.
9. Keener, *A Commentary,* 178.
10. *Gen. Rab.* 10:1—"Everything has its end, the heaven and the earth have their end; only one thing is excepted which has no end, and that is the Law."

21:1);[11] still others, not until the prophecies of Scripture have been fulfilled in Jesus' life, death, and resurrection.[12] That "until heaven and earth pass away" (Mark 13:31; Rev 21:1; 1 Cor 7:31) and "until all is accomplished" (Mark 13:30; Rev 1:1, 19; 4:1) are synonymous expressions in Matthew 24:34–35 favors the second option. This option is very much that verbalized by Philo. "But Moses is alone in this, that his laws, firm, unshaken, immovable, stamped, as it were, with the seals of nature herself, remain secure from the day when they were first enacted to now, and we may hope that they will remain for all future ages as though immortal, so long as the sun and moon and the whole heaven and universe exist" (*Moses* 2.14). It is this option that is followed in this book.

Verse 19. In form, it is a logion in antithetical parallelism. "Whoever relaxes one of the least of these commandments[13] . . . and teaches . . . so, shall be called least in the kingdom of heaven" is the antithesis of "Whoever does them and teaches them will be called great in the kingdom." This saying is addressed to teachers. The danger faced is teachers' tendency to evade the clear intent of the Scriptures (cf. Matt 15:1–9 for a clear example). Non-Christian Judaism knew the problem. In *j. Sotah* 19a the "plagues of the Pharisees" refers to scholars who give counsel, apparently in the strict form of Law, by which the Law may be circumvented. Also *j. Sotah* 3.4 speaks against one who applies lenient rulings to himself and strict rulings to others and against one who latches onto the lenient rulings of Hillel and the lenient rulings of Shammai. According to Matthew 5:19, teachers of the Scriptures are bound by Jesus' interpretation of the Law and the prophets, if they are to have status in the kingdom of heaven.[14]

Verse 20. Formally, this verse is a conditional judgment. "*Unless* your righteousness exceeds that of the scribes and Pharisees, you will never enter the kingdom of heaven." In order to understand what an ancient auditor would have heard, it is necessary to know what righteousness meant in Matthew's milieu.

What does Matthew understand by a surpassing righteousness (5:20)? We may begin with a foray into the Hebrew and Greco-Roman worlds. The Hebrew term *sedaqa,* the Greek word *dikaiosune,* and the Latin noun *iustitia* are the focus of our attention. One may translate in English either *justice* (from the Latin) or *righteousness* (from the Anglo-Saxon). Since the Hebrew *mishpat* (to get what one deserves)

---

11. E.g., Hagner, *Matthew 1–13,* 108; Betz, *Essays on the Sermon,* 45, and *The Sermon,* 183.
12. E.g., Meier, *Vision of Matthew,* 222–39; Guelich, *The Sermon,* 134–74.
13. The rabbis sometimes spoke of "the least of the commandments." The law of the bird's nest (Deut 22:6–7) is so designated in *j. Qidd* 1.61b, 58, and *Deut. Rab.* 6:2. M. Johnson, "The Least," 205–15). Matthew 5:19 speaks not of one commandment that is the least but of multiple commandments that fall into that category. Cf. Matt 23:23–24.
14. The Matthean Jesus apparently did not challenge the validity of the ritual law (Matt 23:23, 26; 24:20); thought justice, mercy, and faith were chief and that tithing (23:23) was a minor matter; and saw the love command as central and all others as subordinate to it.

is normally translated *justice* in English translations, I opt for *righteousness*. In the Greco-Roman world *dikaiosune* was one of the cardinal virtues, along with prudence, temperance or self-control, and courage (Aristotle, *Ethics*, Bk 3.5–6). Although the term is used this way in Wisdom of Solomon 8:7, "righteousness" in the Greek Bible normally functions as *sedaqah* does in the Hebrew Bible. It is this distinctive meaning that we need to explore.

The Meaning of Righteousness in Matthew's Bible

In ancient Israel, *righteousness* was a relational term (i.e., covenant term). It meant faithfulness to a covenant relationship. *Dikaiosunē* could be used in the LXX to translate *hesed* (e.g., Gen 19:19; 20:13; 24:27) and *emeth* (e.g., Gen 24:27; Isa 38:19; 39:8), both covenant terms. It is used in the LXX as a synonym for steadfast love and faithfulness (LXX Ps 88:15), truth (Gen 24:27; LXX Ps 95:13), goodness (LXX Ps 144:7; Prov 2:20), justice (LXX Amos 5:24), and mercy (Bar 5:9), all covenant terms.

Righteousness in Israel's Scriptures is applied to God as well as to humans. What does it mean for God to act with righteousness (to be loyal to the covenant)? It involves such things as finding the right wife for Isaac (Gen 24:27); blessing Jacob materially (Gen 30:10); giving military victory to Israel (Judg 5:11); saving deeds from Exodus through Conquest (1 Sam 12:7); judgment for the faithful Israelite against his enemies (Ps 9:4–8); judgment with equity (Pss 98:9; 99:4); protection of the fatherless and oppressed (Ps 10:18); deliverance of a faithful man in answer to prayer (Ps 31:1); causing the land to yield its increase (Ps 85:9–13); salvation of people from exile (Isa 45:8).

What does it mean for humans to act with righteousness? When expressing righteousness toward God, it involves, for example, worshiping only Yahweh (Ps 106:3, in context); loving the Lord faithfully (Ps 15:2–3); and worshiping and serving only the Lord (Josh 24:14). When acting with righteousness toward other humans, it includes, for example, cleanness of hands (2 Sam 22:21, 25); speaking the truth, not slandering, doing no evil to a neighbor, swearing to one's own hurt, not taking a bribe (Ps 15:2–3); saying nothing twisted or crooked (Prov 3:8); being generous (Ps 37:21); acting charity (Tob 1:3; 2:14; 4:6–7); defending the cause of the poor, the needy, crushing the oppressor (Ps 72:1–4); judging for the poor with righteousness, judging with equity (Isa 11:4); not being partial to the poor or deferring to the great, deciding with equity (Lev 19:15); delivering from the oppressor the one who has been robbed, doing no wrong to the alien, the fatherless, the widow, not shedding innocent blood (Jer 22:3); if one has a covenant with someone, being loyal (Gen 21:23—Abraham and Abimelech).

Only a glimmer of the recognition of human need for divine assistance to enable human righteousness is seen in the Old Testament. Psalm 72:1–2 prays: "Give the king thy justice, O God, and thy righteousness to the royal son! May he judge thy people with righteousness, and thy poor with justice."

The Meaning of Righteousness in Matthew's Gospel
In Matthew, the meaning of *righteousness* from the Hebrew Bible and LXX is carried over (covenant faithfulness). The question is, In Matthew does *righteousness* refer to right conduct by humans or to God's gift of salvation or both? Some think it refers to right conduct by humans throughout; others think 3:15, 5:6, and 6:33 refer to God's salvation while 5:10, 5:20, and 6:1 refer to right conduct by humans (21:32 is unclear). Either way, the references to human conduct involve both vertical (6:1ff) and horizontal (5:20) dimensions. Insofar as 5:20 is concerned, we do not have to settle the larger debate. Matthew 5:20 clearly belongs to the righteousness (covenant faithfulness) expected of humans by God. In 5:20 two types of covenant faithfulness are contrasted. There is a *deficient* righteousness: that of the scribes and Pharisees.[15] There is a *surpassing* righteousness: that of those who will enter the kingdom of heaven (presumably, Jesus' disciples).

Matthew refers to Pharisees thirty times. Eighteen references are peculiar to the First Gospel; ten come from the triple tradition; and two are from the double tradition. In Matthew, Pharisees rely on their birth instead of observance of God's will; they teach but do not practice (23:3); they focus on minor things and neglect the major things (23:23–24); they do what they do for human approval (23:5, 27–28); they seek to evade the intent of the Law (23:16–22; 15:1–9); they persecute God's messengers (23:29–36; 12:14), failing to recognize God's Spirit (9:34; 12:24) or to understand the meaning of Jesus' ministry (9:11, 14; 12:2, 38; 15:12; 16:1, 6, 11–12; 19:3; 21:45; 22:15, 34, 41; 27:62).[16]

What is the surpassing righteousness? There are four large thought units in the heart of the Sermon: 5:17–48, 6:1–18, 6:19–34, and 7:1–12. They are held together by an inclusion (5:17 and 7:12). The first two units have introductory material that marks them as separate units (5:17–20 and 6:1). The last two units share a similar organization. Each has two subunits, each is controlled by a prohibition, and each is composed of three components. Each of the four thought units contrasts the higher righteousness with that of the scribes and Pharisees. With 5:21–48, one should compare 15:1–9 (you break the command of God for the sake of your tradition);

---

15. Glasson, "Anti-Pharisaism," 316–20, argues that Matthew has exaggerated the anti-Pharisaic element. The conflict between Matthew's community and the establishment synagogue in the latter part of the first century colors the presentation in the First Gospel of Jesus' relations with the Pharisees.

16. What were the historical Pharisees like? Scholars disagree. Rivkin, *The Hidden Revolution* and "Pharisees," 657–63, regards the Pharisees as a scholarly class of teachers of the twofold Law. Neusner, *From Politics to Piety,* sees them as a group concerned with ritual purity that tries to extend it to the whole population. Modern scholars generally regard them as the best of the Judaism of their time. The rabbis sometimes criticized some Pharisees in ways similar to Matthew's depiction of them (e.g., *j. Ber.* 14b; *b. Sotah* 22b; *Avot R. Nat.* [A] 37; [B] 45): e.g., the ostentatious Pharisee (= the one who wears his good actions ostentatiously on his shoulder). Cf. Matt 6:1–18.

with 6:1–18, compare 23:5 (they do all their deeds to be seen by others); with 6:19–34, compare 15:1–12 and 23:25 (you cleanse the outside of the cup and plate, but inside you are full of greed); with 7:1–12, compare 9:11, 12:2, 15:2, and 23:2–4 (they judge but do not practice what they teach).

If one asks what the surpassing righteousness is in the Sermon on the Mount, it is found in these four thought units. Matthew 5:21–48 asks: What is the purpose of your Bible reading? It advocates a radical, as opposed to a formal, obedience to Scripture. The surpassing righteousness does not seek to evade the intent of the Law. Matthew 6:1–18 asks: Whose attention are you trying to get? It advocates a piety that avoids ostentatious displays because they are directed to the wrong audience. The surpassing righteousness does not seek for human approval. Matthew 6:19–34 asks: How do possessions function in your life and why? It advocates a piety that is neither greedy nor anxious because it trusts God's providential goodness. The surpassing righteousness does not act out of either greed or anxiety with reference to possessions. Matthew 7:1–12 asks: When you exercise your critical function, where do you direct it first? It advocates a lifestyle in which one walks the talk, directing one's critical faculties first toward oneself. Together with 7:15–27, in 7:1–12 the surpassing righteousness practices what it verbally advocates.

How is the surpassing righteousness possible? In Matthew, one is able to live this way only because of God's grace or enablement. One gets into Jesus' community by his summons or attraction (Matt 4:18–22; 4:23–25). One lives in line with Jesus' call because one is "with Jesus"; because Jesus is "with one"; because one can call on the name of Father, Son, and Holy Spirit; and because one has been blessed by Jesus and given promises by him. These are ways Matthew speaks about the divine enablement of a disciple's righteousness.

In conclusion, one may say that for Matthew, living with a surpassing righteousness means living faithfully within a covenant relationship that encompasses both vertical and horizontal dimensions, and is only possible if such a life is divinely enabled. Left to our own resources, we cannot be faithful. So living justly is as much a matter of receiving as it is of giving.

The expression "will not enter the kingdom of heaven" (5:20) is an eschatological judgment uttered by the Matthean Jesus. In *m. Sanhedrin* 10:1 we hear the rabbinic judgment: "All Israelites have a share in the world to come. . . . And these are they that have no share in the world to come: he that says there is no resurrection from the dead prescribed in the Law, and he that says the Law is not from heaven, and an Epicurean, etc." In Matthew 5:20 we hear the Matthean Jesus' judgment: only those with a surpassing righteousness have a share in the Age to Come.

This thought unit, 5:17–20, serves as an introduction to the material that follows. In 5:21–48, the Matthean Jesus shows that he is not abolishing the Scriptures but rather properly interpreting them and indicates what the greater righteousness looks like. Eric Franklin summarizes: Matthew "sees the Law and its outlook as exerting a continuing control upon the way the Christian dispensation is understood. Christians for Matthew are the right observers of the Law as they follow the way of the Messiah who himself interpreted its teachings and propounded a way in which its obligations were to be correctly pursued. In Matthew the Christian way is the legitimate way of pursuing the Law and, since it is the way the Jewish Messiah unfolded, it declares the illegitimacy of any alternative. Hence the strong attack upon the Pharisees and scribes."[17]

There is, moreover, within 5:17–20 an implicit portrait of Jesus. Two things stand out. First, the one who speaks claims to be the true interpreter of the Law and the prophets. This continues the theme found in 4:1–11 (Jesus interprets the Scriptures correctly and in opposition to the way Satan interprets them) and that continues in 28:16–20 (having all authority given to him by God, Jesus is the greatest teacher in the kingdom of heaven; cf. 5:19). Second, the one who speaks assumes he is the End Time judge who can pronounce in the present the standards of the Last Judgment. This thread we have already seen in 5:3–12; we will meet it again in 7:21–23 and later in 19:28 and 25:31–46.

Hans Dieter Betz has argued, as part of his claim that the Sermon is a pre-Matthean unit taken up entire into the First Gospel, that the Sermon on the Mount has "no christology at all, if by christology we mean the saving event of the death and resurrection of Jesus."[18] Betz provides a list of criteria required for a christology that are lacking in the Sermon. "There is no reference to Jesus's crucifixion and resurrection. No christological titles are affirmed, and there is no specifically Christian soteriology, no doctrine of the holy spirit, no reference to church, baptism, or imitation of Christ."[19] In the Sermon, he argues, Jesus is "an authoritative teacher of the Torah, nothing more."[20] His self-reference in the words "I say unto you" asserts only his role as teacher.[21] Unlike the Gospel of Matthew, which depicts Jesus as the eschatological judge, the Sermon portrays him as an advocate only at the judgment, a role that coheres with the Jewish eschatology of that time.[22] The soteriology of the Sermon is based on keeping the Torah as Jesus taught it, not on his atoning death and resurrection, as in the First Gospel as a whole.[23]

---

17. Franklin, *Luke*, 211. To cite this summary of Matthew's position is not to agree with Franklin's overall thesis. In Luke, Jesus is also the true interpreter of the Law.

18. Betz, *Essays on the Sermon*, 76. Cf. "The Problem of Christology," 191–209, and *The Sermon*, 554–55.

19. Betz, "The Problem of Christology," 193.

20. Betz, "In Defense of a Hypothesis," 76.

21. Betz, "The Problem of Christology," 193.

22. Betz, *The Sermon*, 554.

23. Betz, "In Defense of a Hypothesis," 76; *The Sermon*, 554–55.

Responses to Betz's thesis that the Sermon on the Mount is a completely separate entity incorporated into the First Gospel without Matthean editing have indicated stiff resistance from New Testament scholars.[24] Compositional techniques, vocabulary, and themes shared by both the Sermon and the rest of Matthew point to editing by the First Evangelist. If so, then the christology of the sermon must be read in light of the Gospel in its entirety. If read in the context of the whole Gospel, then Jesus' authority in the Sermon depends on his christological identity prepared for in Matthew 1–4 and continued in the rest of the narrative (e.g., 11:25–27; 25:31–46; 28:18).[25]

Even if the Sermon is looked at on its own, Betz's critics claim, it contains more christology than he is willing to acknowledge. In particular, 7:21–23 indicates that Jesus is more than just a teacher or advocate. In this text set at the Last Judgment, Jesus is depicted as a judge who makes decisions. "The sentence is pronounced 'I never knew you; depart from me, you evil-doers.' That is an exclusion formula expressive of Matthew's valuation of Jesus as the eschatological judge."[26] Matthew 5:3–10 provides for disciples depicted in the Beatitudes a proleptic pronouncement of the evaluation of them at the Last Judgment by the judge of the Last Day, Jesus. Matthew 5:20 states who will and who will not make it into the kingdom of heaven. Again, Jesus is assumed to be the judge of the Last Day, the eschatological judge. Matthew 6:14–15 portrays Jesus as the one who knows whom the Father will forgive and whom he will not; in 6:18 and 6:33 Jesus is said to know whom the Father will reward; in 7:1 Jesus knows who will be judged; in 7:7–11 he knows that the Father will answer a certain prayer; and in 7:19 the fate of those who do not bear good fruit. It is proleptic judgment pronounced throughout by the judge of the Last Day. Even if Jesus were depicted only as advocate, however, this picture also occurs in Hebrews 7:25, 1 John 2:1, and Revelation 3:5 as an example of early Christian christology.[27]

The Sermon on the Mount certainly does not reflect the criteria Betz associates with christology. It does, however, reflect a christological pattern that has been called "two foci christology," a christological pattern that focuses on two points: Jesus' authoritative word during his ministry and his return as eschatological judge.[28] These are precisely the two dimensions of christology that we encounter in the Sermon on

---

24. E.g., Allison, "A New Approach," 405–14; Carlston, "Betz on the Sermon," 47–57; Luz, *Matthew 1–7*, 211–13; Stanton, *A Gospel*, 307–25.

25. Topel, review of H. D. Betz, 370–72.

26. Saunders, "A Response to H. D. Betz," 86.

27. Carlston, "Betz on the Sermon," 54–55.

28. Fuller, *The Foundations*, 243–44. Brown, *An Introduction*, lists Acts 3:19–21, 1 Corinthians 16:22, Revelation 22:20, and the Son of Man sayings in Q as reflections of this type of christology.

the Mount. Jesus' authoritative word is heard in such utterances as "But I say to you." His identity as eschatological judge is conveyed in his proleptic pronunciation of the judgment of the Last Day. These two aspects of Jesus' role and identity are, moreover, those found elsewhere in the First Gospel. Our conclusion, then, must be that there is a christology in the Sermon on the Mount but it is not the one Betz was looking for.

Matthew 5:21–26

The Context

Matthew 5:21–48 is a large thought unit usually called "the antitheses." How this unit functions is best understood in light of the polemic in the First Gospel against scribes and Pharisees. In Matthew the scribes and Pharisees are portrayed as teaching but not practicing (23:2–3) and as teaching in a way that evades the intent of the Law (15:1–9). What one finds in 5:21–48 is a situation analogous to that in 15:1–9. The religious leaders, scribes and Pharisees, use their interpretative tradition to evade the true intent and meaning of the Scriptures. Jesus recognizes the evasion and in his reading focuses on God's intent in the Scriptures. In 5:21–48 either a stated or an implied interpretation of Scripture that attempts to evade the full intent of the demands of the Law is opposed by Jesus' own, which aims to set forth the true intent of the Scripture. In none of the six antitheses is the Matthean Jesus annulling the Law. He is rather interpreting the Law through the lenses of the double love command, mercy, and the golden rule.[29] "The refutation . . . is not directed against what God has *in fact* said but against what he has *allegedly* said."[30]

Some scholars think that while some of the antitheses do not annul the Law, some of them do. John Meier is representative.[31] He thinks that the first (murder), second (adultery), and sixth (love of enemy) antitheses do not annul the Law but rather radicalize it. The third (divorce), fourth (oaths), and fifth (retaliation), however, he thinks annul the Law.[32] Annulment is all right because all of the prophecies have been fulfilled in Jesus' death and resurrection, bringing the Law to an end. So the righteousness that exceeds that of the scribes and Pharisees consists of doing all that Jesus commanded, including that which annuls Scripture. Two arguments render this reading suspect. First, in ancient Judaism "the law was believed totally, but it was also assumed that the meaning of the law is ambiguous and must be debated.

---

29. Gerhardsson, "Hermeneutic Program," 134, 140–41; Snodgrass, "Matthew and the Law," 99–127.

30. Betz, *The Sermon*, 208.

31. Meier, *Law and History.* Suggs, *Wisdom, Christology, and Law,* 113, views the third, fourth, fifth, and sixth antitheses as abrogating the Law; Schweizer, *The Good News,* 110, views the third, fifth, and sixth as abrogations.

32. Meier, *Law and History,* 140–59.

. . . Sometimes one passage of scripture is quoted as justification for not obeying another passage. . . . abrogation of specific precepts of the written torah was not unusual in Jesus's milieu."[33] Such behavior was not regarded as abolishing the Law. Second, in ancient Judaism "it is not against the law to be stricter than the law requires."[34] Taking these two arguments together, most scholars regard the antitheses not as an annulment of the Law but as a struggle for the right interpretation of it.[35] It is in this way that they will be read in this volume.

There are six antitheses laid out in terms of two groups of three. The beginning of the second series is signaled by *palin* (again) in verse 33. The first antithesis is 5:21–26.

Matthew 5:21–26
Formally, the unit looks like this:

You have heard (v. 21):	[You shall not kill = Exod 20:13//Deut 5:17] + [whoever kills shall be liable to judgment = Exod 21:12; Lev 24:17; Num 35:12];
But I say (v. 22):	Everyone who is angry + shall be liable to the local court, Whoever insults his brother + shall be liable to the Sanhedrin, Whoever says "You fool" + shall be liable to the hell of fire.
Two illustrations	(Take the initiative to restore broken relations) 1) Making an offering to God while being at odds with a brother (vv. 23–24). Cf. *m. Yoma* 8:9; *m. B. Qam.* 9:12 2) Making amends with a legal adversary before going to court (vv. 25–26)

It is now necessary to focus on the content of the first antithesis. We will take up each verse in order.

Verse 21. How should the formula "You have heard that it was said to those of ancient times" be understood? "You" refers to the disciples who are auditors; "have heard" probably refers to what was taught in the synagogue; "it was said" likely refers to God or Torah; and "those of ancient times" to the Sinai generation and the successive chain of teachers. This, then, is referring to a traditional interpretation of Scripture. The text reads like a combination of apodictic (You shall not murder) and

---

33. Snodgrass, "Matthew and the Law," 119; cf. Sanders, *Jesus and Judaism*, 248–49.
34. Sanders, *Jesus and Judaism*, 10, 260.
35. Martin, "Matthew on Christ," 53–70.

casuistic law (whoever murders shall be liable to judgment). Taken together, however, the result is casuistic. *If* this is done, *then* this will follow. Murder will bring one before the human court.

Verse 22. This is a patterned response. There are three members describing first the *behavior* (ongoing anger with a brother or sister, insulting a brother or sister by calling him or her "empty head" or "fool") and then the *consequences* (liable to judgment, liable to the Sanhedrin, liable to Gehenna—in increasing intensity or severity of punishment).

The values echo Jewish sentiment about behavior. Compare, for example, Sirach 22:24—"The vapor and smoke of the furnace precede the fire; so insults precede bloodshed"; *Testament of Levi* 4:2—Hatred does not want to hear repeated his commands concerning love of neighbor; 4.6—Hate wants to kill the living; *2 Enoch* 44:2–3—"Whoever insults a person's face, insults the face of a king, and treats the face of the Lord with repugnance. The one who treats with contempt the face of any person treats the face of the Lord with contempt. The one who expresses anger to any person without provocation will reap anger in the last judgment"; *m. Abot* 3.12 —R. Eleazar of Modiim said: "If a man profanes the hallowed things and despises the set feasts and *puts his fellow to shame publicly,* and makes void the covenant of Abraham our father, . . . even though a knowledge of the law and good works are his, he has no share in the world to come"; *b. Baba Mesia* 58b—A teacher of Mishnah taught before Rab Nahman ben Isaac: "If anyone makes the face of a companion pale before a crowd, it is as if he shed blood."

The consequences of the behavior, however, are disproportionate. Although this looks like casuistic law, it is only as parody of such. This is confirmed by the fact that, if Law, the Matthean Jesus is in violation of his own injunction (Matt 21:12— anger; 23:17—calling another "fool"). Furthermore, anger is not the type of misstep that can be judged by a human court. One is, therefore, not to take verse 22 as wooden casuistry.[36] Rather, verse 22 seems to be offering an interpretation of the divine intent behind the Law cited in verse 21.

If so, what reading of the divine intent behind the prohibition against murder would need to be present to make verse 22 an appropriate response? Verse 21 would need to assume that the destruction of a relationship among God's people is limited to the physical act of murder. Verse 22 would then counter by saying that relationships can be destroyed by ongoing anger and by public humiliation of another as well as by murder. So God's intent behind the Law is that one not destroy relationships among brothers and sisters by whatever means.[37] This, then, offers a new way

---

36. Boring, "Matthew," 190.

37. This seems to be the type of argument used when a case involves a written document. Disagreement occurs when one party follows the exact words that are written and the other directs his pleading to what he says the writer meant. (Cf. Cicero, *Inv.* 42.121–22.)

of *seeing* the divine intent: God's will is that there be no destruction of relationships that is your doing.

Verses 23–24 (Mk 11:25). This is the first of two illustrations that speak about taking the initiative to restore broken relationships. It refers to making an offering to God while being at odds with a brother or sister. Its sentiment expresses the values of its ancient Jewish context. For example, consider Leviticus 5:14–16— restitution is required before sacrifice; Sirach 34:29—"When one prays and another curses, to whose voice will the Lord listen?"; *m. Yoma* 8.9—"For transgressions that are between a man and his fellow, the Day of Atonement effects atonement only if he has appeased his fellow. This did R. Eleazar b. Azariah (T2) expound"; *b. Baba Qamma* 9.12—If a person brings what he has stolen before he makes his guilt offering, he has fulfilled his obligation; but if he has brought his guilt offering before he brought what he had stolen, he has not yet fulfilled his obligation.

This cannot be a literal case. If one is worshiping in the temple in Jerusalem and remembers a problem with another, it is not literally possible to leave the temple, go several days to Galilee, be reconciled with the other, go back several days to Jerusalem, and pick up where one left off.[38] This is hyperbole designed to make a point.

Verses 25–26 (Lk 12:58–59). This is the second illustration. It refers to making amends with a legal adversary before going to court. Do it quickly before bad consequences occur. It is the type of situation envisioned by Proverbs 6:1–5 and 25:7b– 10. The two illustrations speak about one's taking the initiative to restore broken relationships. They oppose the assumption that it is possible to be right with God without being reconciled to one's brother or sister. The divine intent is seen to be: Let there be no broken relationships that you do not seek to mend.

Taken together, verses 21–22 and 23–26 say that the divine intent in the prohibition in the Law against murder is that there be no broken relationships among God's people, either that I cause (v. 22) or that I fail to restore when I have been at fault (vv. 23–24, 25–26). Verse 22 also challenges the claim in verse 21 that the wrong interpretation of the Law came down through an authoritative chain of tradition.[39]

This new way of seeing challenges a reading of the Law as limited to the destruction of a relationship by murder (the physical termination of a life). Rather than functioning as a law prohibiting anger and insults, the antithesis aims to shape the disciple's character in the direction of concern for the health and wholeness of relationships among God's people. The material functions as a verbal icon through which one sees into the divine will. To speak of a verbal, as opposed to a pictorial,

38. Boring, "Matthew," 190.
39. Betz, *The Sermon*, 217.

icon would be no stretch for ancient Mediterranean peoples. Lucian, in his *Essays in Portraiture* 8, for example, thinks Homer the best of all painters! Lucian, moreover, uses the same language to characterize a painting on a wall as he does his painting of word pictures (*egrapsamen;* 17–18). Greek Orthodox theologians virtually equate icons and Scripture. John of Damascus argues that Scripture seeks to speak of the "unknowable" (God), "imaging it in verbal form." There are, therefore, two types of images, verbal and visual.[40] Theodore the Studite in speaking about the Gospels says that Christ's image was drawn in writing by the apostles. So icons and Scripture are two sides of the same coin.[41] Leonide Ouspensky contends that "One single content is witnessed in two different ways—with words or with images—conveying the same revelation in the light of the same sacred and living Tradition of the Church." He specifically says "the Gospel is a verbal icon of Christ, the image of spiritual perfection."[42] Like the painted icon, the verbal icon provides a window into divine reality, making possible the perception of the spiritual world. In the Sermon on the Mount the words of Jesus function as verbal icons enabling disciples to *see* into the divine reality of God's unconditioned will. Character is then shaped as the disciple comes to see differently. This is the primary function of Matthew 5:21–26, the shaping of character. The pericope can be used also in the process of decision making. It is to that task that we now turn.

The Contribution of Matthew 5:21–26 to Decision Making

If Matthew 5:21–26 aims not to give a law prohibiting the emotion of anger and insulting acts but to shape the character of a disciple by enabling a new way of seeing the divine intent, what does the material in this pericope have to do with the formulation of a normative Christian stance about anger (and insults as expressions of anger)? In order for Matthew 5:21–26 to function as part of a normative guide for Christian decision making, the pericope must be read in context. Actually there are three contexts that are a required part of this reading: in the context of Matthew as a whole,[43] in the context of the New Testament as a whole,[44] and in the context of the biblical plot as a whole.[45] We begin with the first.

---

40. John of Damascus, *On the Divine Images*.

41. Theodore the Studite, *On the Holy Icons*.

42. Ouspensky, *Theology of the Icon*, 165.

43. Allison, *The Sermon*, 9, says: "The Sermon on the Mount belongs to a book apart from which it was never intended to be read. This matters because so often interpretation has gone astray by ignoring the Sermon's context."

44. Hagner, "Ethics and the Sermon," 55, contends that an adequate hermeneutic must take into consideration the whole of the NT with the love command as its guide.

45. McArthur, *Understanding the Sermon*, 120–22, critiques the "analogy of scripture view" because it reduces all of Scripture to the same level and undermines the radical character of Jesus' demands. Appeal to the biblical plot avoids this criticism because within the overall plot of the Bible there are different levels of authority.

Reading in the context of Matthew as a whole requires one to consider passages such as Matthew 21:12–17, which assumes anger on Jesus' part, and Matthew 23:17, which has Jesus call the scribes and Pharisees "blind fools." Should we follow Allison and focus on the discontinuity between Jesus' teaching in 5:21–26 and his behavior, when necessary, in chapters 21 and 23?[46] Probably not. Since Matthew depicts Jesus as the one who fulfills all righteousness (3:15), this does not seem like a fruitful avenue of approach. Further, since Matthew regards Jesus as faithful to Torah (8:4; 9:20; 12:1–8; 14:36; 15:1–9; 23:23–24) and Jesus' teaching as fulfilling, not relaxing, the Law and the prophets, granting him the highest status in the kingdom (28:18), a focus on discontinuity seems out of place. The Matthean Jesus' life and teaching are depicted by the First Evangelist as corresponding to one another. We must wait until it becomes clear how all these pieces fit together with regard to anger and the address of others as fools.

Reading 5:21–26 in the context of the New Testament as a whole confronts us with texts such as Mark 1:41 and 3:5, where Jesus is angry, and Ephesians 4:26–27, in which verse 26a echoes Psalm 4:4a, verse 26b explains what verse 26a means, and verse 27 provides a basis for the action: Do not hold on to anger. This is similar to Plutarch, *De amicitia fratrum* 488BC, who says the Pythagoreans taught that anger should not extend beyond sunset. Compare also Ephesians 4:31–32, whose "put away anger" means "forgive one another" (i.e., do not hold on to your anger); Colossians 3:8, which refers to orientations to life, so the anger referred to is that which is held on to; 1 Timothy 2:8, which refers to anger and quarreling, assuming anger that is held on to; Luke 11:40, where Jesus says "You fools"; Luke 12:20, which has God say "You fool"; 1 Corinthians 15:36, where Paul says "You fool"; and Galatians 3:1, in which Paul addresses his readers as "O foolish Galatians."

Reading in terms of the Bible as a whole enables one to see that in the Old Testament there are two foci in its reflections on anger. The first focus is on anger for a righteous cause: for example, God's anger for a just cause (e.g., Exod 4:14; Num 11:10; 12:9; 22:22; 25:3; Deut 4:25; 6:15; 7:4; 9:18; 29:20; Josh 23:16; Judg 2:12; 2 Sam 6:7; 24:1; 1 Kings 14:15; 16:2; Ps 106:32); Moses' anger (Exod 32:19), Jeremiah's anger (Jer 6:11), and Sirach's unrighteous anger (1:22) cannot be justified. (It is this stream of thought that produced the textual variant ["for any cause"—*eike*] in Matt 5:22.) The second focus of Old Testament reflection on anger is that one refrain from anger that is held on to (that issues in revenge, etc.). Consider such examples as Psalm 37:8 ("Refrain from anger and forsake wrath") and Sirach 27:30 ("Anger and wrath, these also are abominations, yet a sinner holds on to them"). In no place in the threefold context of the Sermon is the emotion of anger ever prohibited

---

46. Allison, *The Sermon*, 71.

in an absolute way. What is prohibited is the holding on to anger and the expression of anger in negative ways.

Does this mean that Matthew 5:22 stands alone in prohibiting absolutely the emotion of anger? A close reading of Matthew 5:22 shows that *pas ho orgizomenos* is a present participle that quite naturally yields the meaning "every one who is angry in an ongoing way," that is, who holds on to his or her anger and expresses it in acts of insult toward a brother or sister. In this case, Matthew 5:22 fits into the larger biblical stream of prohibition against one's holding on to his or her anger and expressing it in harmful ways toward others. At this point, but not until this point, is one ready to use Matthew 5:21–26 in Christian ethical decision making.[47]

Matthew 5:27–30

The second antithesis comes in Matthew 5:27–30. In form it looks like this.

You have heard (v. 27): You shall not commit adultery (Exod 20:14// Deut 5:18).

But I say (v. 28): Everyone who looks at a woman lustfully has already committed adultery with her in his heart.

Two illustrations (Be whole!)

1) If your right eye offend (v. 29)

2) If your right hand offend (v. 30)

Let us examine the contents of the second antithesis by looking at each verse in order.

Verse 27. You have heard that it was said + "You shall not commit adultery" (Exod 20:14//Deut 5:18; cf. Matt 19:18). This is apodictic law. No human court punishes this sin. It is God's responsibility. No explicit interpretation is given of the biblical command, but in order for the following contrast (v. 28) to make sense it has to be assumed that the accepted interpretation of the command in Matthew's milieu is that the physical act of sex with another man's wife is what is prohibited. (Remember a similar line of reasoning in Matthew 5:21.)[48]

Verse 28. But I say + everyone who *ho blepōn* (goes on looking at) the *gynaika* (the wife of another man—so the context) *pros to epithumēsai* (for the purpose of coveting her—in the LXX this verb translates the Hebrew *covet* in Exod 20:17) has

---

47. The Greco-Roman world regarded anger as dangerous, potentially destructive, needing careful regulation, if not elimination. The *Iliad* begins with Achilles' anger, an anger that is held onto. He becomes for later Mediterranean culture the archetype of the excessively angry man. The major philosophical schools spoke with one voice about the moral priority of dispassion. All wanted to avoid the madness of anger held onto like that of Achilles. The Matthean Jesus spoke in a cultural context sensitive to the issue at hand. Cf. Harris, *Restraining Rage.*

48. Betz, *The Sermon*, 231.

already committed adultery with her in his heart (cf. Matt 15:19—out of the heart come evil intentions . . . adultery).

Adultery in an ancient Jewish context, by convention, refers to a married woman's having sex with a man other than her husband. Both woman and man were guilty of adultery whether or not the man was married.[49] The Matthean Jesus' interpretation of the prohibition against adultery goes deeper. The phrase "everyone who looks at a woman with lust" from the NRSV needs clarification. First, "who looks" translates a present participle whose natural meaning is conveyed by the paraphrase "who goes on looking." Second, "woman" translates a term that ought to be rendered "wife of another man."[50] Third, "with lust" needs two clarifications. On the one hand, "with" translates a preposition that ought to be translated "for the purpose of."[51] On the other hand, "lust" renders an infinitive whose verb in the LXX translates the Hebrew "covet" (Exod 20:17//Deut 5:21, the latter placing first, after "You shall not covet," "your neighbor's wife"). Taken together, these clarifications yield a translation that runs: "I say to you that everyone who goes on looking at another man's wife for the purpose of coveting her for his own has already committed adultery with her in his heart."[52] "Jesus does not, of course, refer to passing attraction, but the deliberate harboring of desire for an illicit relationship."[53]

Ancient courts did not assess liability for mere intention.[54] Consider the following data. Justinian, *Digest* 47.2.1.1–2, says that the bare intent to commit theft does not make a man a thief. Josephus, *Antiquities* 12.358, says that merely to wish a thing without actually doing it is not deserving of punishment. The rabbis distinguished three categories: intention (not triable); intention + unsuccessful attempt (triable); and act (triable). "You shall not covet," dealing with intention, was not enforced by human courts but by the power of God under the terms of the covenant.

On occasion, however, Jews and pagans regarded adultery as involving act and intent. Consider the following examples: 1QpHab 5.7—whoring originates behind the eyes; Sirach 9:8—"Turn away your eyes . . . and do not gaze at beauty belonging to another"; *Testament of Issachar* 7:2—"I have not had intercourse with any woman other than my wife, nor was I promiscuous by lustful look"; *Apocalypse of Moses* 19:3—"Lust is the root of every sin"; *Testament of Issachar* 4:53—"Do not look at a woman with a lustful eye"; *Leviticus Rabbah* 23:12—"You must not suppose that only he who has committed the crime with his body is called an adulterer, if he

---

49. Boring, "Matthew," 190.

50. Luz, *Matthew 1–7*, 294.

51. Arndt and Gingrich, *Greek-English Lexicon*, 710; Bruner, *Matthew 1–12*, 183, says that Jesus condemns looking "in order to lust."

52. Allison, *The Sermon*, 74.

53. Keener, *A Commentary*, 189.

54. Jackson, "Liability for Mere Intention," 192–255.

commits adultery with his eyes he is also called an adulterer"; *Numbers Rabbah* 8:5—
"The moment a man contemplates sinning it is as though he has committed as tres-
pass against the Omnipresent"; 2 Peter 2:14—"They have eyes full of adultery,
insatiable for sin"; Aelian, *Variae historiae* 14.42—Xenocrates, the companion of
Plato, said that it made no difference whether one set one's eyes in a strange house
or placed one's feet there, for the one who looks on forbidden places is guilty of the
same sin as the one who goes there; Epictetus, *Dissertations* 2.18.15; Cicero, *De
finibus* 3.9.32.[55] Of course, no human court could try a person for intent. The lustful heart is a matter for God or the gods to judge.

Verse 29. The first illustration: If your right eye causes you to stumble, tear it out
and cast it from you, for it is better for you that one of your members perish and
your whole body not go into Gehenna. (Cf. Matt 18:9; Mk 9:47; Num 15:39; Ezk
20:7–8.)

Verse 30. The second illustration: If your right hand causes you to stumble, cut
it off and cast it from you, for it is better for you that one of your members perish
and your whole body not go into Gehenna. (Cf. Matt 18:8; Mark 9:43.)

These two illustrations are hyperbole;[56] they are not to be taken literally.[57]
Together they call for a radical integration of the self. Whatever does not fit into the
self's integration around God's will is to be jettisoned, whether it be eye (intent) or
hand (action). The sentiment is reflected in Philo, *Planting* 36–38, where he says
the soul needs to be cultivated, protected, pruned, and even have parts cut off if necessary in pursuit of moral development. "The maiming that moral life requires will
be a thousandfold repaid with the wholeness of selfhood and the life of God that
comes with amputation."[58]

The point of 5:27–30 is that the divine intent behind "do not commit adultery"
is that one not violate another's spouse. Such violation may be due to covetousness
as well as the physical act. Here the Matthean Jesus interprets the seventh Commandment by the tenth. (Cf. Matt 19:1–9, where Jesus appeals to Gen 1–2 in his interpretation of Deut 24, for the same type of argument.) The second member is, therefore,
unfolding the true meaning of the first member, not sweeping away the first.[59] The
Matthean Jesus' argument is be whole in your relationships. This enables the auditor to *see* God's intent in a new way. So, if some part of you is not integrated, eliminate the unintegrated part. This enables the auditor to *see* his or her responsibility

---

55. "Pittacus of Mitylene, on being asked if anyone escapes the notice of the gods in commit-
ting some sinful act, said: 'Not even in contemplating it'" (Hock and O'Neil, *The Chreia*, 331).
56. Hagner, *Matthew 1–13*, 121.
57. As, for example, Origen's castration (Eusebius, *Church History* 6.8).
58. Bruner, *Matthew 1–12*, 186.
59. Davies, *The Setting*, 102. So the antitheses are not antithetical at all. So Jack Levison, "A
Better Righteousness," 171–94.

clearly. The position being opposed is a reading of the commandment "Do not commit adultery" that assumes adultery is limited to the physical act of intercourse. The position being proposed is a reading that calls for a person's being whole in avoidance of adultery.[60]

What kind of statement is this? It is not law that is subject to a human court. Such courts cannot deal with intent. Like Exodus 20:17//Deuteronomy 5:21 ("You shall not covet"), this is subject to God's judgment, for God is the one who looks on the heart. It is not a fence about the Torah. It does not say "do not look lustfully" in order to prevent the violation of the law against adultery; it says rather that looking lustfully is adultery. The assumption is that adultery is something that involves the whole person, not just his/her body. The statement is a verbal icon through which one is able to view the unconditioned divine will. It is a catalyst for a new way of seeing.

Such perceptions of the divine will lead to different dispositions and intentions. Character is being formed. On the first level of reading, then, Matthew 5:27–30 functions as a catalyst for character formation. How is it possible to hear this antithesis, or the previous one for that matter, as other than a new law?

There are two very different ways that one can read such material. On the one hand, it is possible to read this text as a "new law" with a more stringent demand than the old law. One then tends to see the Sermon in a context of covenantal nomism. One has gotten into Jesus' community by his call and grace, but now it is necessary, out of gratitude, to be obedient to the new law. On the other hand, it is also possible to regard the text as a "verbal icon." If so, then one looks through the lens of the command into the divine will behind the text. Such a vision of God and the divine will is transformative for those who see. To see God—in this case through the medium of a verbal icon—always changes the self. One is changed as one contemplates the divine will and is drawn into it. When one reads this way one sees the Sermon in the context of new covenant piety in which God's grace enables the disciples' lives moment by moment from first to last.

Matthew 5:27–30 and Decision Making

How can Matthew 5:27–30 be used in Christian decision making? One must look at its threefold context.

Reading in the context of Matthew as a whole requires one to take account of a text like Matthew 15:19 ("For out of the heart come evil intentions . . . adultery"). The Matthean Jesus looks at human beings as wholes, inner and outer, intention and act. He perceives God's intent to cover the whole.

---

60. Just as in the case of the first antithesis, the issue here seems to be a controversy involving a written document in which one party follows the exact words that are written and the other directs his pleading to what he says the writer meant. (Cf. Cicero, *Inv.* 42.121–22.)

Considering the evidence in the New Testament as a whole involves passages such as Romans 2:22 ("You that forbid adultery, do you commit adultery?") and 13:9 ("The commandments, 'You shall not commit adultery . . . you shall not covet'; . . . are summed up in this word, 'Love your neighbor as yourself.' Love does no wrong to a neighbor; therefore love is the fulfilling of the law"); 1 Corinthians 6:9–10 ("Do you not know that wrongdoers will not inherit the kingdom of God? Do not be deceived! . . . adulterers . . . none of these will inherit the kingdom of God"); James 2:10–11 ("For whoever keeps the whole law but fails in one point has become accountable for all of it. For the one who said, 'You shall not commit adultery,' also said, 'You shall not murder.' Now if you do not commit adultery but if you murder, you have become a transgressor of the law"); Mark 10:19//Luke 18:20 ("You know the commandments: . . . You shall not commit adultery"). In his negative attitude toward adultery, the Matthean Jesus is one with the rest of the New Testament. In his emphasis on the intention as well as the act, he offers a more comprehensive perspective.

When reading in light of the Bible as a whole, one must consider texts such as Leviticus 20:10 ("If a man commits adultery with the wife of his neighbor, both the adulterer and the adulteress shall be put to death") and Proverbs 6:32 ("He who commits adultery has no sense; he who does it destroys himself").

The context speaks with one negative voice. Adultery is prohibited by God; God judges adulterers. The Matthean Jesus' teaching is a part of this unified voice. He also belongs to that stream of ancient thought that held adultery to involve the whole person: intent as well as physical act. With this in mind, it is possible to proceed to use Matthew 5:27–30 in one's decision making.

The data surveyed in this thought unit raises a further question: How original is the Matthean Jesus' teaching, given the parallels? It is clear that Jesus' originality cannot be understood in terms that preclude others from having said many or most of the same things he said. There is, in fact, a parallel for almost all of what is said in the Sermon on the Mount. The Jewish and Greco-Roman parallels mean "that any interpretation of the Sermon that sees it as altogether a bolt from the blue, as something fundamentally unprecedented, is mistaken. . . . [T]he truth of Jesus's teaching cannot in any way depend on its novelty."[61] Jesus' distinctiveness rather lies in what he chose and what he omitted from his culture, and in the relative importance each teaching was given in his overall hierarchy of values.[62]

---

61. Allison, *The Sermon*, 7, 8.

62. Cf. the comments by Klauck, *The Religious Context*, 2–6. Klauck speaks to the issue of the thought content of the NT as a whole. His remarks are applicable to the question of the Matthean Jesus' teachings as well: "The critical eye will see clearly that the specific characteristic of Christianity in many cases is to be found less in the details and the individual aspects than in the total

Matthew 5:31–32

Matthew 5:21–48 consists of six antitheses in two groups of three. The third and last of the antitheses in the first group is 5:31–32. It is linked with the previous antithesis by the key word *adultery.* In form 5:31–32 looks like this.

It was said (v. 31):	Whoever divorces his wife, let him give her a certificate of divorce (Deut 24:1 as interpreted in the Matthean Jesus' time).
But I say (v. 32):	1) Everyone who divorces his wife, except for *porneia,* makes her an adulteress. 2) Whoever marries a divorced woman commits adultery.

Matthew 5:31–32 as a Catalyst for Character Formation

In form, 5:31–32 is casuistic law. In these circumstances, if one acts this way, then this is the result. Its content, moreover, deals with an act (divorce), not an intention, and so it could involve a court. It has, as a result, often been treated as ecclesiastical or civil law.[63] Given the context, however, it is more likely that the third antithesis should be treated as the first two and the last three: not as case law but as a prophetic saying that functions as a catalyst for character formation.[64] A focus on the content of this antithesis should lend support to this reading. We will examine the text following each verse in sequence.

Verse 31. "Whoever divorces his wife, let him give her a certificate of divorce." This is a reference to Deuteronomy 24:1–2 as understood in Jesus' time. Divorce was assumed to be permissible in a Jewish context. The issue was, on what grounds was divorce possible (cf. Matt 19:3)? The interpretation of Deuteronomy 24:1–2 assumed by Matthew 5:31 holds divorce is permissible. Among the teachers there was disagreement about what constituted grounds for divorce. Philo (*Spec. Laws* 3.30–31) assumed divorce was permissible "for any cause whatsoever." Josephus likewise (*Ant.* 3.276–77; 4.253) took it to be acceptable "for whatever cause." *Targum Jonathan* radically refashioned Malachi 2:16 ("For I hate divorce, says the Lord, the God of Israel") by rendering it "If you hate her, divorce her." The school of Shammai said only unchastity was a legitimate ground for divorce. The school of Hillel

---

pattern and in the unifying centre-point, which gives structure to the Christian universe of meaning" (5).

63. Allison, *The Sermon,* 7, 11, says that Matthew 5:31–32 "is the exception to the rule that the Sermon is not legislation."

64. Keener, *And Marries Another,* 23–27. Beare, *The Gospel,* 155, says: "there is no room to hold that Jesus intended such sayings to be taken as legislation, even for his followers, much less for the state."

said even if she spoiled a dish for him (*m. Git.* 9.10) the wife could be divorced by her husband. Some claim that CD 4.19–5.6 forbids divorce. A careful reading in context makes it more likely that this is only a prohibition of polygamy (cf. the reference to Deut 27:17 about the king not multiplying wives to himself). In Matthew 5:31 the assumed interpretation opposed by the Matthean Jesus apparently is that divorce is permissible on any grounds so long as a bill of divorce is given to the woman. The essential formula in the bill of divorce was "Lo, you are free to marry any man" (*m. Git.* 9.3). It was a writ of emancipation. The woman now belonged to herself. The purpose of the bill of divorce was to protect the woman and the man who might marry her from the charge of adultery. The assumption was that the bill of divorce sundered the marital relation with the divorcing husband.

Whether or not a Jewish woman also had the right to divorce her husband is a debated issue in the present time. There is evidence that, in some circles at least, the woman could indeed give her husband a writ of divorce.[65] Philo (*Spec. Laws* 30) assumes a woman is able to get divorced from her husband for any cause. In Jewish marriage contracts from Elephantine, women have a right to divorce equal to that of men.[66] Salome, King Herod's sister, sent her husband a bill of divorce (Josephus, *Ant.* 15.259–60). Papyrus Se'elim 13 is a divorce bill sent from a wife to her husband, dated about 134–35 C.E. It is written in Aramaic, in a fully Jewish court of law, at the time of the Bar Kokhba revolt. Do these examples reflect Jews' rejection of Jewish practice or do they reflect Jews' rejection of Pharisaic practice? By mid second century C.E. the possibility of a woman divorcing her husband was apparently accepted by some rabbis (*j. Ket.* 5.8).[67] In Matthew, the sayings of Jesus assume Pharisaic or majority rabbinic practice. It is only the man who can divorce the woman. The argument makes sense only on this presupposition.

Verse 32. "Anyone who divorces his wife . . . causes her to commit adultery; and whoever marries a divorced woman commits adultery." This logion operates within the framework of adultery as a violation by a man's spouse and of a man's spouse. It says the divorcing husband causes the divorced wife to commit adultery when she remarries. The second husband also is involved in adultery when he marries the divorced woman. Since the bill of divorce was intended to protect both the divorced wife and the next husband from any charges of adultery, the logion must assume that the bill of divorce did not free the woman from her first marriage. The assumption by the Matthean Jesus must be that the woman is still the first man's wife. Matthew

---

65. Ilan, "On a Newly Published Divorce Bill," 195–202; Brewer, "Jewish Women Divorcing," 349–57.

66. Porten and Yardeni, *Textbook of Aramaic Documents,* 30–33, 60–63, 78–83.

67. There were always exceptional cases where the wife could sue for divorce (e.g., *m. Ketub.* 5:5; 7:2–5, 9–10), but in these instances the man still did the putting away.

19:4–5 says God's intention in creation was one man and one woman in permanent union. Matthew 5:32 assumes a human bill of divorce does not cancel the permanent union intended by God. After all, Deuteronomy 24:1–4 stands in a tradition tending to limit divorce.[68] The Matthean Jesus would be saying that the correct interpretation of the intent of Deuteronomy 24:1–2, then, was the protection of the wife and the other man from charges of adultery. But this protection is given not by issuing a bill of divorce but by foregoing divorce altogether.

Verse 32. ". . . except on the ground of unchastity." *Porneia* means "adultery" in its Matthean context. Some scholars, however, have argued for it being a reference to incest.[69] The arguments against include: *porneia* is not the term for incest that would have been familiar to a Jew reading Leviticus 18 in the LXX;[70] an illicit marriage would not have required a divorce; there is no evidence that Matthew is specifically concerned about the lives of Gentile converts.[71] The arguments for *adultery* are threefold: both *moichea* and *porneia* can be used of adultery (cf. Jer 3:8ff. LXX), the former used more of men, the latter of women;[72] Matthew 1:19 speaks of Joseph as a righteous man who aimed to divorce Mary quietly when he believed she was pregnant by means other than himself;[73] and the evidence from ancient Near Eastern culture favors it.[74]

Jewish (e.g., Jer 3:8–9; Hos 2:4; *m. Sot.* 6.1), Greek (e.g., Demosthenes, *Neaer.* 115), and Roman law (e.g., *Lex Julia de adulteriis* of 18 B.C.E.)[75] mandated divorce in the case of adultery. Unfaithfulness was not only sufficient grounds for divorce; it was something that necessitated it. Consider 2 Samuel 20:3, where after Absalom had had intercourse with David's ten concubines, David did not go in to them again. *Testament of Reuben* 3:10–15 says that after Reuben had been with Bilhah, Jacob had no further relations with her. 1QapGen 20.15 has Abraham in Egypt entreat God that Pharaoh not be able to violate Sarah, whom he had taken away from her husband: "May he not be able to defile my wife *away from me* tonight." In *m. Sotah* 5:1, an adulteress becomes sexually forbidden to her husband and to her lover. The early Christian *Shepherd of Hermas* reflects on the issue of whether or not it was sinful for a husband to live with a wife who had committed adultery. Hermas's

68. Betz, *The Sermon,* 246.
69. E.g., Fitzmyer, "The Matthean Divorce Texts," 197–226; Witherington, "Matthew 5:32 and 19:9," 571–76.
70. P. Segal, *The Halakah of Jesus,* 97.
71. Hagner, *Matthew 1–13,* 123–24.
72. Luz, *Matthew 1–7,* 306; Davies and Allison, *Matthew 1–7,* 531. This dual usage explains the repetition of the terms in the vice list of Matthew 15:19.
73. Allison, "Divorce, Celibacy, and Joseph," 3–10.
74. Janzen, "The Meaning of PORNEIA," 66–80.
75. Corbett, *The Roman Law,* 133–46, says that according to the Julian law in Rome, a man who failed to divorce his wife caught in adultery was guilty of the offense of condoning.

answer is that the husband is not guilty as long as he does not know about it, but he must put her away if he is aware of it and she does not repent of her sin ("Mandate," 4.1.4–10). This widespread tradition was evidently the assumption by Matthew, as reflected in Matthew 1:19 where Joseph is called a righteous man when he resolves to put Mary away, assuming she has been unfaithful. So there was the idea that any sexual interference with an existing marriage bond produces a state of impurity that precludes the resumption of that marriage.[76] Given the way of thinking in Matthew's context, a woman who had been unfaithful to her husband had already dissolved the marriage bond. The husband in divorcing her could not be causing her to commit adultery. She had already done that herself.[77] The intent of the language, then, is that the husband, insofar as it depends on him, not be responsible for adultery.

Assuming God's intent of a permanent marriage union, the Matthean Jesus addresses the husband who assumes he may divorce his wife for any reason on the basis of Deuteronomy 24:1–2. Jesus says that the intent of the Law was the protection of the divorced woman and the man who would then marry her from any charge of adultery. This cannot be done by a bill of divorce. The marriage is still intact in God's eyes. To protect her and the other man, therefore, requires one to stay married. So the husband is to see to it that he is not responsible for adultery.

What kind of language is this? It is not the kind of law that a human court can deal with. It is too specific. It does not speak about a woman seeking divorce, the remarriage of the divorcing husband, or remarriage after adultery. It is also too extreme. Marriages end. What then? Its enforcement, moreover, is not by human hands. It is "in God's eyes" that the relation is permanent. So this is a prophetic statement enabling the auditors to *see* the unconditioned divine will that marriages be indissoluble and to hear the call for the disciple to be a person who does not violate the indissoluble marriage bond. The disciple is formed so that he or she determines that he or she will not be the cause of adultery. The language functions not like law but like a verbal icon. It is a window into the divine will behind the words. The logion aims at shaping the character of the disciples, because they *see* differently, are disposed differently, and have different intentions.

Matthew 5:31–32 in Decision Making
Of what relevance is Matthew 5:31–32 for Christian decision making? It must be read in a threefold context.

Reading 5:31–32 in Matthew as a whole takes one to chapter 19, where the issues are raised again. Matthew 19:3–8 distinguishes between God's intention in creation (apart from sin) and God's conditioned will (in light of sin). The Matthean Jesus'

---

76. Bockmuehl, "Matthew 5:32; 19:9," 291–95.
77. Betz, *The Sermon*, 250.

position is that of God's unconditioned will. Matthew 19:9 turns the tables on the man who divorces his wife and marries another. In this case, he is the one who commits adultery, except in the case of unchastity on the part of his spouse. This is presumably for the same reason as in 5:31–32: the divorce does not annul the marriage in God's eyes.

Reading 5:31–32 in the context of the New Testament as a whole involves one with the multiple divorce texts in the canon. Mark 10:2–9 distinguishes between God's unconditioned and conditioned wills, identifying Jesus' stance with the former. The former is against divorce; the latter permits it. Mark 10:11–12 broadens the adultery of remarriage after divorce to include both men and women. Luke 16:18 broadens the adultery of remarriage by the man to include marrying a divorced woman. 1 Corinthians 7:10–11 says if people are married they should stay that way; if the wife does separate, then she should remain unmarried or be reconciled with her husband. 1 Corinthians 7:12–16 qualifies the previous prohibition by saying that if the non-Christian partner wants to separate, the Christian partner should not oppose it.

Reading 5:31–32 in the context of the Bible as a whole introduces divorce texts from the Old Testament. In certain texts divorce is mandated to protect the wife (Exod 21:11; Deut 21:14). Deuteronomy 24:1–2 would probably belong here. In other texts divorce is prohibited to protect the wife (Deut 22:19, 29). Malachi 2:16 would probably belong here.

The material, in context, is overwhelmingly opposed to divorce.

There are instances where divorce is permitted as part of God's conditioned will: as an act with a humane intent, as an act in keeping with the Law and prophets, and as an act designed to protect the church's reputation.

God's unconditioned will is that there be no divorce. Given human sin, however, divorce is sometimes a part of God's conditioned will as the lesser of the evils.

At this point one is able to begin using Matthew 5:31–32 in formulating a stance for Christian decision making.

Matthew 5:33–37

The six antitheses of Matthew 5:21–48 fall into two groups of three each (5:21–26, 27–30, 31–32 and 5:33–37, 38–42, 43–48), the second being introduced by the term *again* (*palin*) in the beginning of verse 33 and the repetition of the full formula ("you have heard that it was said to those of ancient times"—cf. v. 21 and v. 33). The first of the second group is 5:33–37, concerning oaths. An overview of the form of the unit will assist our interpretation.

You have heard (v. 33):	[You shall not swear falsely = Lev 19:12] + [but carry out the vows you have made to the Lord = Deut 23:21, 23; Num 30:2; Ps 50:14b]

But I say (v. 34a):   Do not swear at all.
    Four examples of swearing to be avoided (vv. 34b, 35, 36)
           1) heaven (Cf. *m. Sebu.* 4:13)
           2) earth (Cf. *m. Sebu.* 4:13)
           3) Jerusalem (Cf. *m. Ned.* 1:3)
           4) your head (Cf. *m. Sanh.* 3:2)
Concluding admonition (v. 37): Let your word be "Yes, Yes" or "No, No."

Matthew 5:33–37 as a Catalyst for Formation of Character
The content of 5:33–37 may be explored in a verse-by-verse fashion. Each verse will be taken up in order.

Verse 33. "You shall not swear falsely" is a summary of Leviticus 19:12. Matthew 5:33, however, uses a term not used by Leviticus 19:12. It is *epiorkēseis* (cf. 1 Esd 1:48, in context—making an oath using God's name; Wis 14:28, idolaters lightly swear falsely). "You shall carry out the vows you have made to the Lord" is a summary of Psalm 50:14b; Deuteronomy 23:21, 23; and Numbers 30:2. The question is: Are these two statements to be taken as separate or together as one? In the first antithesis (5:21) the two parts went together, with the second explaining the implication of the first. If the two parts of 5:33 belong together as parts of one whole, then the second should most likely be taken as developing the first: e.g., Do not lie under oath; rather be truthful, because using the name of God makes the oath equivalent to a promissory vow.[78]

A variety of ancient texts make clear what is involved in an oath. Leviticus 19:11–12 names "swearing falsely by my name" in connection with lying. Cicero (*De off.* 3.104) says "an oath is an assurance backed by religious sanctity; and a solemn promise given, as before God as one's witness, is to be sacredly kept." An ancient rhetorical text (*Rhet. ad Alex.* 17.34, 1432a33–34) says: "An oath is an unproved statement supported by an appeal to the gods." Philo (*Spec. Laws* 2.10) agrees: "For an oath is nothing else than to call God to bear witness in a disputed matter." In Mediterranean culture oaths were understood alike, whether it be in Jewish or non-Jewish circles.

The words of 5:33 would have been understood by a Greek-speaking Jew of Matthew's time as an interpretation of the third Commandment in Exodus 20:7 and Deuteronomy 5:11. Philo (*Spec. Laws* 2.1–30), for example, interprets the third Commandment as referring to perjury (*epiorkēseis*). Ps-Phocylides 16–17 paraphrases the third Commandment: "And do not commit perjury (*mē d' epiorkēses*), neither

---

78. Betz, *The Sermon*, 266; Pink, *An Exposition*, 99, says the leaders had restricted the Mosaic precepts on oaths to the single prohibition against perjury. They also invented the practice of swearing by a creature as a way of leaving an escape hatch from truthfulness.

ignorantly nor willingly. The immortal God hates a perjurer, whosoever it is who has sworn." Why? Philo (*Spec. Laws* 2.10) says "to invoke God to witness a statement which is not true is the most impious of all things." The Matthean Jesus says: You have heard, "Do not perjure yourself; if you have invoked God's name, do what you have said." If this was understood as an interpretation of the third Commandment, then "Do not take the name of the Lord in vain" means telling the truth when you have invoked God's name in an oath. The meaning of the commandment is restricted to a very narrow slice of life.

Verse 34a. "But I say . . . Do not swear *holōs*" (*holōs* with a negative may mean "not at all" but it also may mean "not generally, not regularly").[79] In this context the meaning is probably, but not certainly, "not at all." The sentiment echoes what various advocates of the same position said at the time. Suspicion about oaths was widespread in antiquity. Jewish examples are prevalent. For example, Philo, *On the Decalogue* 84, says that to swear truthfully is only second best "because the mere fact of swearing casts suspicion on the trustworthiness of the person."[80] *On the Decalogue* 92 says: "From much swearing springs false swearing." Josephus, *War* 2.135 says about the Essenes that any word of theirs has more force than an oath; they avoid swearing, regarding it worse than perjury. *Sifre* Deuteronomy 23.23 says: "It were good . . . that you vow not at all." Greco-Roman expressions of the same position can also be found. For example, Sophocles opposes oaths (*Phil.* 811–12; *Oed. col.* 650); Epictetus (*Ench.* 33.5) encourages his auditors to refuse, if they can, to take an oath at all; Plutarch (*Quaest. rom.* 44, 275C–D) contends that oaths are unworthy of the wise man; Diogenes Laertius (*Lives* 8.22) says of the Pythagoreans that they intended "not to call the gods to witness, man's duty being rather to strive to make his own word carry conviction." Early Christians shared the same conviction: for example, James 5:12a ("Above all, my beloved, do not swear, either by heaven or by earth or by any other oath, but let your 'Yes' be yes and your 'No' be no, so that you may not fall under condemnation") and Irenaeus, *Against Heresies* 2.32.1 (Jesus "enjoined them not only not to swear falsely but not to swear at all").

Verses 34b–36. The four examples are of oaths that were considered not binding by some: "By heaven and by earth" (*m. Sebu.* 4.13—If a man said, "I adjure you" or "I command you" or "I bind you," they are liable; but if he said "By heaven and earth," they are exempt [cf. Matthew 23:22]); "By Jerusalem" (*m. Ned.* 1.3—If he says, "May it be by Jerusalem," he has said naught); "By your head" (*m. Sanh.* 3.2— If a man take an oath before his fellow, and his fellow said to him, "Vow to me by

---

79. Liddell and Scott, *A Greek-English Lexicon,* 2:1218, sect. III.3.
80. Patte, *The Gospel,* 78, takes a similar line. Swearing attributes to someone or something else the trustworthiness and validity of what one says and wants to do. This is to deny one's own responsibility.

the life of your head," R. Meir says he may retract). The Matthean Jesus says that each of these oaths thought to be nonbinding actually is binding because all involve God.

The question is this: When the Matthean Jesus says one should not swear at all, is the prohibition specifically against oaths that function as loopholes for escape from truthfulness? Or is he against oaths in general because they allow people to attempt to evade the truth? Either way, the higher righteousness does not look for loopholes.

Verse 37. "Let your word be 'Yes, yes,' 'No, no,' and what exceeds this is of the Evil One." Be truthful.

The Matthean Jesus has said that the divine intent behind the prohibition against swearing falsely is that humans be truthful. The pericope both assumes and states that in practice swearing is often a means of avoiding what is promised rather than a guarantee that the promise will be fulfilled. Hence the Matthean Jesus both rejects the possibility of such oaths being nonbinding and dispenses with their use, urging a simple yes or no spoken truthfully. This pericope causes the auditors to *see* speech entirely differently. God's intent is that we be truthful persons. This alters the auditors' dispositions and intentions. Character is being formed.

Matthew 5:33–37 in Decision Making

How may this pericope be used in Christian decision making? It must be examined in three contexts.

When reading in the context of Matthew as a whole, there are two matters to consider: oaths and truthfulness. On the one hand, let us consider how oaths are treated elsewhere in the First Gospel. In Matthew 14:7 Herod Antipas is trapped by an oath; in 15:5 children cheat their parents by means of an oath; in 26:72, 74 Peter denies Jesus with an oath. In Matthew 23:16–22 Jesus attacks the use of oaths by the scribes and Pharisees to evade truthfulness. He does not, however, prohibit oaths as such. In Matthew 26:29 Jesus makes a promise but does not use an oath. On the other hand, in Matthew 12:7 and 22:36–40 the Matthean Jesus who supports truthfulness sets up love and mercy as the primary norms for the interpretation of Scripture. Everything must be seen in light of mercy and love.[81] Gerhardsson puts it this way: "In Matthew Jesus follows a generally accepted juridical axiom: that fundamental law takes precedence over all other law; that each individual statute and paragraph must give expression to the demand and spirit of that fundamental law."[82] If so, then even the value of truthfulness must be subordinated to the overriding value of love and mercy.

---

81. Bornkamm, "Das Doppelgebot der Liebe," 85–93; Gerhardsson, "Hermeneutic Program," 129–50; Donaldson, "The Law That Hangs," 689–709.
82. Gerhardsson, *The Ethos,* 41.

When reading in the context of the New Testament as a whole it is also necessary to consider both oaths and truthfulness. In the New Testament God uses oaths (Luke 1:73; Acts 2:30; Heb 6:13); an angel uses an oath (Rev 10:6); and Paul uses oaths (Rom 1:9; 9:1; 2 Cor 1:23; Gal 1:20; Phil 1:8; 1 Tim 2:7). Truthfulness is held up as a good thing: Titus 1:2; Hebrews 6:18—God does not lie (but the devil does—John 8:44); Ephesians 4:25—Let all of us speak the truth to our neighbors; Ephesians 4:15—speaking the truth in love; Acts 5:4—Christians are not to lie to God; Matthew 26:64a//Luke 22:70b, Luke 23:3, and John 18:37a show Jesus, while on trial, being evasive in his answers to questions from authorities. This reflects a mainline Jewish value. When one is facing the possibility of death at the hands of the authorities, one is not obligated to speak the absolute truth; one may be evasive.[83] To do otherwise would be to manifest a lust for martyrdom. Such a lust for death was frowned upon by pagans (Seneca, *Ep.* 24:25), the rabbis (*Gen. Rab.* 82), and early Christians (*Mart. Pol.* 4) alike. From the New Testament as a whole, the example of Jesus conditions the call for truthfulness in a certain context.

When reading in the context of the Bible as a whole one notes that both God (Gen 22:16; 26:3; Exod 6:8; 33:1; Num 32:11; Deut 34:4; Josh 21:34; Ps 89:49; Isa 45:23) and the patriarch Abraham use oaths (Gen 14:22–23). Regarding the general issue of truthfulness, God's people are not to lie in court (Prov 6:19; Isa 59:3–4), to a neighbor or to one another (Lev 6:2–3), or to God (Ps 78:36). The obligation to speak the truth, however, may be qualified by the need to protect someone's life (Exod 1:19; Josh 2:4–6; 1 Sam 16:2–3; 2 Sam 17:14, 20; Jer 38:27).

Regarding oaths—Since the Matthean Jesus addresses the issue of oaths in 23:16–22 and does not prohibit oaths as such, it may be that 5:34a, 37 should be read as hyperbole. It was not taken as such by some in the early church, however, as James 5:12, Justin (*1 Apol.* 16.5), and Irenaeus (*Adv. Haer.* 2.23.1) make clear. That it is hyperbole is almost required by the use of oaths by God, angels, patriarchs, and apostles elsewhere in both Old and New Testaments.

Regarding truthfulness—Truthfulness is a basic value because relationships depend upon it. Lying is a vice because it undermines relationships. Truthfulness, however, is not the ultimate value. Love and mercy are. Truth may need to be subordinated to love and mercy under certain circumstances. Hilary of Poitiers, *Homilies on Psalms* 10, speaks to the issue. He says: "there is a lie that is most necessary, and sometimes falsehood is useful, when we lie to a murderer about someone's hiding place or falsify testimony for a person in danger or deceive a sick person with respect to the chances for recovery." A story that I heard in my youth makes the same point.

---

83. Daube, *Civil Disobedience*, 112–14.

Suppose you are in your house and hear a frantic knocking on your door. You open it to find a young woman, blood-smeared, eyes wild with fright, who says: "Let me in, hide me! I am being chased by a maniac who wants to kill me!" You hurriedly let her in and motion her to the back room where she can hide. Then there is more pounding on your door. You open it and see a wild-eyed man, breathing heavily, with a huge knife in his hand. He asks: "Did you see a young woman run this way?" Is Jesus' disciple obligated to tell the truth regardless of the circumstances? If the pericope is understood as setting forth a rule or law to govern human decision making, then the answer is yes. If, however, the text aims at character formation and if the disciple acts out of a hierarchy of values in which what is central to Jesus' teaching, love and mercy, is primary, then the answer is no.

At this point, one may begin to use Matthew 5:33–37 in one's decision making, but not before.

Matthew 5:38–42

The fifth antithesis, the second of three in the second series, is found in Matthew 5:38–42. An overview of its organizational form is the place to begin our reading. The arrangement of the pericope looks like this.

You have heard (v. 38):   An eye for an eye and a tooth for a tooth (Exod 21:23–24; Lev 24:17, 19–20, 21; Deut 19:21 LXX).

But I say (v. 39a):   Do not retaliate against one who is evil (cf. Prov 20:22).

    Four illustrations of non-retaliation (vv. 39b–42)

        1) whoever strikes you on the right cheek (v. 39b)

        2) whoever sues to take your coat (v. 40)

        3) whoever forces you to go one mile (v. 41)

        4) whoever begs from you (v. 42)

Matthew 5:38–42 as Character Formation

Our focus on the content of 5:38–42 will take up each verse in order in order to determine the function of the language.

Verse 38. "An eye for an eye and a tooth for a tooth" echoes Exodus 21:24, Leviticus 24:20, and Deuteronomy 19:21. These Old Testament commands were intended as an official regulation (as opposed to an individual's taking the law into his own hands) to prevent vengefulness blinded with rage. In its time it was a social advance. It ended vendettas, blood feuds, which permitted unlimited retaliation. The *lex talionis* continued into the New Testament period in some circles (cf. 11QTem 61.10–12; *Jub* 4:31–32; Philo, *Spec. Laws* 3.182; Josephus, *Ant.* 4.280; *b. B. Qamma* 84a). In other circles contemporary Jewish Law provided monetary restitution as an alternative to maiming the offender (Josephus, *Ant.* 4.280). Apparently some among those who continued its strict usage took the principle as justification for personal acts of vengeance by the one wronged. Such an assumed interpretation seems necessary if one is to make sense of the response by the Matthean Jesus that follows.

Verse 39a. "But I say to you, Do not retaliate against the evil one." If the Matthean Jesus here is following the same practice as before, this statement must be understood as his interpretation of the divine intent behind the *lex talionis.* The true intent of the principle, he says, was to limit revenge. Tertullian (*Marc.* 4.16) says this very thing about the *lex talionis.* So if God's intent was to limit revenge, then that intent is realized best through non-retaliation, not the literal application of the principle of an eye for an eye in personal relations. The issue in the fifth antithesis, therefore, is how to understand the *lex talionis* properly.

Several details need attention. First, the verb *antistenai* in the passive means "to resist" and in the active "to retaliate."[84] The context makes clear that here it means "do not render evil for evil."[85] The "do not resist" of the NRSV should, therefore, be translated "do not retaliate against." Second, non-retaliation was part of the Jewish tradition and could also be found also among some pagans. Jewish evidence includes Exodus 23:4–5; Leviticus 19:18; Proverbs 20:22; 24:29; 1QS 10.17–20; *Joseph & Aseneth* 23:9—"It does not befit us to repay evil for evil"; *b. Shabbat* 88b; *2 Enoch* 50:3–4—"And every assault and every wound and burn and every evil word, if they happen to you on account of the Lord, endure them; and being able to pay them back, do not repay them to your neighbor, because it is the Lord who repays, and he will be the avenger for you on the day of the great judgment." Pagan evidence includes the Socrates of Plato's *Crito,* who says: "One must not even do wrong when one is wronged, which most people regard as the natural course"; Seneca, *On Anger* 2.34.5; Epictetus, *Enchiridion* 42; Plutarch, *Pericles* 5—Pericles accepted in silence for an entire day a hooligan's abuse and reviling and, afterwards, when darkness fell, commanded his servants to take a torch and escort the man home; a Pythagorean maxim recorded by Iamblichus in his *Life of Pythagoras* 155, 179, runs: "It is much more pious to suffer injustice than to kill a person; for judgment is ordained in Hades." Early Christian sources continue the emphasis on non-retaliation: e.g., 1 Thessalonians 5:15; Romans 12:17; 1 Peter 3:9; Polycarp, *Philippians* 2:2–3 (do not render evil for evil); *Didache* 1:4 (turn the other cheek); Clement of Alexandria, *Instructor* 1.8 (do not take revenge).

Verses 39b–42. These verses include four illustrations of the renunciation of retaliation. "If anyone strikes you on your right cheek, turn the other also" (v. 39b). Striking the cheek was a way of humiliating a person (Job 16:10; Lam 3:30; 1 Esd 4:30 LXX) that carried a heavy penalty among the rabbis. (Cf. *m. B. Qam.* 8.6—If a man cuffed his fellow, he must pay him a sela [4 zuz]. R. Judah says: If he struck him with the back of his hand, he must pay him 400 zuz.) The Matthean Jesus

---

84. Betz, *The Sermon,* 280.
85. Hagner, *Matthew 1–13,* 130.

advocates offering the other cheek instead of retaliating. "And if anyone wants to sue you and take your 'inner garment' (John 19:23; Josephus, *Ant.* 17.136), give your 'outer garment' (1 Sam 28:8, 14; Matt 9:20–21) also" (v. 40). Whereas in Luke 6:29b the situation assumed is robbery (so one takes possession of the outer garment first), in Matthew it is the courtroom. Exodus 22:25–27 and Deuteronomy 24:10–13 did not allow the suer to demand the outer garment that was used as a blanket at night. According to law, the outer garment belonged as one's inalienable possession and could be taken only until sunset (Exod 22:25–26; Deut 24:12–13; cf. *m. B. Qam.* 8:6). Hence the suer is demanding the inner garment.[86] The Matthean Jesus advocates giving the second garment as well; so, no retaliation. "And if anyone forces you to go one mile, go also the second mile" (v. 41). Epictetus (*Diss.* 4.1.79) reflects the situation when he says: "If a soldier commandeers your donkey, let it go. Do not resist or grumble. If you do, you will get a beating and lose your little donkey just the same." Apuleius (*Metam.* 9.39–42) gives an example of the practice, as does also Matthew 27:32. Faced with conscription, do not retaliate but go beyond what is required, the Matthean Jesus urges. "Give to everyone who begs from you, and do not refuse anyone who wants to borrow from you" (v. 42). Some think this has only the loosest connection with the theme of non-retaliation,[87] that it seems to demand that one surrender one's possessions to whomever requests them[88] (as perhaps Deut 15:7–11 commands). Does this belong to the series on non-retaliation? If so, how? Consider the situation posed in *b. Yoma* 23a: "But is it not written: Thou shalt not take vengeance nor bear any grudge (Lev 19:18). That refers to monetary affairs, for it has been taught: What is revenge and what is bearing a grudge? If one says to his fellow: Lend me your sickle, and he replied No, and tomorrow the second comes to the first and says: Lend me your axe! And he replies: I will not lend it to you, just as you would not lend me your sickle, that is revenge." If one assumes that some such tradition circulated in Matthew's time, then verse 42 makes sense within the pattern of the previous three illustrations.[89] All four focus on non-retaliation.

Note that these illustrations are very specific (how often is one backhanded on the right cheek, sued for one's underwear, or forced by a soldier to carry his gear?). They are also extreme (if one did as v. 40 advocates, one would stand naked in court, a practice eschewed by Jewish tradition [Gen 3:7, 10–11; 9:22; *Jub.* 3:21–22, 30–31;

---

86. Gundry, *Matthew*, 95.

87. Beare, *The Gospel*, 159.

88. Keener, *A Commentary*, 201–2.

89. If it does belong to the series, it shows the point of the pericope is non-retaliation, not non-violence. Only one of the four examples involves violence, and that only minor physical force. Two are about legal situations and one about borrowing. Contra Wink, "We Have Met the Enemy," 15, and "Beyond Just War and Pacifism," 197–214; Garland, *Reading Matthew*, 72–73; and Hays, *The Moral Vision*, 326.

7:8–10, 20; 1QS 7:12; *Sifre* Deut 320.5.2]). They are part of a series. The effect of such a series is to establish a pattern that can be extended to other instances. The pattern invites the auditor to extend and adapt the pattern to other situations. As such the series is open-ended. The meaning of the text, therefore, cannot be restricted to what it says literally. In each of the four cases, the action commanded runs counter to our natural tendency, reversing it. The pattern is experienced as a general, fundamental attack. The pericope, then, does not consist of legal rules. Legal rules must state everything explicitly and can never do justice to the complexities of unique situations. The language of this pericope gives a shock that arouses the moral imagination, enabling the auditor "to *see* his/her situation in a new way and to contemplate new possibilities of action." "The hearer is invited to lay the saying alongside his own situation and, through the imaginative shock produced, to *see* that situation in a new way."[90] An element of "insight," of seeing things in a new way, is involved. Tannehill calls this kind of language "focal instance";[91] Crossan calls it "case parody."[92] I am calling it a "verbal icon" through which one sees the divine will and in the contemplation thereof is changed. Whatever one's categories, this type of language functions to form moral character. It is a catalyst for one's becoming a person who does not retaliate.

Matthew 5:38–42 in Decision Making

Can this pericope be used in Christian decision making? Eugene Boring's comments are to the point. "These commands of Jesus must be taken with the utmost seriousness, but any attempt to take them literally as casuistic law leads to absurdity. Obeyed literally, 5:40 results in public nudity and arrest. The literal practice of these injunctions would result in anarchy and the multiplication of all the evil held in check by the legal system, a system that in our fallen world operates by violence or the threat of violence. Literal obedience can also result in suffering and oppression of those one is charged to protect."[93] It seems obvious that 5:38–42 is not, in the first instance, capable of being used as a norm for decision making. Can it be so used at all? If so, how? It must be read in three contexts.

When reading 5:38–42 in the context of Matthew as a whole, Matthew 5:39 must be taken in connection with 22:39–40. We have already argued in previous segments of this commentary that the hermeneutic of the Matthean Jesus placed love

90. Tannehill, *The Sword,* 74, 75.

91. Ibid., 67–77, and "Tension in Synoptic Sayings," 138–50. In the latter source he says: "It is not a rule of behavior which can be followed mechanically but rightly works through the imagination. . . . When the moral imagination is awakened in this way, these words have had their intended effect" (143).

92. Crossan, "Jesus and Pacifism," 195–208. He contends that this logion is not case law and does not enjoin pacifism.

93. Boring, "Matthew," 197.

and mercy as the overriding concerns in terms of which everything else is to be interpreted. If so, then love for the neighbor would override the value of non-retaliation.

When reading Matthew 5:38–42 in the context of the New Testament as a whole, two things must be noted. First, Romans 12:17, 19; 1 Thessalonians 5:15; and 1 Peter 3:9 continue the theme of non-retaliation. Second, Matthew 5:39 must be heard in connection with Romans 13:1–7, where the state is given the power of the sword (power of life and death) to deal with wrongdoers. In fact, if Romans 12:19 exhorts individual Christians never to avenge themselves but to leave it to God's wrath, Romans 13:4 says the state is ordained by God to execute wrath on the wrongdoer in this age before the resurrection. "Christians . . . live in both Romans 12 and Romans 13 at the same time; both texts are Holy Scripture."[94]

When reading 5:38–42 in the context of the Bible as a whole, attention must be paid to texts like Leviticus 19:18 and Proverbs 20:22, which represent the stream of thought taken up in the New Testament about the desirability of non-retaliation.

There may be occasions when love of neighbor trumps one's commitment to non-retaliation. Confronted by an evildoer, the disciple, whose character incorporates both love of the neighbor and non-retaliation but privileges the former as more basic, would likely respond if necessary to defend, protect, and vindicate the neighbor. Variations on the Good Samaritan story illustrate two options open to Jesus' disciples. Suppose, on the one hand, the Good Samaritan had come upon the robbers attacking a fellow traveler on the road to Jericho, and suppose he had earlier heard Jesus' words "Do not retaliate against an evil doer" and had taken them as a law, then he would likely have waited until the attack was over, the robbers gone, and then have made his way to the victim, bound up his wounds with oil and wine, and set him on his animal and taken him to the inn to provide care for him. He would have thereby satisfied the two commands: do not retaliate and love the neighbor, in that order. Judged by the Matthean Jesus' value system, however, he would have acted improperly, because love of the neighbor was not central to his behavior. If, on the other hand, the Good Samaritan, with a character shaped by the Matthean Jesus' priorities, had come along when robbers were attacking someone else on the road to Jericho, he would likely have taken his staff, cuffed the robbers about their ears and driven them off, and then gone to the man. In so doing he would have made his ethical decision out of a character that gave mercy and love for the neighbor the priority. He remained a non-retaliatory person, but he was a loving person above all.[95] It is from this reading that the Just War tradition emerges.[96]

---

94. Bruner, *Matthew 1–12*, 213.

95. In light of the Matthean Jesus' hermeneutic, the claim that "There is no foundation whatever in the Gospel of Matthew for the notion that violence in defense of a third party is justifiable," by Hays, *The Moral Vision*, 324, is puzzling, to say the least.

96. Major points of Christianity's Just War doctrine taken from the U.S. Roman Catholic bishops' 1983 letter, "The Challenge of Peace," include (1) Justifications for waging war (*jus ad bellum*):

A Christian who works for the State may find it necessary to retaliate in that role. Even a pacifist, like Richard B. Hays, admits that "there is nothing within the New Testament itself that explicitly excludes or forbids such careers (= serving as a soldier). Thus, of the texts we have examined that might seem to stand in tension with the New Testament's central message of peacemaking, these narratives about soldiers provide the one possible legitimate basis for arguing that Christian discipleship does not necessarily preclude the exercise of violence in defense of social order or justice."[97] Personal non-retaliation, therefore, does not relieve one of the responsibility of defending the neighbor and does not negate the State's role as bearer of the sword. Having recognized this, one is ready to use Matthew 5:38–42 in decision making.

Matthew 5:43–48

The last of the six antitheses is 5:43–48. Formally the pericope looks like this.

You have heard (v. 43): [Love your neighbor = Lev 19:18 LXX] + [hate your enemy. Cf. Deut 7:2; Ps 26:5; 139:21–22; 1QS 1:10–11; 9:21–23; ARN 16; Josephus, *J. W.* 2.139.]

But I say (v. 44): Love your enemies. (Cf. Exod 23:4–5//Deut 22:4; Prov 25:21; *2 Bar.* 52:6)

Two rhetorical questions (vv. 46–47)

1) If you love those who love you . . .
Do not the tax collectors do the same? (v. 46)
2) If you salute only brethren . . .
Do not the Gentiles do the same? (v. 47)

It is now time to turn to an examination of the contents of this pericope.

Matthew 5:43–48 as a Catalyst for Character Formation
We will explore the content of 5:43–48 by taking each verse in order.

Verse 43. You have heard that it was said: "Love your neighbor" (Lev 19:18 LXX; cf. Matt 19:19; 22:39) + "hate your enemy." The second member functions as the interpretation of the first: loving the neighbor implies the hatred of the enemy. This second phrase is not a quote from Scripture, though it could be a paraphrase of

---

(a) just cause—Warfare is necessary to confront real danger, protect innocent life, or secure human rights; (b) right intention—It is waged solely for a "just cause," not aggression or retribution; (c) competent authority—It is declared by authorities responsible for public order, not private groups (though revolution is sometimes allowable); (d) comparative justice—Justice falls clearly enough on one side of a conflict to override the general presumption against war; (e) proportionality—The good that war is intended to achieve outweighs expected destruction; (f) probability of success—The cause is not futile and will not require violations of proportionality to succeed; (g) last resort—All peaceful alternatives to war have been exhausted. (2) The rules for conduct in war (*jus in bello*): (a) discrimination—Noncombatant civilians and nonmilitary property are not attacked directly and indirect harm to them is minimized; (b) proportionality—The means are limited to military necessity and avoid disproportionate damage.

97. Hays, *The Moral Vision*, 335–36.

sentiments like those in Deuteronomy 7:2; 2 Chronicles 19:2; Psalm 26:5; and 139:21–22. It could also be an echo of general sentiment, Jewish and pagan, near the time of Matthew.[98]

From the Jewish context one should note that explicit commands to hate the enemy do appear in the Qumran literature (e.g., 1QS 1.3–4, 9–10—"Seek God . . . and do what is good and right before him . . . , love all the sons of light, each according to his lot in God's design, and hate all the sons of darkness, each according to his guilt in God's vengeance"; cf. also 1QS 10.17b–18; 1QM 9.21; 11QTem 61.12–14). Josephus (*J.W.* 2.139) says of the Essenes that they swear oaths, for example, that they will forever hate the unjust. Tacitus (*Hist.* 5.5) and Juvenal (*Sat.* 14.102) had the impression that Jews held that hatred of everyone except Jews was part of their religion. *Avot of Rabbi Nathan* 16 says: "No man should think of saying, 'Love the sages but hate the disciples'; or 'Love the disciples but hate the '*am ha-aretz*.' On the contrary, love all these. But hate the sectarians, apostates, and informers."

From the pagan side one should consider examples like Plato, *Republic* 1.7–8, 332b–336a, which attributes to the poet Simonides the saying "Benefit your friends and harm your foes." Xenophon, *Memorabilia* 2.6.35, says Plato condemned this popular maxim as ethically unacceptable. Earlier it was contested by Socrates (Plato, *Crit.* 49a–e; *Rep.* 1, 332d–336a). The *Rhetorica ad Alexandrum* 1.38–40, 1421b, says: "What is just (*dikaion*) is the unwritten custom of the whole or the greatest part of mankind, . . . to honour one's parents, do good to one's friends and repay favours to one's benefactors." In 1.38–39, 1422a, it says: "We are not alone in hating and doing harm to our enemies."

Verse 43, then, is a quotation from the Old Testament followed by an interpretation of its meaning. The interpretation (hate your enemies) reflects popular sentiment at the time, Jewish and pagan.[99]

Verse 44. But I say: "Love your enemies." The Matthean Jesus here sets forth his interpretation of "Love your neighbor."[100] The roots for this sentiment may be found in Exodus 23:4–5; Deuteronomy 22:4; and Proverbs 25:21. Post-biblical Judaism sometimes voiced a similar perspective (cf. *T. Benj* 4:3—"The good man loves all those who wrong him as he loves his own life"; *2 En.* 50:4; *2 Bar.* 52:6—"Why do you look for the decline of your enemies?"). Occasionally pagan people express a similar refrain. For example, Epictetus, *Dissertations* 3.22.54, says: "For this too is a very pleasant strand woven into the Cynic's pattern of life; he must

98. Reiser, "Love of Enemies," 411–27.
99. For the pagan world, see Blundell, *Helping Friends*.
100. It is not a fence around the law of love, making the demands more stringent than the law itself in order to protect the command. Contra Keener, *A Commentary*, 204. It is rather an interpretation of the law of love that brings out its divine intent, as in all six of the antitheses.

needs be flogged like an ass, and while he is being flogged he must love the men who flog him, as though he were the father or brother of the all." Seneca, *De Otio* 1.4, speaks about giving aid even to our enemies (cf. also *De Ben.* 4.26.1; 7.30.5; 4.28.1).

The second phrase, "pray for those persecuting you," also has parallels in Jewish teaching. Consider, for example the following: Psalm 35:11–14 (although treated horribly by others, the Psalmist prayed for his oppressors when they were sick); *Testament of Joseph* 18:2—"If anyone wishes to do you harm, you should pray for him"; 1QapGen 20:28–29—Abraham prays for the king who took his wife. The sentiment continues in early Christianity (e.g., Luke 23:34; Acts 7:60; Rom 12:14; 1 Cor 4:12; 1 Pet 3:9 [note that the Matthean Jesus does not pray for his persecutors; it is the Lukan Jesus who does that]). Others, however, in laments, complained to God about the divine failure to defend them against their enemies (e.g., Pss 10, 13, esp. 22). Still others, moreover, prayed that God would destroy their enemies (e.g., the imprecatory Psalms in the Old Testament [e.g., Pss 17:13–14; 137:7–9]; *Ps. Sol.* 2:25—"Do not delay, O God, to repay them"; 12:4—"May the bones of the slanderers be scattered far"; 17:21–24—"Lord, raise up the son of David. Undergird him to destroy unrighteous rulers, to purge Jerusalem of gentiles, to smash the arrogance of sinners, to shatter all their substance, to destroy the unlawful nations").

Verse 45. ". . . so you may become sons of your father in heaven, because he causes his sun to rise on the evil and the good and causes it to rain on the righteous and unrighteous." This sentiment was regarded as strange by some in antiquity, both Jew and Greek. For example, the Jew Josephus, *J. W.* 5.407, says: "It is surely madness to expect God to show the same treatment to the just and the unjust" (cf. *Ant.* 4.180–83); the pagan source, *Theognis* 373ff, addresses the deity: "Dear Zeus, I wonder at Thee: Thou art the lord of all. . . . How then . . . dost thou think fit to deal the same measure to sinful and just alike, careless whether their hearts are turned to moderation or to insolence?"

The sentiment would have been affirmed by others, both Jewish and pagan. Note Jewish sources like Psalm 145:9—"The Lord is good to all, and his compassion is over all that he has made"; Proverbs 29:13—"The poor and the oppressor have this in common: the Lord gives light to the eyes of both"; *Exodus Rabbah* 26:2 to Exodus 17:18. Note also pagan examples like Seneca, *De Beneficiis* 4.26.1—"If you are imitating the gods, you say, 'then bestow benefits also upon the ungrateful; for the sun also rises upon the wicked, and the sea lies open also to pirates'"; 7.31.2, 4—"Do as the gods . . . do; they begin to give benefits to him who knows them not, and persist in giving them to those who are ungrateful. . . . Let us imitate them"; *Odyssey* 6.186–90—"It is Zeus himself, the Olympian, that gives happy fortune to men, both to the good and the bad, to each man as he will."

The hope that the disciples might be children of their heavenly Father reflects cultural conventions. Children were assumed to act like their parent. Consider examples like Sirach 4:10—"Be like a father to orphans, and instead of a husband to their mother, you will then be like a son of the Most High"; Philo (*Virt.* 195) says: "Kinship is not measured only by blood, but by similarity of conduct and pursuit of the same objects"; *Targum Pseudo-Jonathan*, Lev 22:28—"My people, children of Israel, as I am merciful in heaven so shall you be merciful on earth"; *b. Kiddushin* 36a—"When you behave as sons, you are sons"; cf. 1 John 4:7–12.

Verses 46–47. The two rhetorical questions ("If you love those who love you, what reward do you have? Do not the tax collectors do the same?" and "If you greet your brothers only, what more are you doing? Do not even the Gentiles do the same?") ask how anyone with such values is different from their culture. For the cultural values, consider the *Rhetorica ad Alexandrum* 1.38–40, 1421b—"What is just (*dikaios*) is the unwritten custom of the whole or the greatest part of mankind . . . to honour one's parents, do good to one's friends, and repay favours to one's benefactors." The injunction "Do good to those who do good to you" was a commonplace of Greek thought (e.g., Hesiod, *Works* 352; Xenophon, *Mem.* 4.4.24; Epictetus, *Diss.* 2.14.18). The Matthean Jesus says that there is no surpassing righteousness here. It is a righteousness of the lowest common denominator.

Verse 48. "Be therefore perfect (*teleioi*) as your heavenly father is perfect (*teleios*)." In what sense should this exhortation be taken? Parallels assist our understanding. In *Targum Neofiti*, Deuteronomy 18:13 is paraphrased as "My people, sons of Israel, be ye perfect in good work as the Lord your God." The philosopher Epictetus, *Dissertations* 2.14.13, says: "The man who is going to please and obey them (the gods) must endeavor as best he can to resemble (*eksomoiousthai*) them. If a deity is faithful, he must also be faithful; . . . if high-minded, he also must be high-minded, and so forth; therefore, in everything he says and does, he must act as an imitator of God." "Perfect" in this Matthean context, then, must mean "inclusive in one's love." Behind such a call is the conception of imitation of God in Matthew's Mediterranean milieu.

Imitation of God in Mediterranean Antiquity
Let us begin with Plato.[101] Plato uses certain terminology interchangeably: *homoiosis theo* (*Theaet.* 176a, f)—being made like; *mimoumenos* god (*Phaedr* 252d; also 253b)—imitator of; *theoeides te kai theoeikeon* of God (*Rep.* 501b)—in image and likeness of; *paraplēsia heauto* (*Tim.* 29e)—resemblance to himself; *ton akolouthesonton tō theō* (*Laws* 716bc, f)—those following God. The Greek anthologist Stabaeus says the phrase "follow after God" derives from the Pythagorean school. Of the founder, Iamblichus said that the whole of his and his disciples' lives was directed toward "following after God." The philosopher believed that contemplation brings knowledge of God and results in likeness to him (cf. *Phaedrus*). Each person is fashioned by

---

101. Rutenber, *The Doctrine.*

what he/she contemplates. The imitator of God will be good because God is good (*Gorg.* 470e).

The Hellenistic Jew, Philo, may be considered next. Although "imitation of God" is not found in the LXX, Philo uses it. Indeed, it is the great theme of Philonic ethics. It was part of the thought-world of Hellenistic Judaism before Philo (cf. *Let. Arist.* 187–88, 210, 281). Philo uses it in several ways. Kings and rulers are imitators of God (*Spec. Laws* 4.187–88) In *On the Embassy to Gaius* 79, 95, Philo says the good king does not imitate God by dressing up in a costume to look like Herakles with his lion's skin or Apollo with the sun's rays encircling his head. Rather one attains likeness to God by imitating God's virtues. Parents are also believed to be imitators of God (*Decal.* 51 and 120). Furthermore, all humans ought to be imitators of God (*Alleg. Interp.* 1.48; 4.73; *Det.* 160; *Sacr.* 68; *Virt.* 168; *Spec. Laws* 2.225; 4.72–73).

First-century C.E. philosophers used the concept. For example, Seneca (*Prov.* 1.5.7–8 [cf. 6.1]) says that the good person is God's pupil, his imitator and true offspring. Epictetus (*Diss.* 2.14.12–13) says: "It is of prime importance for those who would please and obey the deities to be as much like them as lies within their power. If fidelity is a divine characteristic, then they are to be faithful; if generous, they are to be generous; if beneficent, they are to be beneficent; if magnanimous, they are to be magnanimous. In brief, they are to do and say everything in imitation of God."

In the New Testament only Ephesians 5:1 uses the language of imitation of God. (Paul in 1 Cor 11:1 says: "Be imitators of me as I am of Christ." 1 Thess 1:6–7 speaks of the readers being imitators of us and the Lord; 1 Pet 2:21 speaks about "following" in Jesus' steps.)

Second-century Christians used the concept in several ways. Imitation of God by Christians was one (Ignatius, *Rom.* 6:3; *Eph.* 1:1; *Tral.* 1:2; *Diogn.* 10:4, 5, 6—one cannot imitate God through injustice; one imitates God through goodness). Imitation of God by Jews is another. The Christian apologist Aristides of Athens, c. 120 C.E., writes: "The Jews imitate God's goodness by beneficence." Imitation of God by Jesus is yet another usage (Ignatius, *Phil.* 7:2—be imitators of Jesus Christ as he was of the Father). Imitation of Jesus Christ by Christians is still another (Ignatius, *Phil.* 7:2; *Eph.* 10:3; Polycarp, *Phil.* 8:1–2, referring to 1 Pet 2:22, 24, says: "Let us be imitators of his [Jesus'] endurance . . . for this is the example [*hupogrammon*] he gave us"; *Mart. Pol.* 1:2 speaks of Christians being imitators of the Lord [Jesus]).

Rabbinic sources attribute the concept of imitation of God to second- and third-century rabbis.[102] The second-century teacher Abba Saul is said to have used the category (*Sifra* on Lev 19:2: Of Abba Saul it is said—It was he who used to comment on the word of God, "You shall be holy; for I the Lord your God am holy," by

---

102. Kirschner, "Imitatio Rabbini," 70–79.

explaining: "It behooves the royal retinue to imitate the King"; *Mek.* 37a—Abba Saul said: "Be like God; as God is gracious and merciful so be thou gracious and merciful"; *Sifre* on Deut 11.22, 49—Abba Saul speaks of the one who imitates the qualities of God). To the third-century teacher Rabbi Hama is attributed similar speech (*b. Sotah* 14a—R. Hama b. Hanina says that the imitation of the love and mercy of God finds expression in clothing the naked, caring for the sick, comforting the mourners, and burying the dead).

Imitation in Mediterranean antiquity had a character a bit different from views of it circulating among modern theologians and biblical scholars. Two differences stand out. First, imitation was not regarded as a copying of specific acts. For example, Isocrates, *Evagoras* 73–77, speaks about imitating the character of someone, that is, the person's thoughts and purposes. Ps-Isocrates, *Demonicus* 11, says: "I have produced a sample of the nature of Hipponicus, after whom you should pattern your life as an example (*paradeigma*) . . . striving to imitate and emulate your father's virtue." Brant captures the essence of the practice in antiquity. "In the classical world *mimēsis* is a process whereby one expresses the essential characteristics of the object one imitates. The imitator is involved in the conscious effort to bring an idea to expression. Imitation is not mimicry or rote repetition. The imitator is not a mirror reflection of the object. The product of *mimēsis* is not necessarily a copy."[103] Second, imitation was not something that was done without aid. Plutarch, *Pericles* 1.3–4, says: Virtuous deeds "*implant* in those who search them out a great and zealous eagerness which leads to imitation." They dispose those who admire them to emulate those who did them (2.2).

It is in this kind of thought-world that the Matthean Jesus speaks of being like God. His focus, of course, is on the hope that his disciples be as inclusive in their love as their heavenly Father is.

The Matthean Jesus, in 5:43–48, responds to what he regards as a misinterpretation of the Old Testament command to "love the neighbor." Instead of a meaning that leaves open room for hate of the enemy, the Matthean Jesus says the divine intent behind the command is that one love one's enemy also. One is called to love in the way that God loves—perfectly (inclusively). Bruner says this means "looking at every person we meet and saying, at least to oneself, 'I will never, God helping me, do anything to hurt you': neither by angrily lashing out at you, lustfully sidling up to you, faithlessly slipping away from you, verbally oiling you up, protectively hitting you back, or even justifiably disliking you."[104] This new way of *seeing* through the verbal icon into the unconditioned will of God is a catalyst for new dispositions and intentions. Character is being formed.

---

103. Brant, "The Place of *mimesis*," 287–88.
104. Bruner, *Matthew 1–12*, 225.

The Contribution of Matthew 5:43–48 to Decision Making

How can this pericope be used in Christian decision making? It must, of course, be read in a threefold context. Also, two questions arise about the use of this pericope in ethical decision making. First, does loving enemies mean that one is unfailingly accepting, unceasingly affirming, and never demanding of changes in the behavior of others? Second, when is it appropriate to ask one to pray for his/her enemies? We may consider Matthew 5:43–48 in context in terms of these two questions.

Question One. Reading 5:43–48 in the context of Matthew as a whole, we note that the Matthean Jesus made distinctions between those inside and those outside (e.g., 13:11; 25:31–46; chap 23). He also advocated moral discernment (7:1–12).

Reading 5:43–48 in the context of the New Testament as a whole, one notes that the Johannine Jesus made distinctions among people and pronounced critiques on others' behavior (e.g., 8:39–47). The disciples also made moral distinctions and pronounced critiques (e.g., Acts 8:22–23).

Reading 5:43–48 in the context of the Bible as a whole, one notes also that the prophets made moral distinctions and offered critiques both of God's people and those not part of Israel (e.g., Amos 1:2–2:16).

This data indicates that loving the enemy does not mean that one is unceasingly affirming of the enemies' behavior or that one does not demand change. Loving the enemy does not mean passivity in the face of evil.

Question Two. Reading 5:43–48 in the context of Matthew as a whole yields the following: the Matthean Jesus complained to God about God's desertion of him (Matt 27:46); he also engaged in the equivalent of the imprecatory Psalms when he pronounced woes on his enemies (Matt 23:13, 16, 23, 25, 27, 29).

Reading 5:43–48 in the context of the New Testament as a whole yields the following: the Markan Jesus complains to God about God's desertion of him (Mk 15:34); the martyrs in Revelation 6:9–10 complain to God about their lack of vindication; the Lukan Jesus engaged in the equivalent of imprecatory prayer when he pronounced woes on opponents (Lk 6:24, 25, 26; 11:42, 43, 44, 46, 47, 52); the Apostle Paul pronounced a double anathema on his opponents (Gal 1:8, 9); the Lukan Jesus prayed for his enemies (Lk 23:31), as did his disciple Stephen (Acts 7:60).

Reading 5:43–48 in the context of the Bible as a whole causes us to be aware that the Psalmists complain (Ps 22:1–2) and engage in imprecatory prayer (Ps 17:13–14), as well as praying for enemies (Ps 35:11–14).

This data indicates that all three forms of prayer (lament, imprecatory prayer, and intercessory prayer) are part of the life of a disciple of Jesus. That being so, when is prayer for enemies appropriate? When might the exhortation to pray for one's enemies function as psychological repression of one's anger and denial of one's pain as opposed to enabling one to transcend one's hurt and anger? Could it be that the prayers of complaint and imprecation are a (necessary) preliminary stage before prayers for one's enemies?

Walter Brueggemann looks at the imprecatory Psalms like Psalm 109 and contends they are cathartic; they enable "self-discovery"; they enable "reality-discovery" (words and feelings do not destroy the enemy, nor do they bring judgment from heaven on us); they are a prelude to the real agenda, namely, the yielding of the full rage and bitterness to God's wisdom and providential care. Rage is transformed by the double step of owning it as our own and yielding it to God. Vengeance is God's business, not ours. There may be a way beyond the Psalms, but it is not around, but rather through, them.[105]

At this point one is ready to begin reflection on the relevance of Matthew 5:43–48 for Christian decision making.

In the light of 5:21–48, what does 5:17 mean by "fulfill the law and the prophets"? In the context of 5:21–48, "to fulfill the law and the prophets" means to clarify and affirm the divine intent of Scripture over against other interpretations that cloud or attempt to evade it.

In the light of 5:21–48, what does 5:20 mean by the "higher righteousness"? In this context the higher righteousness of 5:20 is that which fulfills the Law and the prophets. To use Bultmann's terms,[106] it is a *radical obedience* rather than a *formal obedience*. Formal obedience is concerned with doing the outward regulations while leaving free play to a person's self-will in areas beyond the regulations; radical obedience is focused on one's being completely obedient. Radical obedience is another way of speaking about character formation.

Davies and Allison conclude their examination of Matthew 5:21–48 with these words: "Matthew 5:21–48 does, without question, contain absolute and impractical commands, and their literal observance would land one in hopeless confusion. But then one must ask, what is the passage all about?"[107] It is the contention of this book that in 5:21–48 Jesus' teachings function as verbal icons through which one may see into the divine will. As such they are a catalyst for the formation of the character of the disciples around the higher righteousness of radical obedience. This involves:

> 5:21–26—being a person who neither breaks nor fails to restore relationships;
>
> 5:27–30—being a person who does not violate another's marriage partner, either by act or by thought;

---

105. Brueggemann, *Praying the Psalms*, 69.
106. Bultmann, *Jesus and the Word*, 89–92.
107. Davies and Allison, *Matthew 1–7*, 566.

5:31–32—being a person who does not violate the indissoluble marriage
　　bond;
5:33–37—being a truthful person;
5:38–42—being a non-retaliatory person;
5:43–48—being a person who does not exclude enemies from the love
　　shown to friends.

Jesus' disciples who are so formed in their character will be influenced or affected thereby in their decisions about ethical actions. The disciples, however, will, in so doing, have to reconcile multiple values that are a part of their character in their decision making. For example,

being a truthful person will have to be reconciled with no broken
　　relationships and love of the neighbor;
no divorce or remarriage will have to be reconciled with the fact that there is
　　only one unforgivable sin (Matt 12:31);
no retaliation will have to be reconciled with the fact that the state has been
　　given the power of the sword and with one's responsibility for one's neighbor;
love of everyone will have to be reconciled with the fact that the Matthean Jesus
　　makes distinctions between insiders and outsiders and advocates making
　　moral distinctions.

The fact that this kind of tension goes on in the disciples' decision-making process is yet another indication that the Sermon on the Mount is not a compilation of laws for disciples to follow. It is not ethical guidance for decision making, except in an indirect way.

EIGHT

True Piety

Matthew 6:1–18

Matthew 6:1–18

In 5:20 the Matthean Jesus spoke of a righteousness that exceeds that of the scribes and Pharisees. In 5:21–48, in six antitheses, he showed what such a righteousness looked like in terms of one's relationship to others as discerned in the process of interpreting Scripture. Now in 6:1–18 Jesus continues his elaboration of the higher righteousness by focusing on three acts of the disciples' piety done before God. The spotlight is trained on the necessary "inwardness" in the practice of these three external acts of piety.

Matthew 6:2–4, 5–6, 16–18 is usually viewed as a unity into which verses 7–15 have been inserted at some point and to which verse 1 has been added as an introduction. Verses 1–4, 5–6, 16–18 make one point (appropriate piety is done *for* God: to be seen by God and rewarded by God), while verses 7–15 make another (appropriate piety is done in line with God's character). Consequently, in our discussion verses 1–4, 5–6, 16–18 will be taken up separately from verses 7–15, although in their present form verses 1–18 are a Matthean unity. The unity can be seen if one notes the form of 6:1–18 as a whole.

The unit consists of a statement of principle (6:1) followed by four paragraphs with the same basic arrangement. The three acts are typical of Jewish piety.

The principle: 6:1, "Beware of practicing your righteousness before people to be seen by them."

The illustrations: 6:2–18, four paragraphs following the same basic arrangement. The acts are typical of Jewish piety (e.g., Tob 12:8).
>   1) Matthew 6:2–4—almsgiving
>   a) The act—"when you give alms" (cf. Tob 12:8; Acts 3:2; 24:17)
>   b) The prohibition + basis—"Sound no trumpet before you" + "they have their reward"

c) The prescription + basis—"Let your alms be in secret" + "your Father will reward you"

2) Matthew 6:5–6—prayer

    a) The act—"When you pray" (cf. Tob 12:8; Acts 3:1)

    b) The prohibition + basis—"Do not pray so as to be seen by others" + "they have their reward"

    c) The prescription + basis—"Pray in secret" + "your Father will reward you"

3) Matthew 6:7–15—prayer

    a) The act—"in praying"

    b) The prohibition + basis—"Do not heap up empty phrases" + "your Father knows what you need before you ask"

    c) The prescription + basis—"Pray like this" + "if you forgive, then . . ."

4) Matthew 6:16–18—fasting (Tob 12:8; Acts 13:3)

    a) The act—"When you fast" (cf. Tob 12:8)

    b) The prohibition + basis—"Do not look dismal to be noticed" + "they have their reward"

    c) The prescription + basis—"anoint your head and wash your face" + "your Father will reward you"

Remember, in this current section of commentary the focus is on verses 1, 2–4, 5–6, 16–18; in the next section it will be on verses 7–15. This division is for the sake of analysis only.

Matthew 6:1, 2–4, 5–6, 16–18 and Character Formation

A first-level examination of the content of verses 1, 2–4, 5–6, 16–18 may be done by focusing on the function of the content of the material in these four subunits.

Verse 1. "Be careful not to do your righteousness before others for the purpose of being seen by them." In its Matthean context this is a continuation of the criticism of Pharisees in the First Gospel. (Cf. Matt 23:5—"They do all their deeds to be seen by others." This is similar to *j. Ber.* 14b [*b. Sotah* 22b], which describes seven types of Pharisees, one of which is the "shoulder Pharisee" who packs his good works on his shoulder [to be seen by others]. The critique in Rom 2:28–29 does not limit the problem to Pharisees but applies it to all Jews.) Why should the disciples avoid the proscribed behavior? It is because "then you have no reward from your Father in heaven." This principle introduces verses 2–18. Like 5:21–48, 6:1–18 deals with the righteousness that exceeds that of the scribes and Pharisees. Verses 2–4, 5–6, 16–18 argue that it involves piety done for God, not for our status before other humans. Otherwise "it is theater, not worship."[1] (That this was a problem in early Christianity, cf. 1 Cor 12–14.)

Verses 2–4. They provide the first illustration of the principle enunciated in verse 1. The act is specified by the phrase "when you give alms." Almsgiving was integral to Jewish piety.[2] For example, consider LXX Daniel 4:27/MT 4:24 ("O king, let my counsel please you. Redeem your sins by almsgiving and your iniquities by compassion on the poor. It may be that God will be long-suffering of your trespasses"); LXX Proverbs 15:27a/MT 16:6 ("By almsgiving and faithfulness sins are purged away"); Tobit 12:8b–9 ("It is better to give alms than to lay up gold. For almsgiving saves from death and purges away every sin") and 4:7–11 ("for all who practice it, almsgiving is an excellent offering in the presence of the Most High"); Sirach 3:30 ("almsgiving atones for sin") and 35:4 ("One who gives alms sacrifices a thank offering"); cf. Acts 3:2; 9:36; 10:2, 4, 31; 24:17. The importance of almsgiving was heightened in post-70 C.E. Judaism. In *Avot of Rabbi Nathan* [A] 4 there is a story of Johannan ben Zakkai's reaction to the destruction of the Jerusalem temple. Rabbi Joshua cried out: "Woe unto us that this place where the iniquities of Israel were atoned for is now laid waste!" Rabbi Johannan replied: "Do not fret. We have another atonement as effective as the sacrificial system. It is acts of loving kindness (almsgiving)." So in the period after 70, when Matthew was written, almsgiving was understood as the equivalent of an atoning sacrifice. Its focus was on the vertical relationship with God.

The prohibition runs: "do not sound a trumpet before you, as the hypocrites do in the synagogues and in the streets, so they may be praised by others." Mark 12:41–44 indicates that it was possible to observe people's gifts made in the temple and to compare them. Sirach 31:11b indicates that almsgiving was often of public note ("the assembly will proclaim his acts of charity"). The *Epistle of Aristeas* 168 exhorts humans to "practice righteousness before all people." This Matthean language (one gives alms after a trumpet has announced the forthcoming act) is so extreme that it must be hyperbole or satire. *Hypocrite* originally designated actors (Aristotle, *Poet.* 18.19 1456a; Diodorus Siculus 37.12.1) but had come to designate moral pretense (Epictetus, *Diss.* 2.9.20; Plutarch, *Educ.* 17). The basis for the prohibition is "They have received their reward." The Greek (*apechousin*) appears elsewhere in commercial language and on receipts for completion of payment.[3] So one might paraphrase: "They have been fully compensated."

The prescription runs: "when you give alms, do not let your left hand know what your right hand is doing, so that your alms may be done in secret." Rabbinic traditions speak about the virtue of giving alms secretly. Consider *m. Shekalim* 5:6 (There were two chambers in the Temple, one the chamber of secrets, into which the devout

1. Betz, *The Sermon*, 353.
2. Garrison, *Redemptive Almsgiving.*
3. Gundry, *Matthew*, 102.

used to put their gifts in secret and the poor of good family received support therefrom in secret); *t. Shekalim* 2:16 (Just as there was a chamber of secret donations for the poor in the Jerusalem temple, so there was such a chamber in each and every town); *Koheleth Rabbah* 12:14 (R. Yannai once saw a man give money to a poor man publicly; he said: "It would have been better to give him nothing than to have given it to him and put him to shame"); *b. Baba Batra* 9b ("The one who gives *zedeqah* in secret is greater than Moses"); *b. Pesah* 113a, b ("There are three things whose virtuousness the Holy One proclaims every day: the bachelor who lives in a big city and does not sin; the poor who turns over a find to its owner; and a rich man who gives the tenth of his fruits in secret"). The sentiment is one with which a philosopher like Epictetus had sympathy (*Diss.* 4.8.17, "That which I did well I did not in order to be seen but for my own sake . . . to please myself and God").

The phrase about the left and right hands is used to say that the donor's knowledge of the gift should not be used to let others know of it. Keep it secret. This again is extreme language, hyperbole. The basis is once again the same: "your Father who sees in secret will reward you."

Verses 5–6. These verses offer the second illustration of the principle enunciated in verse 1. The act is specified by the phrase "when you pray." It is an act of importance to ancient Judaism. Consider Tobit 12:8a ("Prayer with fasting is good"); *m. Berakoth* 1:4 ("In the morning two Benedictions are said before [the Shema] and one after; and in the evening two Benedictions are said before and two after"); Sirach 39:5 (the ideal scribe is one who rises early to seek the Lord and to petition the Most High); cf. also Acts 3:1; Didache 8:3. Prayer by Jews was assumed.

The prohibition runs: "do not be like the hypocrites; for they love to stand and pray in the synagogues and at the street corners, so that they may be seen by others." This is again hyperbole or satire. The basis echoes the now familiar refrain: "They have received their reward."

The prescription is offered: "Whenever you pray, go into your room and shut the door and pray to your Father who is in secret." There was a tradition within Judaism of praying in secret. One might mention 2 Kings 4:33–34 (Elisha goes in, closes the door, and prays); Daniel 6:11 (Daniel prays in his upper chamber); Philo (*Contempl. Life* 25—the Therapeutae hid themselves away in private rooms); *Testament of Joseph* 3:3 (the patriarch prays after retiring to his own quarters); *Testament of Jacob* 1:9 (Jacob had a secluded place that he would enter to offer his prayers); *Mekilta* Exodus 15:25 (You call in secret, but I answer you in public). The basis is the now familiar "your Father who sees in secret will reward you." Bruner sums up: "Prayer must be vertical to be honest. Directing an activity that is supposed to be directed to God into an activity that can also make a good impression on others, Jesus calls phony."[4]

---

4. Bruner, *Matthew 1–12,* 234.

Verses 16–18. They offer the third illustration of the principle enunciated in verse 1. The act is indicated by the phrase "whenever you fast." Fasting was a common Jewish practice, both personal (Tob 12:8; Dan 9:3; Mark 2:18; Luke 18:12; *Did.* 8:1) and public (Lev 16:29–31; Num 29:7; *m. Taan.* 1:6—"If these days passed by and their prayers were not answered, the court enjoins on the congregation three more days of fasting"). Fasting was so characteristic of Jews that Augustus could boast that he fasted even more than a Jew (Tacitus, *Ann.* 5.4). The practice referred to here in verses 16–18 is private fasting.

The prohibition runs: "Do not look dismal, like the hypocrites, for they disfigure their faces so as to show others that they are fasting." By practicing fasting in an extreme way, one could acquire the reputation of a saint. Josephus, *Life* 11–12, indicates as much in his remarks about the hermit Bannus. There are, moreover, references to private fasting being accompanied by sackcloth and ashes (Dan 9:3; Josephus, *Ant.* 20.89—Izates fasted with ashes on his head) as well as public fasts (Jonah 3:5, 8—sackcloth; 1 Macc 3:47—sackcloth, ashes, torn clothes; *m. Taan.* 2:1—ashes on heads, forbidden to wash or anoint themselves). Again this is hyperbole or satire. Behavior with such a tendency has been blown up into an extreme form to make a point. The basis is once again the familiar "they have received their reward."

The prescription reads: "put oil on your head and wash your face, so that your fasting may be seen not by others but by your Father who is in secret." What is being said? 2 Samuel 14:2 refers to anointing and washing as everyday practices (so they are being told to appear as usual); *Testament of Joseph* 3:3–4 reflects the same spirit: "For those seven years I fasted, and yet seemed to the Egyptians like someone who was living luxuriously, for those who fast for the sake of God receive graciousness of countenance." No one knew of his fasting. The basis is the familiar "your Father who sees in secret will reward you."

Sometimes modern readers demean the language of reward. Some explanation is in order. A. M. Hunter contends that there are two kinds of rewards: those that have a natural connection with the activity being rewarded and those that do not. For example, money is not the natural reward of love, so a man who marries a woman for her money is mercenary. Marriage is the natural reward for love, so a man is not mercenary for desiring it. "The proper rewards are not simply tacked on to the activity for which they are given, but are the activity itself in consummation."[5] A rabbinic tradition reflects the Jewish tradition of rejecting rewards that have no intrinsic connection with the activity. In *m. Abot* 1:3 Antigonos of Soko says: "Be not like servants who serve the master on condition of receiving a gift, but be like servants who serve the master not on condition of receiving." The Roman Stoic

---

5. Hunter, *A Pattern for Life*, 38–39.

philosopher Seneca also reflects Hunter's perspective. In *On the Happy Life* 9.4, Seneca says: "Do you ask what it is that I seek in virtue? Only herself. For she offers nothing better—she herself is her own reward." This logion rejects rewards that have no intrinsic connection with the activity.

The point of these three examples is that piety before God is done for God alone and not for oneself, to enhance one's standing before other humans. In terms of honor-shame categories, Matthew 6:1, 2–4, 5–6,16–18 is promoting honor virtue and opposing honor precedence. Some scholars portray Mediterranean society in monolithic terms. Honor, they say, was conferred in the eyes of an evaluating public, was to be aggressively pursued, and was competitively safeguarded.[6] Others, however, distinguish honor precedence and honor virtue.[7] Honor precedence is worldly honor that validates itself before an evaluating public and is based on power, wealth, and other indicators of status. Honor virtue is gained before one's own inner being or before an omniscient divine figure. In the Mediterranean world people could attain honor and reputation not only through bold masculine daring and aggression but also by virtuous living and adhering to affiliate norms, like hospitality, kindness, and justice. The Jewish tradition ideally honored the latter. Yet in the First Gospel the Pharisees pursue honor precedence rather than honor virtue. The Matthean Jesus rejects the former in favor of the latter.[8]

Note that the language is very specific. For example, in verses 2–4 only two possibilities of action are mentioned: sounding a trumpet and not letting the left hand know what the right hand is doing; in verses 5–6 only two possibilities are mentioned: standing in synagogues or on street corners and hiding in a closed room; in verses 16–18 only two possibilities are mentioned: disfiguring one's face on the one hand and putting oil on one's head and washing one's face on the other. The language is also extreme and striking. Sounding a trumpet to announce one's gift, doing one's praying on street corners, and disfiguring one's face to announce one's fasting are hyperbole, caricatures revealing a tendency in human nature. In a caricature an inclination is magnified so that we may see it in its most blatant and ridiculous form. This specific and extreme language belongs to a pattern. The repetition makes the forcefulness of the words increase, "increasing the chance that we will recognize the danger to which we are normally blind."[9] This is what Tannehill calls a "focal instance." It produces an imaginative shock that sets the hearer thinking about many other situations. The extreme makes one aware of a "tendency which

6. E.g., Malina, *The New Testament World.*
7. Pitt-Rivers, "Honor," 503–11.
8. Lawrence, "'For truly, I tell you,'" 687–702.
9. Tannehill, *The Sword,* 88.

likes to conceal itself but which can be recognized once we have had a clear view of its undisguised form."[10] This thought unit is not case law. It is rather a verbal icon that shapes the character of the auditors by enabling us to *see* differently.

Matthew 6:1, 2–4, 5–6, 16–18 and Decision Making

How then does this material function in Christian decision making? It must be read in three contexts. The question it raises is, Must Christian piety be totally private and never public?

Reading 6:1, 2–4, 5–6, 16–18 in the context of Matthew as a whole yields helpful insight. Regarding Matthew 5:16 ("let your light shine before others, so they may see your good works"), Hans Dieter Betz says that Matthew 5:16 and 6:1–18 "come from different traditions and thus express different concerns. These concerns are, however, not incompatible. Verse 16 is concerned about the visibility of good deeds because otherwise the people will not be moved to praise *God* (not to praise *the doers* of those deeds!), while 6:1–18 emphasizes that good deeds, in order to be worthy of merit, must be done in such a way that premature praise of the doer is avoided."[11] Matthew 10:32–33 ("Everyone therefore who acknowledges me before others, I also will acknowledge before my father in heaven; but whoever denies me before others, I also will deny before my Father in heaven"), moreover, calls for public confession. In Matthew 11:25–27, furthermore, Jesus prays before his disciples; 26:36–46 may also be read the same way.

Reading Matthew 6:1, 2–4, 5–6, 16–18 in the context of the New Testament as a whole is also helpful. In Luke 9:29–32 the disciples see Jesus' glory; in Luke 11:1 Jesus prays before his disciples; in 1 Thessalonians 1:8 we hear that in every place your faith is spread abroad; in 2 Corinthians 9:2 Paul says your zeal has stirred up very many of them (other Christians); in Colossians 4:5–6 there is the exhortation to conduct yourselves wisely before outsiders, making the most of the time; in 1 Peter 2:12 a similar exhortation runs: "Conduct yourselves honorably among the Gentiles, so that, though they malign you as evil doers, they may see your honorable deeds and glorify God when he comes to judge" (cf. also 3:15–16; 4:3–4).

Reading this text in the context of the Bible as a whole is the final task. There one finds, for example, that in Genesis 41 Joseph's actions are witnessed by Pharaoh; and in Daniel 6:11 Daniel is seen at his prayers by his enemies.

The aim in Matthew 6:1–18 is not the privatization of piety but the purification of motive in one's relating to God. Piety may be public, but when it is, it should be for God's sake.

---

10. Ibid., 86.
11. Betz, *The Sermon*, 164.12. E.g., Betz, *Essays on the Sermon*, 62; Gerhardsson, *The Shema*, 84–87.

Matthew 6:7–15

Matthew 6:7–15 is an integral part of 6:1–18. It is cast in the same formal pattern as verses 2–4, 5–6, 16–18. Because of a break in rhythm and because it makes a different point, however, 6:7–15 is widely regarded as an interpolation into an older unit.[12] In order to allow undivided attention to its distinctive focus, it will be treated separately in this volume. Formally, the pericope is organized into the act, the prohibition + basis, and the prescription + basis, just as are verses 2–4, 5–6, 16–18. The discussion that follows will follow this pattern.

Matthew 6:7–15 as a Catalyst for Character Formation
Let us begin with the act: "when you are praying" (v. 7). The assumption is that Jesus' disciples pray. There is no exhortation to pray; that is assumed. So the Matthean Jesus speaks about the practice of doing what they normally do. The issue is how they pray.

The prohibition runs: "do not heap up empty phrases as the Gentiles do; for they think they will be heard because of their many words" (v. 7b). Its basis is "Do not be like them, for your Father knows what you need before you ask him" (v. 8). The focus here shifts from Jewish ostentation (vv. 5–6) to Gentile babbling (vv. 7–8). The stereotypical pagan prayer was long and flowery. In 1 Kings 18:26–29 the prophets of Baal prayed all day but received no answer. Catullus (*Poems* 34) provides a poem to the goddess Diana in which many words are used by way of invocation, to flatter the goddess and raise the probability that she will answer the petition. Whether it is flattery in the invocation or elaborate presentation of the petitions, the assumption is that an answer to one's prayer depends on one's own ability to get control of God or to persuade the deity to do one's bidding. This, says the Matthean Jesus, runs counter to the character of God. God knows what is needed before one asks and, it is assumed, wants to do one good.

There was both a Jewish and a pagan tradition about short prayers. Jewish examples include 1 Kings 18:36–38, where Elijah's prayer is short and effective; Ecclesiastes 5:2 exhorts, "Let your words be few"; Sirach 7:14 says: "Do not babble in the assembly of the elders, and do not repeat yourself in prayer"; Judith 8:16 states: "God is not like a human being, to be threatened, nor like a mere mortal, to be won over by pleading"; *t. Berakoth* 3:2 reads: If one is traveling in a place of danger or of robbers, he should pray a short prayer. What is a short prayer? R. Eleazar says: "Perform your will in heaven and bestow satisfaction on earth upon those who revere you, and do that which is good in your sight. Blessed are you who hears prayer"; *m. Berakoth* 4:3 has R. Gamaliel say: A person should pray the Eighteen Benedictions every day. R. Joshua says: The substance of the Eighteen; *b. Berakoth* 61a says: A

---

12. E.g., Betz, *Essays on the Sermon*, 62; Gerhardsson, *The Shema*, 84–87.

person's words should always be few toward God; *Mekilta* on Exodus 15:25 states: The prayer of the righteous is short. The sentiment favoring short prayers is found outside Judaism as well. For example, Marcus Aurelius, *Meditations* 5.7, counsels people to pray in a simple and frank fashion.

The basis for short prayers is given in verse 8: "Do not be like them, for your Father knows what you need before you ask." Jewish tradition assumed the omniscience of God. For example, Psalm 139:3–4 says of God: "You are acquainted with all my ways. Even before a word is on my tongue, O Lord, you know it completely"; *Exodus Rabbah* on 14:15 is explicit: Before a person speaks, God knows what is in that person's heart. On the basis of such knowledge Isaiah 65:24 can have the Lord say: "Before they call I will answer." Philosophers expressed similar sentiments. For instance, Xenophon (*Mem.* 1.3.2) tells us that Socrates prayed simply "Give me what is best for me," for he knew that the gods know what the good things are. Philostratus, in his *Life of Apollonius* 1.11, has the philosopher say that because of the God's omniscience, short prayers are recommended.

The prescription reads: "Pray then in this way." What follows is a prayer ascribed to Jesus, a similar form of which is also found in Luke 11:2–4 and *Didache* 8:2. The prayer consists of an address to God (v. 9b), three Thou-petitions (vv. 9c–10), and three Us-petitions (vv. 11–13). Our examination of the prayer will follow this pattern.

The Address is: "Our Father in heaven." God is often addressed as Father in prayers in Mediterranean antiquity. From the Ancient Near East we may consider:

The prayer of Rameses II has the pharaoh address the god, Amon, as Father. "What then, O my Father Amon? Does a father forget his son? I call upon you, O my Father Amon, I am in the midst of enemies without number whom I do not recognize."

In a hymn to the moon god, addressed by his Sumerian name, Nanna, god is addressed as Father.
"O Lord, hero of the gods, who in heaven and earth is exalted in his uniqueness, Father Nanna, lord Anshar, hero of the gods . . .
Begetter, merciful in his disposing, who holds in his hand the life of the . . . land,
O father, begetter of gods and men . . .
Father begetter. . . .
O Lord, decider of the destinies of heaven and earth, whose word no one alters."

The Greco-Roman world offers its share of examples as well:

Homer pictures humans calling on Zeus in prayer as Father. For example, *Iliad* 3.320–23 has Greeks and Trojans joining in prayer:

"Father Zeus, that rulest from Ida, most glorious, most great, whichsoever of the twain it be that brought these troubles upon both peoples, grant that he may die and enter the house of Hades, whereas to us there may come friendship and oaths of faith."

Euripides, *Helen* 11.1441–45, gives a prayer to Zeus as Father:
"Zeus, Father art thou called, and the Wise God:
Look upon us, and from our woes redeem;
And, as we drag our fortunes up the steep,
Lay to thine hand: a finger touch from thee,
and good-speed's haven long-desired we win."

Cleanthes, *Hymn to Zeus,* addresses Zeus as Father:
"Deliver men from their dark ignorance; drive it away, O Father, far from their soul, and grant that they may attain the thought that guides thee in governing everything with justice."

Odysseus and Herakles call god Father in Epictetus, *Dissertations* 3.24.13–16.

Jewish prayers also involve the invocation of God as Father on occasion:

Psalm 89:26—"He (the Davidic king) shall cry to me, 'Thou art my Father, my God, and the Rock of my salvation.'"

Isaiah 64:8—"Yet, O Lord, thou art our Father; we are the clay, and thou art our potter."

Sirach 23:1, 4, in a prayer for self-control (22:27–23:6), has the man cry out: "O Lord, Father and Ruler of my life, do not abandon me. . . . O Lord Father and God of my life, do not give me haughty eyes, and remove from me evil desire."

Sirach 51:10 has the individual say:
"I cried out, 'Lord, you are my Father; do not forsake me in the days of trouble.'"

Wisdom of Solomon 14:3, has a navigator pray to God:
"It is your providence, O Father, that steers its course, because you have given it a path in the sea."

3 Maccabees 6:1–15 gives Eleazar's prayer. In verses 2–3, 8–9, we read: "King, great in power, Most High, All-conquering God, who governs the whole creation with mercy, look upon the seed of Abraham. . . . When Jonah was pining away unpitied in the belly of the monster of the deep, you, Father, restored him uninjured to all his household."

4Q372, 1:16, has Joseph pray to God:
"My Father and my God, do not abandon me in the hands of gentiles"
(cf. also 4Q460, 5:6).

Blessing 4 of the Eighteen Benedictions from the Cairo Genizah—"Favor us with your knowledge, our Father."
Blessing 6—"Forgive us, our Father."

In the Ahabah Rabbah (Great Love), part of the morning worship in the Jerusalem temple, as well as part of the morning worship in the synagogue, the prayer begins:
"With great love hast thou loved us, O Lord, our God, with great and exceedingly great forbearance hast thou ruled over us. Our Father, our King, for the sake of our fathers . . . be gracious also to us and teach us. Our Father, Merciful Father, have pity on us and inspire us to perceive and understand."

The Litany of the New Year beginning and ending, as quoted by R. Akiba (b. Taan 25b), runs:
"Our Father, our King, we have no other king but thee; our Father, our King, for thine own sake have mercy on us."

In the Kaddish—"Father who is in heaven."

In the third section of the Grace after festive meals—"Our God, our Father, tend and nourish us."

Jesus and his followers in the canonical Gospels reflect the common practice:

Jesus is depicted as teaching his disciples to address God as Father (Matt 6:9–13; Luke 11:1–4).

Jesus is depicted as believing that God was his Father and that he was God's Son (Luke 10:21–22//Matt 11:25–27; Mark 13:32; 14:36; John 12:27–28; 11:41–42). Jesus addresses God as Father in his prayers (Matt 11:25–27; 26:39, 42).

The "Abba" prayer reflects the Aramaic tradition from the earliest Christians. It was taken up and used in Gentile Christian congregations (Rom 8:15–16; Gal 4:6).

The Matthean Jesus' prayer begins with an invocation of God that would have been regarded with favor by his Mediterranean auditors.

One of the most sensitive issues confronting Christians today is that of the traditional language for God.[13] Some Christians are offended by Trinitarian language

---

13. For what follows, see Talbert, *Romans*, 49–53; also "The Church," 421–39.

(Father, Son, and Holy Spirit) and by the Lord's Prayer (Our Father). This language, it is felt, has been used to support patriarchy, subjugate women, and deprive them of their full participation in home and church. There is no doubt that the language has at times functioned in this way in the history of the church and continues to do so in the present. As a result, some Christians have called for a replacement of the traditional language for God, deleting all references to God as Father. The more basic question that must be faced has to do with the origins of the language.

Let us look at the two very different views of religious language operative in Christian churches in our time: a relational view and a political view. On the one hand, the relational view of religious language assumes that such speech arises out of reflection on an ongoing relationship between God's people and God. It is analogous to speech that arises out of a durable human relationship like marriage. For example, John Doe has been married to Jane Doe for over thirty years. It is a durable personal relationship. As a result of this ongoing relationship John can say certain things. He can say something about Jane (e.g., "Jane is the most interesting person I have ever known"). He can say something about himself (e.g., "I am a different man today than I was before I married; I have been changed"). He can say something about the relationship between the two of them (e.g., "Life together is unpredictable but never dull"). Such talk arises out of his reflection on the relationship. On the basis of an ongoing relationship John simply confesses what is: about Jane, about himself, and about the nature of the relationship between them. This is confessional language. By analogy, a Christian can speak of Jesus' role in the relationship (e.g., Jesus is Lord, Messiah, Son of God), of him- or herself in terms of the relationship (e.g., "I am not the person I was before I met Christ; I have been changed/saved"), and of the nature of the relationship between the two (e.g., "it is one in which God always has the initiative [grace] and I always do the responding [faith]"). This is simple, confessional religious language. It confesses what the Christian senses to be the case about the role of Jesus in the relationship, about what has happened to him or her as a result of the relationship, and about the nature of the relationship between them.

On the other hand, an understanding of religious language as political assumes that religious language originates as a projection of the organization of human relationships on earth onto the canvas of heaven. If so, then any change in the human social order demands a corresponding change in the way one speaks of the heavenly world. Moreover, if one wishes a change in the human social order, this can be facilitated by a change in the language used of heavenly reality. For example, if God is spoken of in masculine terms (e.g., Father), this is a projection onto heaven of a patriarchal social system on the human level. If the social order is egalitarian or if an egalitarian social structure is what one hopes for, then the language for God must also be egalitarian (e.g., either Mother as well as Father, or some name that avoids gender altogether, like "God"). It is assumed that father-language for God is a reflection of the patriarchal world in which the Bible was written. In the crassest terms, the Bible was written by men, so in it God is male. This language is political, that is, it is all about power in relationships.

While it is true that sometimes in antiquity the depictions of the gods were a projection of earth's social order onto heaven, the gendered descriptions of God and other gods do not seem to be so. On the basis of the assumptions of a political view of religious language that holds calling God "Father" is a projection of a patriarchal social system, then where one finds worship of a goddess, the social order should be matriarchal, and where one finds worship of male and female deities together, the social order should be egalitarian. The correlation does not hold. In antiquity, even where a female deity is worshiped, the social order remains patriarchal; where one finds both male and female deities worshiped, the social order remains patriarchal. This disparity is enough to falsify the assumptions of a political view of religious language as it relates to God-language. Note, moreover, that in Matthew 23:9 the distinctive early Christian practice of addressing God as Father has radically egalitarian implications with regard to relationships within the community. "The saying of Jesus uses the 'father' name of God not as a legitimation for existing patriarchal power structures in society or church but as a critical subversion of all structures of domination."[14]

The relational view of religious language assumes that deity transcends sexuality. God is neither male nor female. Yet God is sometimes spoken of in Scripture in gendered terms. Sometimes in the Bible God is spoken of in feminine terms: for example, Isaiah 42:14—God says, "I will cry out like a woman in travail"; 49:15—God asks, "Can a woman forget her suckling child? Even if these may forget, yet I will not forget you"; 66:13—God says, "as one whom his mother comforts, so I will comfort you"; Luke 13:34b—Jesus says, "How often would I have gathered your children together as a hen gathers her brood under her wings." When this is so, it is always as simile. God is compared to a mother but is never named "Mother." This distinction is fundamental. At other times in the Bible God is spoken of in masculine terms: both with simile (e.g., Isa 42:13—"The Lord goes forth like a mighty man, like a man of war he stirs up his fury") and metaphor (e.g., Isa 63:16—"Thou art our Father, . . . thou, O Lord, art our Father, our redeemer from of old is thy name"; 64:8—"Yet, O Lord, thou art our Father; we are the clay, and thou art the potter"; Mark 14:36—Jesus prays, "Abba, Father"). In the Bible God is both compared to a male (simile) and addressed as Father (metaphor).

Why does the Bible reserve a masculine metaphor for God? Two reasons stand out. First, there is the matter of the experience of ancient Israel. The prophets would not speak of God with a female metaphor because such language results in a basic distortion of the nature of God and God's relation to the creation. Creation by a

14. Fiorenza, *In Memory of Her*, 151.

feminine deity was understood as a birthing process and the world consequently as an extension of God. This is pantheism (the world is divine), not theism (the world is created by God but is radically other than God). Israel knew that God acted like a mother as well as a father. She, therefore, occasionally spoke of God as like a mother (simile). She did not use the feminine metaphor for God, however, because she wanted to guarantee that the qualitative distinction between God the creator and the creation be clearly maintained. Since God relates in personal ways, neuter language would not do. Since creation must be distinguished from the Creator, feminine metaphor would not do. Israel spoke of God as Father, not to say God was male but to maintain the otherness of God from the created order at the same time that God was spoken of as personal.

On the other hand, another reason grows out of the practice of Jesus. The canonical Jesus not only spoke of God as Father (Mark 13:32), he also spoke *to* God as Father (Mark 14:36; Matt 11:25–27//Luke 10:21–22; John 11:41; 12:27). Before Easter Jesus taught his disciples to address God as Father (Luke 11:2; Matt 6:9), a practice his disciples continued after Easter (Rom 8:15–16; Gal 4:6). After Easter the canonical Jesus taught his disciples to baptize in the name of the Father, the Son, and the Holy Spirit (Matt 28:19–20). For Jesus before Easter, the name of God was Father; for Jesus after Easter, the name of God was Father, Son, and Holy Spirit. In the New Testament, God is called Father and addressed as Father because Jesus knew God as Father and invited his disciples to so address God.[15] Father (or Father, Son, and Holy Spirit) is God's name (not the only one, but one). This name is made known as revelation by Jesus, the Father's Son. This is a second reason Christians hold on to traditional language for God. Neither reason offered here has anything to do with God as male or the social order as patriarchal.[16]

After the address, there are three Thou-petitions: hallowed be your name; your kingdom come; your will be done on earth as it is in heaven. The three are virtual synonyms. The first two are very similar to the Kaddish, an Aramaic prayer following immediately after the sermon, which ended the synagogue liturgy. The earliest form we know runs:

> Exalted and hallowed be his great name
> > in the world which he created according to his will.
> May he let his kingdom rule
> > in your lifetime and in your days and in the lifetime
> > of the whole house of Israel, speedily and soon.

---

15. Juel, "The Lord's Prayer," 56–70. Juel says that mostly Jesus speaks of God as his Father, and that only in Matthew 6:9 does one hear "our Father." "Others may use the language by invitation, not imitation" (59–60).

16. This fact continued in the patristic period. Widdicombe, *The Fatherhood,* contends that ancient Alexandrians understood divine fatherhood in terms of generativity and relationality, not maleness or sexuality.

Praised be his great name from eternity to eternity.
And to this, say: Amen.[17]

The similarity of Matthew's Thou-petitions to the Kaddish, an eschatological prayer, causes most to take Matthew's petitions as eschatological. They are a prayer for the speedy coming of the eschatological kingdom.

The Us-petitions are also three. They are interpreted in several different ways: either as eschatological prayers, like the Thou-petitions,[18] or as petitions for benefits in the here and now,[19] or as a combination of concern for both future and present.[20] In what follows, we will attempt to present evidence for both future and present readings.

The first Us-petition is found in verse 11. The NRSV translates "Give us this day our daily bread" but has a footnote that reads "our bread for tomorrow." The debated term is *epiousian*. It may be derived from *epeinai/epiousia* or from *epienai*. If the first, it would mean "what is necessary for existence" (e.g., the bread that is necessary for life, give us today). If the second, it would mean something like "coming" or "tomorrow" (e.g., tomorrow's bread, give us today). Jerome (*Com. on Matt.* 6.11) tells us two things about this problem of interpretation. On the one hand, he says that the Gospel of the Nazareans used the Aramaic term *mahar*. On the other hand, he gave us an interpretation of the term: "future bread." By this he meant the bread of life, bread of the time of salvation, bread of the End Time. If so, then the request that it be given this day is a prayer for the speedy coming of the Messianic banquet. That Matthew 8:11–12 speaks of the eschatological banquet helps explain why Jerome's type of reading was the dominant one in the first centuries, both in the East and in the West[21] (cf. Lk 14:15). Nevertheless, "Give us *each day* our daily bread" in Luke 11:3 indicates that some early Christians took this petition as a request for daily sustenance. Did Matthew?[22]

The second Us-petition comes in verse 12: "Forgive us our debts, as we also have forgiven our debtors." Benediction 6 of the Amidah indicates the ancient Jews sensed need for God's forgiveness: "Forgive us, our Father, for we have sinned against thee; Erase and blot out our transgressions from before thine eyes." The Prayer of

17. Jeremias, *New Testament Theology,* 198. For another eschatological prayer with different categories, cf. *2 Bar.* 21:19–25.

18. E.g., Jeremias, *New Testament Theology,* 199–203 (cf. R. E. Brown and K. Stendahl).

19. E.g., Birger Gerhardsson, "The Matthean Version," 215 (cf. F. Beare, R. Gundry, D. Garland, J. Lambrecht, A. Finkel). Tertullian and Cyprian made a distinction between the first three petitions and the last three. The first three concern heavenly things; the last three earthly things. See Froehlich, "The Lord's Prayer," 81.

20. Boring, "Matthew," 8:204 (cf. G. Strecker, *The Sermon*).

21. Jeremias, *New Testament Theology,* 199–200.

22. Luther's *Exposition* takes "daily bread" to refer to the Word of God, Christ, the spiritual bread of the soul. Later in his catechetical writings (*Small Catechism*) he says that "daily bread" referred to everything needed for our physical life. Robinson, "Luther's Explanation," 435–47.

Manasseh 11–13 reflects the same sentiment: "I have sinned, O Lord, I have sinned; and I certainly know my sins. I beseech you; forgive me, O Lord, forgive me." A strong tradition existed in ancient Judaism that focuses on humans' forgiveness of others. For example, *Testament of Gad* 6:3—"If anyone confesses and repents, forgive him"; 6:7—"Even if he is devoid of shame and persists in his wickedness, forgive him from the heart and leave vengeance to God." Certain texts connect humans' forgiveness of others with God's forgiveness of them. For example, note Sirach 28:2—"Forgive your neighbor the wrong he has done, and then your sins will be pardoned when you pray"; *Sifre* on Deuteronomy 13.18—Whenever you have mercy on other creatures, they from heaven have mercy on you. These examples all seem to focus on forgiveness within history. Taken alone, Matthew 6:14–15 seems to fit here. Built upon the prophetic hopes of the exilic period (e.g., Isa 43:25–26; 44:22; Jer 31:34; Ezek 16:63; 36:25; Mic 7:19), however, there was in ancient Judaism also an expectation of eschatological forgiveness (e.g., *b. Ros. Has.* 16b–17a, 17b; *b. Pesah* 54b). Matthew 18:23–35 seems to speak of this eschatological forgiveness and its link to disciples' forgiveness within history. It is difficult to separate eschatological and present dimensions in the second petition.

The third Us-petition comes in verse 13. It has two parts. "Do not bring us to the time of trial, but rescue us from the evil one." The translation in the NRSV of "the time of trial" is preferable to "temptation." Hagner argues the translation should be "testing" because God does not lead into temptation (James 1:13). God does, however, allow his people to be tested. "To be tempted" is to be enticed to sin; "to be tested" is to be brought into difficult circumstances that try one's faithfulness. The two are similar, since sin can result in either case; yet they are also to be differentiated, since the former has a negative purpose, the latter a positive one. "The petition in this instance concerns severe testing that could eventuate in apostasy. . . . The disciple . . . prays not to be led into such a situation, that is, not to be led into a testing in which his or her faith will not be able to survive" (cf. 1 Cor 10:13).[23]

Certain Jewish prayers are very similar to the two parts of the third petition. In 11QPs Col XXIV 10, the prayer is voiced: "Recognize me and do not forget me or lead me into difficulties." In *b. Berakoth* 60a–60b, a prayer to be uttered before going to sleep includes "do not make it my custom to do transgressions nor bring me into the power of sin, violation, temptation, or humiliation. May the impulse to do good control me and may the impulse to do evil not control me." Jeremias says the causative "bring me not" in the Lord's Prayer's closing petition has permissive sense: "Do not let me fall victim."[24] James Charlesworth notes that the Old Syriac means "do not allow us to enter temptation."[25] This, then, is a prayer to be

23. Hagner, *Matthew 1–13*, 151.
24. Jeremias, *New Testament Theology*, 202.
25. Charlesworth, "Jewish Prayers," 48n. 36.

protected from testing in the present time. Matthew 24:4–26, however, speaks of the great testing at the end of history in association with the Eschaton. In Matthew 26:42, "pray that you may not come into the time of trial" is ambiguous and offers little assistance in determining whether this petition is eschatological or related to a disciple's present existence.[26] In *b. Berakoth* 16b, Rabbi, on concluding his prayer, added the following: "May it be thy holy will O Lord our God . . . to deliver us . . . from the destructive accuser." Similar prayers are heard elsewhere in ancient Judaism. For example, 11QPs a 19:15–16—Let not Satan dominate me, nor an unclean spirit; 4QLevi b ar frag 1—Let not any satan have power over me. Matthew 4:1 speaks of Jesus' being tested by the devil. These references all seem to focus on present experience. Matthew 24:4–26, however, is concerned that disciples not be deceived and led astray at the last great time of testing. In all three of the Us-petitions, then, both an eschatological and a present, existential meaning seem to be present.

The Doxology in verse 13b is missing in Sinaiticus, Vaticanus, Bezae, etc. On the basis of manuscript evidence, it is not an original part of the Lord's Prayer in Matthew. Why would it have been added? Jews normally finished prayers with doxologies (e.g., Pss 41:13; 72:18; 89:52; 106:48; 115:18; 150:6; 1 Chr 16:36; 29:11). It was the rule at Jamnia that every benediction had to be responded to with a full doxology (*b. Ber.* 62b–63a): "Praised be his name whose glorious kingdom is forever and ever."[27]

The prescription is followed by its basis in verses 14–15. "For if you forgive others their trespasses, your heavenly Father will also forgive you; but if you do not forgive others, neither will your Father forgive your trespasses" (cf. Matt 18:23–35). Two readings of this text, one ancient and one modern, cast light on its meaning. Martin Luther, in his *Large Catechism,* says that just as baptism and the Lord's Supper are signs of our forgiveness and new life, so also is our forgiveness of others. When we remit the sins of others, we can be assured that God has forgiven us.[28] C. F. D. Moule contends that understanding this text depends on one's distinguishing between earning or meriting forgiveness on the one hand and on the other adopting an attitude that makes forgiveness possible—the distinction between deserts and capacity. Forgiveness can never be earned; it is always an act of undeserved generosity. It cannot be received, however, without repentance. Repentance makes the recipient capable of receiving the forgiveness offered, but the offer remains one of free generosity.[29]

---

26. Grayston, "The Decline of Temptation," 279–95, agrees that Matthew 6:13 refers to testing rather than temptation. He thinks that rather than God's testing humans, however, this refers to humans' testing God.

27. Davies, *The Setting,* 451–53.

28. The *Large Catechism,* in Tappert, ed., *The Book of Concord,* 433.

29. Moule, "'As We Forgive,'" 68–77. Contra Lambrecht, *The Sermon,* 144, who thinks in 6:12 the forgiveness of the other in advance is a condition for receiving God's forgiveness.

In Matthew 6:5–15 there are two pericopes on prayer: verses 5–6, directed to a Jewish issue (which offers the motive for prayer: it is for God, not one's self-glorification), and verses 7–15, focused on a Gentile issue (which offers the model for prayer). The model offered consists of three components:

1. with few words (vv. 7–8), which comes out of a certain view of God;
2. with proper focus (vv. 9–13), which also comes out of a view of God;
3. with right relationships (vv. 14–15), which also comes out of a certain view of God.

So, Matthew 6:5–6 says appropriate piety is done *for* God (to be seen by God and rewarded by God), while 6:7–15 says proper prayer is done in line with God's character.

The Lord's Prayer indicates what God thinks our needs are. As such it causes the auditor to *see* what his or her needs really are, what his or her petitions should really be—that is, to see prayer differently. As such, in effecting changes in one's perceptions, it leads to alterations in one's dispositions and intentions. Character is being changed. Prayer is being purified.

The Use of Matthew 6:7–15 in Decision Making

Does Matthew 6:7–15 provide any norms for one's life of prayer? Let us look at three contexts. The question whose answer is being sought is, What about short prayers?

Reading 6:7–15 in the context of Matthew as a whole yields several observations: in Matthew 11:23–24, Jesus' prayer is brief; in Matthew 14:23–24, Jesus prays all night; in Matthew 26:36–46, Jesus' prayer is short, but he prays it three times (i.e., repetitiously).

Reading 6:7–15 in the context of the New Testament as a whole likewise results in diverse observations: in Luke 6:12, Jesus prays all night; in Luke 18:1, Jesus' disciples are to pray always and not lose heart; in John 17, Jesus prays at length; in 1 Thessalonians 5:17, Christians are exhorted to pray without ceasing.

Reading 6:7–15 in the context of the whole Bible causes our attention to focus on 1 Kings 18:36–37, where Elijah's prayer is a short prayer (in contrast to the priests of Baal [18:26–29]). Their prayers assumed the god was busy or away or asleep, that is, not aware and not involved unless made so by humans.

In the Sermon on the Mount brevity is linked to the assumption that God is aware of our needs and is graciously going to provide for them. Lengthy prayers are linked to the assumption that God will not answer unless humans cause him to do so. The larger context, however, indicates that the call to avoid babbling does not eliminate long periods of time spent in prayer or the repetition of one's requests. At this point one can begin using Matthew 6:7–15 in decision making.

NINE

God and Possessions

Matthew 6:19–34

Matthew 6:19–24

If 5:21–48 and 6:2–18 are clearly defined units of thought in the Sermon on the Mount, each introduced by a heading (5:17–20 and 6:1), what about 6:19ff.? There are no headings in this segment of the Sermon. This has led Krister Stendahl to contend that 6:19–7:29 "offers material which has been brought into the Sermon on the Mount by Mt. in such a manner that we find no clue as to its arrangement."[1] The actual case is quite the contrary.[2] On the one hand, Matthew 6:19–34 is composed of two subunits controlled by two prohibitions: "Do not store up for yourselves treasures on earth" (v. 19) and "Do not be anxious" (v. 25). Each subunit has three parts. Matthew 6:19–24 breaks into verses 19–21 (//Lk 12:33–34), verses 22–23 (//Lk 11:34–36), and verse 24 (//Lk 16:13). Matthew 6:25–34 falls into verses 25–30, verses 31–33 (both //Lk 12:22–32), and verse 34 (no parallel). The first subunit (6:19–24) deals with getting one's priorities straight about possessions. The second (6:25–34) deals with trusting God to provide for one's needs. On the other hand, Matthew 7:1–12 falls into two subunits controlled by two prohibitions: "Do not judge" (v. 1) and "Do not give what is holy to dogs" (v. 6). Each subunit consists of three parts. Matthew 7:1–5 consists of verse 1, verse 2, and verses 3–5. Matthew 7:6–12 consists of verse 6, verses 7–11, and verse 12. The former focuses on judging as condemnation; the latter on judging as discernment. Matthew 6:19–7:12, then, consists of two large thought units (6:19–34 and 7:1–12), each of which is organized in the same way. Following the Evangelist's clues enables the reader to discern the arrangement of the segment. In this section of the commentary we will focus on 6:19–24.

---

1. Stendahl, "Matthew," 779. Guelich, following Bornkamm, thinks 6:19–24 expounds the first three petitions of the Lord's Prayer (*The Sermon,* 324–25). This is not compelling.
2. For a reading very much like what follows, see Davies and Allison, *Matthew 1–7,* 626–27.

Matthew 6:19–24 as a Catalyst for Character Formation

Remember, this segment of the text consists of three logia: verses 19–21, verses 22–23, and verse 24. Like the preceding sections (5:21–48 and 6:2–18), 6:19–24 is cast in antithetical form: for example, the wrong way (v. 19) and the right way (v. 20). In form 6:19–24 looks like this:

The Two Treasures (vv. 19–21)
>Prohibition (v. 19)—"Do not lay up treasures on earth."
>Command (v. 20)—"But lay up treasures in heaven."
>Reason (v. 21)—"Where your treasure is, your heart will be also."

The Two Eyes (vv. 22–23)
>Assertion (v. 22a)—"The eye is the lamp of the body."
>Inferences (vv. 22b, 23a)—"If your eye is sound, your whole body will be full of light; if your eye is not sound, your whole body will be full of darkness."
>Conclusion (v. 23b)—"If the light in you is darkness, how great is the darkness."

The Two Masters (v. 24)
>Assertion (v. 24a)—"No one can serve two masters."
>Reason (v. 24b, c)—"either love the one . . . or be devoted to the one."
>Application (v. 24d)—"You cannot serve God and mammon."

Let us now examine the content of the three sayings in order.

The first logion is 6:19–21. It is composed of a prohibition, a command, and a reason.

Verse 19. It provides the prohibition: "Do not make a habit of storing up as treasure (*thesaurizete*) for yourselves treasures on earth." Such treasures are perishable and vulnerable. Fabrics will be consumed by moths, grain by rust, and precious stones will be stolen by thieves.

Verse 20. This verse contains the command: "Habitually store up as treasure (*thesaurizete*) for yourselves treasures in heaven." How would the Matthean Jesus' auditors have understood this? Consider the following: Tobit 4:8–9, regarding giving of one's possessions, says, "So you will be laying up good treasure for yourself"; Sirach 29:10–12, regarding helping a poor man (v. 9), says, "Lay up your treasure according to the commandments of the Most High"; *4 Ezra* 6:5—"before those who stored up treasures of faith were sealed"; *2 Baruch* 24:1—"the treasuries in which are brought together the righteousness of all, those who have proven themselves to be righteous"; *m. Peah* 1:1—"These are things whose fruits a man enjoys in this world while the capital is laid up for him in the world to come: honouring father and mother, *deeds of loving kindness,* making peace between a man and his fellow; and the study of the Law is equal to them all"; *t. Peah* 4:18:D—"My ancestors stored up treasures for this lower world, but I, through giving charity, have stored up treasures for the heavenly world above." (Cf. Matt 19:21; Luke 12:21; Heb 11:26.) The treasure that is laid up in heaven is one's generosity toward others. This has permanence. Moth, rust, and thieves cannot touch generosity toward others.

Verse 21. It offers the reason for the prohibition and the command: "Where your treasure is, there your heart will be also." (Cf. Epictetus, *Diss.* 2.22.1.) In this logion, the contrast is between acquisition of and hoarding earthly treasures, or greed, and treasure in heaven, or generosity to others. One must choose between the two treasures. The implied exhortation is to choose properly.

The second logion comes in 6:22–23. It consists of an assertion, inferences, and a conclusion. They will be examined in order.

Verse 22a. It provides the assertion: "The eye is the lamp of the body." In this context, *eye* is used metaphorically. In ancient Jewish thought, the eye indicated one's disposition toward others.[3] Consider the following examples: Deuteronomy 15:9—"lest your eye be hostile to your poor brother and you give him nothing"; Tobit 4:7—"Give alms from your possessions to all who live uprightly, and do not let your eye begrudge the gift when you make it"; Sirach 14:9—"A greedy man's eye is not satisfied with a portion"; Sirach 14:10—"A stingy man's eye begrudges bread."

Verses 22b–23a. These verses provide the inferences. The positive inference is "If your eye is sound (*haplous*), your whole body will be full of light." In ancient Judaism a sound eye is a generous eye (a generous intent or disposition). Several examples show this to be the case. In Proverbs 22:9, "he that has a good eye" (MT) becomes in the LXX "he that pities the poor." In the *Testament of Benjamin* 4:2 we hear: "The good man has no dark eye, for he has pity on all." In *b. Shabbat* 74a, a beautiful eye is a generous eye. (Cf. Rom 12:8—the one who gives with generosity [*haploteti*]; 2 Cor 8:2; 9:11; James 1:5.) The negative inference is "If your eye is not sound (*poneros*—evil), your whole body will be full of darkness." What is an unsound eye? Consider the following examples. In Deuteronomy 15:9 LXX, an "eye that becomes evil to one's brother" is a disposition not to give what is needed by the brother. Sirach 14:8 says, "Evil is the man with a grudging eye." Matthew 20:15 asks: "or is your eye evil (*poneros*) because I am good?" In context, the evil eye is a stingy spirit.

Verse 23b. This gives the conclusion: "If the light in you is darkness, how great is the darkness." A statement in the *Testament of Judah* 18:2–3, 6 makes the conclusion clear. "Guard yourselves, therefore, my children against . . . love of money; listen to Judah, your father, for these things . . . blind the direction of the soul. . . . They blind his soul, and he goes about in the day as though it were night." If one's eye (ethical perception) becomes clouded by greed, the result is darkness (selfishness) in the whole self.

---

3. Contra Patte, *The Gospel*, 92, who contends a bad eye is a divided eye, a divided perception of who has authority to establish one's vocation.

Both H. D. Betz and Davies and Allison[4] contrast the two different ways the ancients viewed vision: some thought objects emit images that float into the eye (Epicurus and Lucretius), and others believed vision occurs by means of light passing from the inside out through the eye (Plato and Philo). They argue further that in Matthew 6:22–23 it is the latter view that is assumed. So the eye is not the real cause of sin, but rather the "inner light" when it has turned to darkness is the cause. This would result in the point that if your intent or disposition is not generous, then it is because the self is selfish. The disposition (the eye) reflects the orientation of the self. If, however, the former view is assumed, then if the disposition (the eye) toward the other is stingy, it will cause the whole self to be stingy. Character is shaped by intent or disposition. Context favors this reading.

Verse 24a. The third logion is found in verse 24. It consists of an assertion, a reason, and an application. They will be examined in order. Verse 24a gives the assertion: "No one can serve two masters." At the human level this may not be true (cf. *m. Git.* 4:15, *m. Ed.* 1:13, and Acts 16:16, 19 for examples of slaves with more than one master); at the spiritual level it is acknowledged in antiquity as true (Rom 6:16; Philo, frag. 2:649—"It is impossible for love of the world to coexist with the love of God").

Verse 24b, c. Here the reason is supplied: "for the slave will either hate the one and love the other, or be devoted to the one and despise the other." In Semitic language usage, to love A and hate B means to prefer A over B. Also, Jeremiah 8:2 indicates that "to love" means "to serve" (to be devoted to).

Verse 24d. It concludes with the application: "You cannot serve God and mammon." Here "mammon" is personified as an idol, the service of whom is the rejection of God. Betz interprets: "Materialism . . . is a pseudo-religious way of life, the service of a pseudo-god identified by the name of Mammon."[5] Mammon is not found in the Old Testament. At Qumran it is found with the sense of "property" (1QS 6:2; CD 14:20). It has much the same neutral sense in *m. Pirke Abot* 2:12. In *Targum Onkelos* on Genesis 37:26, it refers to the wicked "gain" of Joseph's brothers. In *Targum Onkelos* on Exodus 18:21, the honest judge is one who "abhors mammon." In the New Testament it is used only in Matthew 6:24 and in Luke 16:9, 11 (modified by *adikia*). (Cf. *2 Clem* 6:1, which reflects dependence on Matthew.)

The sentiment expressed is similar to that of others both in ancient Judaism and among pagan writers. For example, consider the following Jewish sources: *1 Enoch* 94:8—"Woe unto you . . . who have put your trust in your wealth"; *Testament of Judah* 18:2–3—"Guard yourselves, therefore, my children against . . . love of money, . . . for (this) distances you from the Law of God"; 1 Timothy 6:17–19 expresses the

---

4. Betz, *Essays on the Sermon,* 75–87; Davies and Allison, *Matthew 1–7,* 635–41; Allison, "The Eye," 61–83.
5. Betz, *The Sermon,* 458–59.

same point in slightly different words. Some pagan examples include Plato, *Republic* 8.555C; Seneca, *On the Happy Life* 26.1—"In the eyes of a wise man riches are a slave, in the eyes of a fool a master."

This unit consists of three logia dealing with one's relation to possessions. All three are concerned that one's relation to possessions be appropriate. The three sayings are various ways of saying basically the same thing.

The two treasures (v. 21)   One's choice of treasure (greed or generosity) determines the state of one's inner self. So be someone whose heart belongs to God, not to this world. Be generous, not greedy.

The two eyes (vv. 22–23)   One's life-controlling perspective on money affects the spiritual condition of the whole self. So be someone whose intent is generous, not stingy. Be a generous person.

The two masters (v. 24)   One's choice of master (God or mammon) determines one's conduct and service. So be someone who serves God, not money.

Although only the first logion uses an imperative, all three function as exhortations to get one's priorities straight about possessions. They give a new perception of one's relation to possessions. Do not allow wealth to become your functional deity; let God be God. "We are asked . . . to turn our backs resolutely on the god of the world, to be the *real* atheists of our time, to deny the gods to whom most give unquestioning fealty and to serve only the Living God."[6] *Seeing* the divine will about such matters by means of this verbal icon results in the formation of the character of the reader as a non-greedy person.

The Use of Matthew 6:19–24 in Decision Making

How should Matthew 6:19–24 be used in ethical decision making? The text should be looked at in terms of three contexts. The question to be considered is, Does the Matthean Jesus call for the renunciation of all belongings?

Reading 6:19–24 in the context of Matthew's Gospel as a whole is instructive. Consider on the one side, Matthew 6:2–4—only those with possessions can give alms; and Matthew 27:57—Joseph of Arimathea was both a rich man and a disciple. Consider on the other hand, Matthew 4:18–22—when called, four men leave everything and follow Jesus (cf. 19:27); and Matthew 19:16–22, 23–24—the young man with many possessions is asked to sell all he possesses and to follow Jesus.

---

6. Bruner, *Matthew 1–12*, 265. Bruner also writes: "Being a disciple has always required Christians to be cultural atheists, publicly disavowing . . . the myriad . . . gods of popular life" (182).

Reading 6:19–24 in the context of the New Testament as a whole also offers help. Consider, on the one hand, examples like Acts 5:4—the sin of Ananias was not having private property but lying about what he had done; Acts 11:27–30—the church at Antioch sent aid to the poor in Jerusalem, implying that the church had possessions; Acts 16:14–15—Lydia, a well-to-do woman, is a disciple; Acts 24:17—that Paul can bring alms means Paul had possessions; 1 Corinthians 16:1–4—the collection presumes Christians have possessions (cf. 2 Cor 8–9; Gal 2:10); Philippians 4:15–18—the gifts from the Philippians imply that Christians had possessions. Consider, on the other hand, examples like Mark 1:16–20—the men leave their possessions and follow Jesus; Mark 10:17–22, 23–25—following Jesus involves leaving one's possessions; Luke 6:24–25—Woes on the rich and the full; Luke 12:13–21—the parable of the rich fool; Luke 16:19–31—the parable of the rich man and Lazarus; Acts 2:44–45—disciples had all things in common (cf. 4:32).

Reading 6:19–24 in the context of the Bible as a whole is likewise helpful in gaining a balanced perspective. In the Old Testament there were at least three different attitudes toward possessions. Affluence is connected with righteousness and poverty with wickedness (e.g., Deut 28:12ff.; 8:7–10; 26:1–9; Prov 6:6–11; 10:4; 28:19). Affluence is associated with evil, while the poor are associated with the righteous (e.g., Amos 8:4ff.; Mic 2:1–5; Jer 5:28; Prov 28:6; Sir 10:21–23). The ideal was neither poverty nor wealth—because each is subject to perversion—but just enough to meet one's needs (Prov 30:7–9). All three positions assume possessions are appropriate for God's people. The various tendencies can be reconciled if one recognizes that possessions are not inherently evil and are not forbidden to disciples. God provides wealth (2 Cor 9:8, 10–12). Problems, however, often arise at both individual and corporate levels. When they are absolutized by individuals and become idolatrous, then possessions are problematic (interfering with love of God). When they are not shared within the community, they are also problematic (interfering with love of neighbor).

It is not the possession of property as such that is the problem but rather wealth that has become an idol.[7] It is enslavement to earthly possessions that cannot be brought into harmony with service to God.[8] The ethical issue, then, is, Are your priorities straight about possessions?

Matthew 6:25–34

"At the root of the money question is the anxiety question, and thus Jesus moves now to that root."[9] The second subsection on possessions comprises 6:25–34. It deals with trusting God to provide for one's needs. It consists of three paragraphs (vv.

---

7. Schnackenburg, *The Moral Teaching,* 125.
8. Strecker, *The Sermon,* 135.
9. Bruner, *Matthew 1–12,* 265.

25–30, 31–33, 34), each beginning with "Do not be anxious." In the unit, food, drink, and clothing are regarded as the necessities for human life. The unit functions not to offer concrete counsels on what to do with wealth but to reassure believers about God's trustworthiness. Rather than being an ethical text with a horizontal focus, 6:25–34 focuses on the vertical dimension. In terms of its formal arrangement, 6:25–34 looks like this:

Unit One: Matthew 6:25–30—
  Prohibition (v. 25a)—"Do not be anxious about . . ."
  Four Reasons (vv. 25b–30)
    1. (v. 25b)—"Is not life more than food and the body than clothing?"
    2. (v. 26)—"Look at the birds of the air."
    3. (v. 27)—"Who by being anxious can add one cubit to his span of life or stature?"
    4. (vv. 28–30)—"Consider the lilies of the field."
Unit Two: Matthew 6:31–33—
  Prohibition (v. 31)—"Do not be anxious about . . ."
  Two Reasons (v. 32)
    1. (v. 32a)—"The Gentiles seek all these things."
    2. (v. 32b)—"Your heavenly father knows that you need them all."
  Command (v. 33a)—"Seek first God's kingdom and righteousness."
  Promise (v. 33b)—"All these things shall be yours as well."
Unit Three: Matthew 6:34—
  Prohibition (v. 34a)—"Do not be anxious about tomorrow."
  Two Reasons (v. 34b, c)
    1. (v. 34b)—"Tomorrow will be anxious for itself."
    2. (v. 34c)—"Today's trouble is enough for today."

It is now time to examine the contents of this thought unit.

Matthew 6:25–34 as a Catalyst for Character Formation
In an attempt to understand the role of 6:25–34 in character formation, we will focus on the content of the three paragraphs in order.

Unit One (vv. 25–30). The Prohibition (v. 25a) runs: "Do not be anxious about your life . . . or about your body." The cognate noun *merimna* (anxiety) occurs in 1 Maccabees 6:10 and Sirach 42:9, where it is associated with sleeplessness, so the meaning is anxious in the sense of being fearful. It is a "paralyzing anxiety."[10] So the Prohibition is against debilitating anxiety.

10. Hagner, *Matthew 1–13*, 163.

The reasons why one should not be anxious are four (vv. 25b–30). The first (v. 25b) is: "Is not life more than food, and the body more than clothing?" Matthew 4:4 makes a similar point: "One does not live by bread alone." The second reason (v. 26) says: "Look at the birds of the air; they neither sow not reap nor gather into barns, and yet your heavenly father feeds them. Are you not of more value than they?" In both the Old Testament (e.g., Prov 6:6–11) and in Greek philosophy (e.g., Philodemus, *On Methods of Inference*) there is the assumption that human behavior can be learned from animals. That God provides for the animal kingdom is, moreover, a conviction integral to ancient Judaism. Consider Job 38:41—"God provides the raven its prey, when its young ones cry to God, and wander about for lack of food"; Psalm 147:9—"God gives to the animals their food, and to the young ravens when they cry"; *Psalms of Solomon* 5:9–10—"Birds and fish you (God) nourish"; *m. Kaddushin* 4:14—R. Simeon b. Eleazar says: "Have you ever seen a wild animal or a bird practicing a trade?—yet they have their sustenance without care, and were they not created for naught else but to serve me? But I was created to serve my Maker. How much more then ought not I to have my sustenance without care?" The birds are an example not of idleness but of freedom from anxiety. It was also a commonplace to assume that humans are more valuable to God than animals (e.g., Matt 10:31; 12:12). The third reason (v. 27) runs: "Can any of you by worrying add a single hour to your span of life?" Anxiety is ineffectual. The fourth (vv. 28–30) puts it this way: "Consider the lilies of the field. . . . If God so clothes the grass of the field . . . , will he not much more clothe you—you of little faith?"

Unit Two (vv. 31–33). The prohibition (v. 31) repeats a prior command: "Do not be anxious" (about food or drink and clothing). Two reasons are given (v. 32a, b). The first (v. 32a) says: "The Gentiles strive for all these things." The second reason (v. 32b) echoes: "Your heavenly Father knows that you need all these things" (cf. 6:8). The pagans pursued these things because they did not know God as a loving Father. "People, and above all, the religious people of the Hellenistic age, were tormented by anxiety."[11] They feared the future because it was believed to be in the hands of Fate and Fortune. The former was experienced as a crushing burden, the latter as capriciousness, for no one knows how the wheel of fortune will spin. The pagan Trimalco in Petronius's *Satyricon* says: "What comes next you never know, Lady Luck runs the show." Jews also struggled with the same issue. In *Mekilta* on Exodus 16:4, R. Simeon ben Yohai asks: "How can a man be sitting and studying when he does not know where his food and drink will come from nor where he can get his clothes and coverings?"

The command (v. 33a) reads: "Strive first for the kingdom of God and his righteousness." Although some seek to distinguish between kingdom of heaven and

---

11. Betz, *The Sermon*, 105.

kingdom of God,[12] most interpreters regard the two expressions as stylistic variations referring to the same reality.[13] God's righteousness and God's kingdom also
amount to the same thing.[14] Are *kingdom* and *righteousness* here referring to God's
eschatological vindication of saints (e.g., 1QS 10:11), or to the right conduct that
God requires of them (e.g., *T. Dan* 6:10)? Scholars differ.[15] Context seems to indicate that the kingdom of God signifies the divine sovereignty breaking through in
Jesus' ministry (cf. 12:28) and that God's righteousness is the covenant faithfulness
that he is manifesting in Jesus and that can provide for the disciple. If one is recipient of God's intervening rule and covenant faithfulness, then one's priorities are
straight: God first, then God's provision for us.

The promise (v. 33b) says it is so: "All these things will be given to you as well."
The sentiment is Jewish. *Mekilta* on Exodus 16:33 relates that when the prophet
Jeremiah said to the Israelites "Why do you not busy yourself with the Torah?," they
said to him: "If we keep busy with the words of the Torah, how will we get our sustenance?" Then Jeremiah brought forth to them the bottle containing the manna
and said to them: "O generation, see ye the thing of the Lord. See with what your
forefathers, who busied themselves with the words of the Torah, were provided. You,
too, if you busy yourselves with the words of the Torah, God will provide you with
sustenance of this sort." (Cf. Phil 4:6; 1 Pet 5:7.) "For disciples, goods are by-
products not goals. While disciples seek God's kingdom in the front or living room
of their lives, possessions are brought in the back door and deposited in the kitchen."[16]

Unit Three (v. 34). The prohibition (v. 34a) repeats: "Do not be anxious about
tomorrow." This also was a typical Jewish sentiment. Compare *b. Sotah* 48b—
Whoever has a piece of bread in his basket and says: What shall I eat tomorrow?
belongs only to them who are little in faith; also *Mekilta* on Exodus 16:4—He who
has what he will eat today and says, What shall I eat tomorrow? behold, this man has
little faith.

Two reasons are given (v. 34b, c). The first (v. 34b) reads: "Tomorrow will bring
worries of its own." Again, the sentiment is typically Jewish. Compare *b. Sanhedrin*
100b—"Worry not about the worries of tomorrow, for you do not know what the
day will bring forth; perhaps you will be no more, and then you would have wor-
ried about a world that will belong to you no more" (cf. James 4:13–15). The second reason (v. 34c) runs: "Today's trouble is enough for today." Again, this is a typical
Jewish assertion. Compare *b. Berakoth* 9b—"Sufficient is the evil in the time thereof."

12. E.g., Pammet, "The Kingdom of Heaven," 211–32.
13. E.g., Thomas, "The Kingdom of God," 136–46; Foster, "Why on Earth," 487–99.
14. Davies and Allison, *Matthew 1–7*, 661.
15. Luz, *Matthew 1–7*, 407, argues that the kingdom refers to the coming reign of God and
righteousness to the activity of righteousness that humans are to perform. The relation between
the two, he says, is that of human practice and promised reward.
16. Bruner, *Matthew 1–12*, 269.

It was also found among the philosophers. Seneca, *On the Happy Life* 26.4, says, regarding riches, that the wise man ever lives happy in the present and is unconcerned about the future.

The text does not simply command. One does not stop worrying or avoid debilitating anxiety by obeying a command to do so. Indeed, such a command would further complicate the situation. From my youth I remember a ditty that makes the point.

> I've joined the new "don't worry club,"
> In fear I hold my breath,
> I'm so afraid I'll worry,
> I'm worried half to death.

It takes more than a rule or a law to deal with human anxiety. Only divine enablement makes trust in God possible. So Matthew 6:25–34 seeks to make possible what it commands. "Our involvement in these structures of care is too deep to be uprooted by a simple command. . . . a change could only take place if we were to *see* the world in a fundamentally new way."[17] Two structures are set up opposite each other: the structure of care and the world of birds and flowers, in which the structure of care is absent, yet life goes on. Which is the real world, the world of our anxiety or the world of which birds and flowers are images? The text "induces a sense of strangeness about our life and a sense of the presence of something more, something deeper, which offers an alternative for action and makes finally unimportant our structures of care. . . . This opens a new possibility for life, a possibility which the text describes as seeking the kingdom (Matt 6:33)."[18]

If 6:25–34 is taken as moral exhortation, it sounds in its agricultural context like a call to abandon all farming and storage of products and in our context like an obligation to burn all our insurance and retirement policies. Then all sorts of stratagems must be tried to make sense of the material. C. G. Montefiore, assuming it to be ethical material, claimed that Jesus said Matthew 6:25–34 because he believed the End was at hand. If so, why labor to get earthly goods? As a modern man, he was dismissive of a Jesus who gave such exhortation. "We who do not live under this belief can observe and value, at most, the spirit of the counsel here given."[19] As moral exhortation, 6:25–34 does not make sense. If taken ascetically (i.e., as a verbal icon through which one perceives who God is), however, "it leads to common-sense teaching on 'surrender,' abandonment to divine Providence, . . . the sinfulness of anxiety."[20] This text, then, is designed to serve as a catalyst for the formation of the

---

17. Tannehill, *The Sword*, 67.
18. Ibid., 66.
19. Montefiore, *The Synoptic Gospels*, 2:542.
20. Thornton, *English Spirituality*, 33.

character of disciples in the direction of trust in God's providential goodness by enabling them to *see* a different kind of world, one in which creatures live out of their trust in divine providence and are free of debilitating anxiety. This subunit, then, calls for Jesus' disciples to be persons who trust God for their needs.

The Role of Matthew 6:25–34 in Decision Making

How can this text be used in Christian decision making? It must be considered in three contexts. It should also be considered in terms of two questions: Is this text an encouragement of idleness? Is there a difference between being anxious and being irresponsible?

Reading in the context of Matthew as a whole leads one to consider texts like Matthew 25:14–30, where the parable of the talents encourages work and forethought (cf. also 24:45–51 and 25:1–13, both of which encourage forethought).

Reading Matthew 6:25–34 in the context of the New Testament as a whole adds a needed dimension to one's understanding. The first category of texts to consider includes passages like Acts 20:34–35, where Paul works with his own hands; Ephesians 4:28, which exhorts to "Work honestly with one's own hands"; 1 Thessalonians 5:14, which commands "Admonish the idlers"; and 2 Thessalonians 3:6–13, which encourages to "Keep away from believers who are living in idleness." Work is promoted as a positive value in these texts. The second category of texts promotes forethought. Compare Luke 14:28–32—One should count the cost of an action; 2 Corinthians 12:14—Parents ought to lay up for their children; and 1 Timothy 5:8, 16—Whoever does not provide for family members is worse than an unbeliever.

Reading Matthew 6:25–34 in the context of the Bible as a whole continues the emphasis already encountered in favor of work and forethought. A classic text in favor of work is Proverbs 6:6—"Go to the ant, you lazybones; consider its ways, and be wise." In favor of forethought is Genesis 50:20–21, where Joseph tells his brothers that he will provide them and their little ones what they need.

There is a difference between being anxious and being idle. To trust God's goodness does not relieve one of the responsibility of work. This passage does not mean that food, drink, and clothing will come to the disciple automatically without work or foresight. The text addresses only the problem of undue anxiety about these things.[21]

There is also a difference between being anxious and being irresponsible. To trust God's goodness does not relieve one of the responsibility of providing for others in one's care (parents, children, family). "What Jesus condemns here is not a wise forethought for the future but nervous anxiety about it."[22]

At this point one is ready to start using Matthew 6:25–34 in one's decision making.

---

21. Hagner, *Matthew 1–13*, 166–67.
22. Hendrickx, *Sermon on the Mount*, 159.

TEN

Judging—Condemnation and Discernment
Matthew 7:1–12

which righteousness?

Matthew 7:1–12

Matthew 5:20 speaks about a righteousness that exceeds that of the scribes and the Pharisees. In 5:21–48 the Matthean Jesus contrasts the two types of righteousness reflected in the interpretation of Scripture (contra Pharisaic readings that seek to evade the divine intent—e.g. 15:1–12); in 6:1–18 he contrasts two types of righteousness in relation to piety before God (contra Pharisaic practice, which seeks self-promotion—e.g., 23:5); in 6:19–34 he speaks about two types of righteousness in relation to possessions (contra Pharisaic tendencies toward greed—e.g., 15:1–12; 23:25). In 7:1–12 the Matthean Jesus' teaching is again set in opposition to Pharisees who are judgmental (e.g., 9:11; 12:2; 15:1–2) while not practicing what they preach (23:2–4). Again, the higher righteousness is being expounded over and against the Pharisees as Matthew sees them.

Matthew 7:1–12 as a Catalyst for Character Formation
Scholars differ considerably about the arrangement of this segment of the Sermon. The United Bible Societies Greek New Testament, third edition, divides Matthew 7:1–12 into two paragraphs of six verses each; Nestle-Aland's *Novum Testamentum Graece*, twenty-seventh edition, makes separate paragraphs of verses 1–5, 6, 7–11, and 12.[1] The problem is especially acute in verses 6–12. Hagner says about verse 6: "This verse appears to be a detached independent logion apparently unrelated to the preceding . . . or following context, inserted here for no special reason but only as another saying of Jesus." About verses 7–11 he says: "This is another self-contained unit having no connection with the material that precedes or follows it."[2] I suggest, however, that the unit is a two-part whole.[3] This section is composed of two subunits,

---

1. Hendrickx, *Sermon on the Mount,* 161, contends that the four units deal with various themes, the one not seeming to lead to the other.
2. Hagner, *Matthew 1–13,* 171, 173.
3. McEleney, "The Unity and Theme," 490–500, agrees about the unity of the thought unit but reads its particulars a bit differently.

verses 1–5 and verses 6–12, each controlled by an opening prohibition and composed of the same three components. Formally, the unit looks like this.

> Unit One: 7:1–5, deals with judging as condemnation of another by one who has not judged him- or herself (so contra severity). It consists of three parts: vv. 1, 2, and 3–5.
>
> 1) What we are *not* to do: condemn (v. 1)—"Judge not."
> 2) What God will do (v. 2)—"With the judgment you pronounce, you will be judged."
> 3) What we are to do (vv. 3–5)—Reprove oneself first; then one will be able to reprove others.
>> Rhetorical question (v. 3)—"How can you see . . . ?"
>> Rhetorical question (v. 4)—"How can you say . . . ?"
>> Concluding exhortation (v. 5)—"First . . . then. . . ."
>
> Unit Two: 7:6–12, deals with judging as discernment necessary for appropriate action (so contra laxity). It consists of three parts: vv. 6, 7–11, and 12.
>
> 1) What we are *not* to do: do not fail to recognize the difference between holy and unclean things and do not fail to act accordingly (v. 6)—"Do not give dogs what is holy."
> 2) What God will do: supply wisdom to enable discernment (vv. 7–11)—"Ask . . . seek . . . knock. . . ."
>> Exhortation (v. 7)—"Ask and it will be given."
>> Basis (v. 8)—"For every one who asks receives."
>> First example (v. 9)—"If a child asks for bread. . . ."
>> Second example (v. 10)—"If a child asks for a fish. . . ."
>> Concluding inference (v. 11)—"If you . . . how much more God. . . ."
>
> 3) What we are to do: follow the Golden Rule in making judgments (v. 12).

Really?

When examining the contents of 7:1–12, we will follow the outline just proposed.

Unit One. Matthew 7:1–5 focuses on judging as condemnation of another by one who has not judged him- or herself. Verse 1 tells what *not* to do: do not condemn (cf. Matt 12:41–42; 20:18; Rom 2:1, 3 for such a meaning of *krinete*).[4] Verse 2 says what God will do: judge the condemner with the same judgment the condemner has exercised. This was a common Jewish sentiment. Compare Romans 2:1, 3—"in passing judgment on another you condemn yourself, because you, the judge, are doing the very same things. . . . Do you imagine . . . that when you judge those who do such things and yet do them yourself, you will escape the judgment

---

4. Davies and Allison, *Matthew 1–7*, 668.

of God?"; *m. Sotah* 1:7—"With the measure with which a person measures, he will be measured (by God)"; *Mekilta* on Exodus 13:19a—(This is) "to teach you that with the measure with which a man measures, they (God) measure to him"; *Sifre* on Numbers 12:13—"According to the measure with which a man measures, they (God) measure to him"; *b. Rosh ha-Shanah* 16b—R. Abin said: "He who calls down divine judgment on his neighbor is himself punished first for his own sins"; *Genesis Rabbah* 9:11—R. Simeon said in R. Simeon by Abba's name: "All measures have ceased yet the rule of measure for measure has not ceased." R. Huna said in R. Jose's name: "From the very beginning of the world's creation, the Holy One, blessed be He, foresaw that with the measure a man measures, with it they will measure to him"; *Targum* on Isaiah 27:8—"in the measure you were measuring with, they will measure you"; *Palestinian Targum* on Genesis 38:26—"with the same measure by which a person measures on earth, he is measured in heaven." In Matthew 7:2 mention of divine judgment is probably a reference to the Last Judgment.

Verses 3–5 tell what we are to do: Reprove yourself first, then you will be able to reprove others. Verse 3 is a rhetorical question: "Why do you see the speck in your neighbor's eye, but do not notice the log in your own eye?" Verse 4 is another rhetorical question: "How can you say to your neighbor, 'Let me take the speck out of your eye,' while the log is in your own eye?" Verse 5 is a concluding exhortation: "First take the log out of your own eye, and then you will see clearly to take the speck out of your neighbor's eye."

The language is typically Jewish. Consider *b. Arakhin* 16b—R. Tarfon (100 C.E.) said: "I should be surprised if in this generation it were given to anyone to undertake to reprimand another. For if one should say, 'Take the splinter out of your eye,' the latter might very well answer, 'Take the beam out of your own eye.'"

The sentiments are common both to Jewish and to Greco-Roman contexts. On the Jewish side, note Sirach 18:20—"Before judgment comes, examine yourself; and at the time of scrutiny you will find forgiveness" (cf. 2 Sam 12:1–5). On the Greco-Roman side, note Cicero, *Tusculun Disputations* 3.73—"It is a peculiarity of folly to discern the faults of others and to be forgetful of its own"; Horace, *Satires* 1.3.25—"When you look at your own sins, your eyes are rheumy and daubed with ointment; why, when you view the failings of friends, are you as keen of sight as an eagle?"; Seneca, *On the Happy Life* 27.4—"You look at the pimples of others when you yourselves are covered with a mass of sores"; 27.6—"Why do you not rather look about you at your own sins that rend you on every side?"; Plutarch, *How to Profit by One's Enemies* 2.88D, F—"One should not revile an enemy for something in which one is also caught up oneself." The first unit, then, focuses on condemnation of another by one who has not used the same spotlight on oneself.

Unit Two. Verses 6–12 focus on the discernment necessary for appropriate action that avoids laxity. Verse 6 says what *not* to do: Do not fail to discern the difference between holy and unclean things and do not fail to act accordingly. Is this a detached, independent logion unrelated to what comes before or what follows? Or is it placed here to serve as a qualification of the prohibition against judging?[5] The latter, I think. Two sayings, one Jewish and one Pythagorean, aid one's understanding of this very difficult logion. In *m. Temurah* 6:5 a priestly rule about sacrificial meat runs "Do not give to dogs what is holy," meaning in context that one should use discernment and should not act inappropriately. A Pythagorean maxim runs "Do not throw bread into a chamber pot." This was interpreted to mean "do not try to teach those unfit to receive your teachings" (i.e., do not do what is inappropriate under the circumstances).[6] Matthew 7:6 operates out of the same concern for discernment and the requisite appropriate action. One is to make appropriate moral judgments and distinctions and act accordingly.

Verses 7–11 tell what God will do: God will supply wisdom to enable this discernment. Is this another self-contained unit having no connection with the material that precedes or follows it or should it be taken as an integral part of the larger context? The latter is preferable, if possible. The unit is held together by an inclusion (v. 7—ask . . . given—and v. 11—given . . . ask).[7] It opens with an *exhortation* (v. 7): ask . . . be given, search . . . find, knock . . . be opened. This language is typical of speech about prayer. Compare Jeremiah 29:12–14—call . . . hear; search . . . find; seek . . . find; Isaiah 65:1—sought . . . ask . . . found . . . seek; *b. Megillah* 12b—"he knocked at the gates of mercy and they were opened to him." The basis is then given (v. 8): "everyone who asks receives, everyone who searches finds, to everyone who knocks, the door will be opened." Just as all six sentences of the Lord's Prayer are petitions, so here prayer is understood as asking. It is assumed that disciples appear before God as "humble receivers from a generous Father."[8] Is this an affirmation of the efficacy of unrestricted prayer? Or is its meaning more restricted by the context? The latter, I think, in this context. The language is typical of prayers for wisdom. Consider, for example, Proverbs 8:17—Wisdom says: "those who seek me diligently find me"; Wisdom of Solomon 6:12—Wisdom "is found by those who seek her"; James 1:5—"If any of you is lacking in wisdom, ask God, who gives to all generously and ungrudgingly, and it will be given you." The language seems to say that those who ask for divine wisdom will be heard and given this treasure. Two rhetorical questions (vv. 9–10) focus the issue of God's goodness and willingness to answer prayer. They use a "how much more" argument. "Is there any one among you who, if your child asks for bread, will give a stone? Or if the child asks

---

5. So Beare, *The Gospel,* 190; Hendrickx, *Sermon on the Mount,* 165; Davies and Allison, *Matthew 1–7,* 674; Patte, *The Gospel,* 96.
6. Thom, "'Don't Walk,'" 93–112.
7. Garland, *Reading Matthew,* 86.
8. Bruner, *Matthew 1–12,* 278.

for a fish, will give a snake?" The concluding inference (v. 11) runs: "If you then, who are evil, know how to give good gifts to your children, how much more will your Father in heaven give good things to those who ask him?" Reading verses 7–11 in context results in seeing the pericope as an enablement of verse 6. If one needs to discern what is appropriate judging and discerning, ask God for wisdom and God will provide it.

Verse 12 focuses on what we are to do, namely, follow the Golden Rule in making judgments. This verse functions formally as the second member of an inclusion that holds together the material from 5:17 (the Law or the prophets) to 7:12 (Law and the prophets); logically it serves as the conclusion to 7:1–12.[9] If so, then it should be interpreted as part of that train of thought. So far the thought has run: judge appropriately and act rightly; if you do not know how, ask God for wisdom and it will be provided; and when judging and evaluating, do it in the spirit of the Golden Rule. In the *Epistle of Aristeas* 207, the Golden Rule is part of an answer given by a sage to the king's question, "What is the teaching of wisdom?" Just so it functions here in Matthew 7:1–12 as well.

"In everything do to others as you would have them do to you." This ethical guideline was widespread in antiquity in both positive and negative forms (Tob 4:15; *Ep. Aris.* 207; Sir 31:15 LXX; *T. Naph.*, Heb, 1:6; *Ahikar*, Aramaic B, 53; Philo, *Hyp.* [in Eusebius, *Praep. ev.* 8.7.6]; Tg Ps-J. on Lev 19:18; *Ps. Men.* 39; 2 Enoch 61:1–2; *b. Sabb.* 31a; *Avot R. Nat.* 15; Dio Cassius 51.34.39; Isocrates, *Nic.* 49, 61; Herodotus 3.142; Homer, *Ody.* 5.188–89; cf. Acts 15:20, 28, Bezae; *Did.* 1:2; *Apos. Const.* 7.2.1; Ps. Clem. *Hom.* 17.35.5; *Recog.* 8.56.7). Positive and negative forms of the Golden Rule are moral equivalents. One is not superior to the other.

The Golden Rule, says the Matthean Jesus, "is the law and the prophets" (v. 12b; cf. Matt 22:40, where it is the double love command). That is, the Jewish Scriptures are interpreted in terms of the Golden Rule. It was a practice in both Judaism and the Greco-Roman world to attempt to sum up a body of teaching in one general principle. From the pagan world, consider Plutarch, *Consolation ad Apollonium 28* (116 C–D)—"There are two of the inscriptions at Delphi which are most indispensable to living. They are: 'Know thyself' and 'Avoid extremes,' for on these two commandments hang all the rest." Numerous examples from the Jewish world include *b. Makkoth* 23b–24a—the 613 precepts communicated to Moses were reduced to one principle by Habakkuk: "But the righteous shall live by faith"; *b. Berakoth* 63a—Bar Kappara expounded: "What short text is there upon which all the essential principles of the Torah depend? 'In all thy ways acknowledge Him and He will

---

9. Contra Hendrickx, *Sermon on the Mount,* 170, who agrees with NEB and JB (and NRSV) in separating 7:12 from 7:7–11 and regarding verse 12 as the summary of the whole Sermon so far.

direct thy paths'"; *Sifra* on Leviticus 19:18—Thou shalt love thy neighbor as thyself. R. Akiba said: "That is the greatest principle in the Law"; Philo, *Decalogue* 18–19—the Decalogue is the *kephalaia nomon; b. Shabbat* 31a—a heathen came to Hillel. Hillel said: "What is hateful to you, do not do to your neighbor: that is the whole Torah, while the rest is commentary thereon; go and learn it." (Ps. Philo, *L.A.B.* 11:9–13, interprets the Decalogue by the Golden Rule. *Syr. Menander* 246–47 interprets the law of adultery by the Golden Rule.) It is interesting to note that the Matthean Jesus' summation of the Jewish Scriptures has affinities with those of Akiba and Hillel (love of neighbor and the Golden Rule).

The question is, Is the Golden Rule (v. 12) the climax of verses 1–12 or only of verses 6–12? If the former, then one's refusal to judge or condemn others before judging oneself would be motivated by the Golden Rule as well as one's evaluation of others in light of God-granted wisdom. If the latter, then the Golden Rule would apply only to the application of God's wisdom to one's evaluation of good and bad. It seems that verse 12 functions well as the conclusion to the whole of 7:1–12. When one hears Hillel's statement "Judge not thy fellow until thou art come to his place" (*m. Abot* 2:5), one realizes that the Judaism of Jesus' time applied the Golden Rule to topics like that discussed in 7:1–5 and that it would likely have been heard as such by Matthew's auditors.

Matthew 7:1–5 employs a grotesque contrast (splinter . . . log) to provide metaphoric shock. It is presented as a highly personalized attack. The aim is to help uncover what we do not see because we are blind. The extreme picture is able to illumine a whole range of situations that we would otherwise miss.[10] If we are enabled to *see* differently, then we can be different people. Character formation is in view.

The Function of Matthew 7:1–12 in Christian Decision Making

How should Matthew 7:1–12 be used in Christian decision making? It must be read in three contexts. The questions to be addressed are: Does "judge not" mean Christians are to abstain from all moral evaluation of others? Is the Matthean Jesus promising unrestricted efficacy to his disciples' petitions? We will take up these two questions in order.

The first question asks whether Christians should abstain from any and all moral evaluation of others. After all, Jesus said, "Judge not." Reading in the context of Matthew's Gospel as a whole requires one to consider the following: Matthew 7:1–5 must be read together with 7:6–12, which enjoins discernment; Matthew 7:15–20; 10:11–15; 16:6, 12; 18:17–18, all of which require moral distinctions to be drawn by Jesus' disciples; and Matthew 23, which shows Jesus doing that very thing, and

---

10. Tannehill, *The Sword,* 114–18.

with a vengeance. Reading in the context of the whole New Testament involves a consideration of texts like 1 Thessalonians 5:21–22—"Test everything; hold fast to what is good; abstain from every form of evil"; Romans 16:17—"Keep an eye on those who cause dissensions and offenses . . . ; avoid them"; Hebrews 5:14—"Solid food is for the mature, for those whose faculties have been trained by practice to distinguish good from evil"; Luke 12:57—"Why do you not judge for yourselves what is right?"; John 7:24—"Do not judge by appearances, but judge with right judgment." Reading in the context of the Bible as a whole demands recognition of texts like Malachi 3:18—"Then once more you shall see the difference between the righteous and the wicked, between one who serves God and one who does not serve him." Taken in context, the "judge not" of Matthew 7:1–5 cannot be taken to mean abstinence from discernment that evaluates differences between good and bad. There is a legitimate judging in which Jesus' disciples are to be engaged, both in private and in public. "There is thus a limit to not judging."[11]

The second question asks whether Jesus promises unrestricted efficacy to his disciples' petitions. Some have so read 7:7–11.[12] Montefiore's reaction to the text is typical of such readers. He says: "One can, let us hope, have faith, and yet not have this wholesale belief in the efficacy of unrestricted prayer."[13] When one reads in context, what becomes clear? Reading 7:7–11 in the context of Matthew as a whole requires Matthew 7:7–11 to be read together with verse 6 and thus related to discernment; Matthew 18:19, a text that has to do with discernment about disciplinary matters in the church; Matthew 26:39, where Jesus' prayer is answered in the negative. Reading in the context of the New Testament as a whole involves one with passages like Luke 11:13, which uses the same material as prayer for the Holy Spirit; John 14:13–14, whose prayer refers to empowerment for ministry; James 1:5, which speaks about prayer for wisdom; 2 Corinthians 12:8–9, where Paul's prayer is answered in the negative; and Revelation 6:9–11, where the martyrs' prayer is answered "Not yet." Reading in the context of the Bible as a whole causes us to encounter examples like Jonah 4:2–3, where the prophet's prayer is not answered positively; Psalm 22:1–2, where the psalmist complains that God has not answered his prayer; Psalm 42:9–10, where the psalmist feels God has not answered prayer. Reading Matthew 7:7–11 in context, therefore, leads to a certain conclusion. Scripture does not promise that every prayer of God's people will meet with a certain yes. Sometimes God's answer is yes; sometimes it is no; sometimes it is "not yet."

At this point, Matthew 7:1–12 may begin to contribute to Christian decision making.

---

11. Strecker, *The Sermon*, 147.
12. On the history of the use of the saying, see Goldsmith, "'Ask and It Will,'" 254–65.
13. Montefiore, *The Synoptic Gospels*, 2:549.

ELEVEN

Exhortations, Warnings, and Closing

Matthew 7:13–27; 7:28–8:1

Matthew 7:13–27; 7:28–8:1

This section of the Sermon on the Mount is composed of two parts: 7:13–27 and 7:28–8:1. The former (7:13–27) is comprised of three units (vv. 13–14, vv. 15–23, and vv. 24–27), each of which is built around a contrast (two gates, two trees, two houses) and is concerned with judgment (cf. 10:40–42; 13:47–50; 18:23–25; 25:31–46). The first and third units focus on everyone; the second focuses on false prophets. The latter part (7:28–8:1) constitutes the conclusion of the Sermon and forms an inclusion with 4:23–5:2.

Matthew 7:13–8:1 as a Catalyst for Character Formation

Formally, this section, with its two parts (7:13–27; 7:28–8:1), looks something like this.

Part One (7:13–27)
>Paragraph One: (7:13–14)—the two gates, the two roads, the two destinations
>>V. 13a (command)—"Enter through the narrow gate"
>>Vv. 13b–14 (a dual reason)—
>>V. 13b—"for the gate is wide and the road is easy that leads to destruction, and there are many who take it."
>>V. 14—"for the gate is narrow and the road is hard that leads to life, and there are few who find it."
>Paragraph Two: (7:15–23)—the two trees
>>Unit One (vv. 15–20)—
>>>V. 15 (warning against false prophets)
>>>Vv. 16–20 (the basis of recognition)
>>>V. 16a (general principle)—"You will know them by their fruits."

Vv. 16b–18—The *nature* of a tree is revealed by its
fruit.

V. 19—The *destiny* of a tree is determined by its fruit
(cf. 7:21–23).

V. 20 (general principle)—"You will know them by
their fruits."

Unit Two (vv. 21–23)

V. 21a—warning: "Not everyone who says . . . will enter."

V. 21b—basis for entrance: doing the will of my Father in
heaven.

Vv. 22–23—an illustration of the warning and basis

Evidence presented to the judge (v. 22):

Christological confession (but cf. Matt
10:32–33)

Prophecy (cf. 24:11, 24)

Mighty works (cf. Matt 24:23–28)

Sentence pronounced by the judge (v. 23)

Paragraph Three (7:24–27)—The two houses

Vv. 24–25—Promise

Vv. 26–27—Warning

Part Two: 7:28–8:1 (Conclusion to the Sermon on the Mount)

In our examination of the contents of 7:13–8:1 it is this outline that will be followed. In reading 7:13–27, it is important to keep in mind that all of the material is related to the expectation of the End and the prospect of judgment. The warning of catastrophe predominates. We begin with Paragraph One (7:13–14) of Part One. "Enter through the narrow gate; for the gate is wide and the road is easy that leads to destruction, and there are many who take it. For the gate is narrow and the road is hard that leads to life, and there are few who find it." Presupposed here is the ancient conventional image of the two ways. The Jewish roots in Deuteronomy 11:26–27 are elaborated in Jeremiah 21:8 ("Thus says the Lord: See, I am setting before you the way of life and the way of death"). The "two ways" tradition in Judaism is echoed in texts like 1QS 3:13–4:26; *Testament of Asher* 1:3–5; *2 Enoch* 30:15; *m. Abot* 2:12–13; *Mekilta* on Exodus 14:28; *Sifre* on Deuteronomy, Piske 53; and *b. Berakoth* 28b. The Greek roots of the tradition go back at least to the story about Herakles at the crossroads (Hesiod, *Works* 286–93; Xenophon, *Mem.* 2.1.21–34). This conventional form of thought was appropriated by early Christians, of whom Matthew is one. The command (v. 13a) "Enter through the narrow gate" makes the choice clear-cut. The basis for the choice comes in a contrast. On the one hand, "the gate is wide and the road is easy that leads to destruction, and there are many who take it." Jewish and Greek authors spoke this way. Sirach 21:10 says:

"The way of sinners is paved with smooth stones, but at its end is the pit of Hades." Philo, *Special Laws* 4.112, uses the metaphor of the two ways: the way of pleasure and the way of self-control. The road leading to pleasure is easy and downhill. The road leading to self-control is uphill and toilsome. Hesiod, *Works and Days* 286–91, puts it: "Wickedness is easy to choose and plentiful; the way is smooth and near to hand." On the other hand, "the gate is narrow and the road is hard that leads to life, and there are few who find it." Again Jewish and Greek authors spoke in a similar way. *4 Ezra* 7:47–51 says: "the world to come will bring delight to few, but torments to many . . . the righteous are not many but few, while the ungodly abound." Hesiod, *Works and Days* 286–92, contends: "The immortal gods have decreed that we must sweat to win virtue; the path is long, and steep and rough." Elsewhere, the Matthean Jesus puts it: "For many are called but few are chosen" (20:16; 22:14). The image of two ways functions to set before the auditors an either-or choice.

Paragraph Two (7:15–23) utilizes the image of the two trees. There are two units (vv. 15–20 and vv. 21–23) in this segment. In 7:15–20 there is first a warning against false prophets. "Beware of false prophets, who come to you in sheep's clothing but inwardly are ravenous wolves." False prophets were a problem for the early church (cf. 1 John 2:18–27; 4:1–6; Mark 9:38–40; 13:5–6, 21–23; Tit 1:10–16; Acts 20:29–30; Rev 2:20; 2 Pet 2:1; *Did.* 11:3–12:5; Hermas, *Man.* 11; Montanists). Early Christian authors sometimes used the conventional image of wolves (Acts 20:29) for these false teachers. Matthew 7:15, like Aesop's *Proverbs,* 123, speaks of wolves in sheep's clothing (i.e., disguised).

Verses 16–20 provide the basis for recognition of these false prophets. The subunit is held together by an inclusion. Beginning (v. 16) and ending (v. 20) say: "You will know them by their fruits." "Fruits" of course refer to deeds (Ps 1:1–3; Philo, *Spec. Laws* 4.75, compares young people to plants that are cultivated "until they bear the fruit of goodness on their stems"; *Gen. Rab.* 30:6 asks, What is the fruit of the righteous? and answers: good works; Col 1:10 says of its readers, "as you bear fruit in every good work"). Good works are fruits that good trees spontaneously produce.[1]

Verses 16b–18 clarify the thesis statement when they state that the nature of a tree is revealed by its fruit. This again is conventional language (Seneca, *Ep.* 87.25— "Good does not spring from evil any more than figs grow from olive trees"; Epictetus, *Diss.* 2.20.18—"Such a powerful and invincible thing is the nature of man. For how can a vine be moved to act, not like a vine, but like an olive, or again an olive to act, not like an olive, but like a vine? It is impossible; inconceivable"; Plutarch, *Tranq.* 13—"But as it is, we do not expect the vine to bear figs nor the olive grapes"; James 3:12—"Can a fig tree yield olives or a grapevine figs?" The point: deeds emerge out of and reveal one's character.

---

1. Patte, *The Gospel,* 100.

Verse 19 says that the destiny of a tree is determined by its fruit. "Every tree that does not bear good fruit is cut down and thrown into the fire" (cf. Luke 13:9). If the way one walks has consequences, so also does the fruit one bears.

The conclusion reiterates the general principle. "You will know them by their fruits" (v. 20). The Matthean Jesus' criterion for distinguishing between true and false prophets here is behavioral: deeds. A variety of tests were employed by early Christians: for example, 1 Corinthians 12:3 (false prophets do not confess Jesus as Lord); 1 John 4:2 (false prophets do not confess Jesus having come and remaining in the flesh); Matthew 24:24–27 (false prophets do not view the Parousia as a cosmic event); 2 Peter 2 (false prophets have false doctrine and libertine ethics); *Didache* 11:10 (false prophets do not do the truth they teach) and 11:5 (false prophets ask for money); Hermas, *Mandate,* 11.12–13 (false prophets do not go to church and they take money); Ps-Clementine *Homilies* 2.10 (only those whose prophecies come to pass are true prophets). There were behavioral and doctrinal tests. Matthew 7:20 falls into the camp of those who test behavior by its fruits.

Who are these false prophets to whom Matthew's Sermon makes reference? Suggestions include gnostics (Bacon)[2]; Essenes (Daniel)[3]; Zealots (Cothenet)[4]; post-Easter Palestinian enthusiasts (Käsemann, appealing to 24:24)[5]; Jewish Christians who are overzealous for the Law and opposed to a Gentile Christian mission (Guelich)[6]; hellenistic Christian libertines/antinomians (Betz, appealing to 24:11–12)[7]; and no particular group but rather a generic description (Hagner).[8] The difficulty of identifying a specific group makes the generic description attractive.

Unit Two (vv. 21–23) begins with a warning: "Not everyone who says to me, 'Lord, Lord,' will enter the kingdom of heaven" (v. 21a). The basis for entrance into the kingdom comes in verse 21b: "but only the one who does the will of my Father in heaven." This is a conventional Jewish mode of expression (*m. Pirke Abot* 5:22— R. Jehudah b. Thema [mid second century] said: "Be bold as a leopard, swift as an eagle, fleet as a hart, and strong as a lion to do the will of your Father who is in heaven"). The sentiment is echoed in James 1:22: "Be doers of the word and not merely hearers."

Verses 22–23 provide an illustration of the warning and its basis. The scene assumed here is that of the Last Judgment, when various groups appear before the

2. Bacon, *Studies in Matthew,* 348.
3. Daniel, "Faux prophètes," 45–79.
4. Cothenet, "Les prophètes chrétiennes," 281–308.
5. Käsemann, "The Beginnings," 82–107.
6. Guelich, *The Sermon,* 393.
7. Betz, *The Sermon,* 528.
8. Hagner, *Matthew 1–13,* 182–83.

End Time judge, who happens to be Jesus.[9] This group appeals to Jesus because they believe he will look favorably on them. They present their evidence. It includes a christological confession (Lord, Lord), prophecy in Jesus' name, exorcisms, and other mighty works in Jesus' name (v. 22). Jesus, however, refuses even to acknowledge them. "Go away from me, you evil doers" (v. 23). Why? Confession of Jesus is crucial (Matt 10:32–33) but not sufficient. Prophecy can be false (Matt 24:11, 24). Mighty works can be instruments of false prophets and false messiahs (Matt 24:23–28). The Matthean Jesus' crucial test is the bearing of good fruit. A similar logion is found in fragment 6 of the Nazarene Gospel ("If you are at my side and do not do the will of my Father in heaven, I will push you away from me").

Paragraph Three (7:24–27) utilizes the image of the two houses. One finds here a parable with a promise (vv. 24–25) and a warning (vv. 26–27). The stress is on the fate of the two houses. Will they be standing when the storm is over? The thought-world is a conventional one. From the Jewish side, note *The Avot of Rabbi Nathan* 24, where Rabbi Elisha ben Abuyah says: "One in whom there are good works, who has studied much Torah, to what may he be likened? To a person who builds first with stones and afterward with bricks: even when much water comes and collects by their side, it does not dislodge them. But one in whom there are no good works, though he studied Torah, to what may he be likened? To a person who builds first with bricks and afterward with stones: even when a little water gathers, it overthrows them immediately." From the Greco-Roman side, consider Seneca's *Epistle* 52, where the philosopher says: "Suppose that two buildings have been erected, unlike as to their foundations, but equal in height and grandeur. One is built on faultless ground, and the process of erection goes right ahead. In the other case, the foundations have exhausted the building materials, for they have sunk into soft and shifting ground and much labor has been wasted in reaching the solid rock." Both Jewish and pagan comparisons are alike in their stress on proper foundations. So also the parable of the Matthean Jesus.

The Palestinian house had no foundations as such. Its stability depended on the soil on which it was built.[10] The proper soil is specified in the promise (v. 24). "Everyone then who hears these words of mine and acts on them will be like a wise man who built his house on the rock." An improper soil is delineated in the warning (v. 26). "Everyone who hears these words of mine and does not act on them will be like a foolish man who built his house on sand." Luz's words summarize well the function of the final parable in the Sermon. "Like the end of the holiness code (Lev 26), Deuteronomy (30:15–20), the final redaction of 1 Enoch (108), and the Assumption of Moses (12:10–13), the readers are . . . placed before the great alternative. As in

---

9. Contra Betz, *The Sermon*, 554, who claims that in 7:21–23 Jesus does not act as eschatological judge but as the advocate of his disciples, as in 1 John 2:1.

10. Hendrickx, *Sermon on the Mount*, 187.

the discourse on the community (18:23–35) and in the eschatological discourse (24:45–25:46), it is an eschatological parable which puts before the readers the two possibilities."[11]

If the Sermon on the Mount begins with blessings (5:3–12), it ends with warnings of judgment. Like the other large discourses in Matthew (10:40–42; 13:47–50; 18:23–35; 25:31–46), the Sermon of the Mount ends with a focus on the Last Judgment (7:13–27). Indeed, here, as in 5:3–12, Jesus is pronouncing proleptically the verdict of the Last Judgment. In so doing the Matthean Jesus enables the auditors to *see* the true standards by which ultimate evaluations are made. Doing the will of the heavenly Father must surely be related to the "higher righteousness," to the exposition of which the Sermon of the Mount overall (5:17–7:12) has been devoted. The function of 7:13–27 is to move the auditors to act as if they were part of the very few who will enter life. It is a catalyst for the shaping of intentions.

Montefiore regards the Sermon on the Mount as lacking in christology. He says: "If we regard the Sermon on the Mount as the charter of the 'Christianity' of Jesus, it is immensely striking how completely the christological element is lacking. The new Law contains no article of faith concerning the person of its giver. It is silent about his Messiahship. There is no word about his divinity. We can seek to live in the spirit of the Sermon and yet, like every Jew from Jesus's day to this, refuse to acknowledge any MAN as our religious 'Lord.'"[12] Is this so?

The following evidence from the Sermon enables an appropriate evaluation. In Matthew 5:3–10, the Matthean Jesus not only knows the basis of the Last Judgment but also offers a proleptic pronouncement of it. He acts now as eschatological judge. In Matthew 5:17–20, the Matthean Jesus claims to know whether or not one will enter the kingdom of God and how one will be ranked there. In Matthew 5:21–48, the "but I say to you" is the Matthean Jesus' claim to the normative interpretation of Scripture. He claims to know God's intentions. In Matthew 6:9–13, the Matthean Jesus knows how one should address God and for what one should pray. In Matthew 6:33, the Matthean Jesus knows God's priorities for human life. In Matthew 7:21–23, the Matthean Jesus claims he will be the eschatological judge and tells how he will act. In Matthew 7:24–27, the Matthean Jesus claims a person stands or falls depending on his or her relation to his words. What can be deduced from these texts?

In the Sermon on the Mount Jesus functions as both *revealer* and *judge*. Taken together, these two functions point to what has been called a "two foci christology."[13] Jesus in his earthly career is the one who speaks God's authoritative word. This is

11. Luz, *Matthew 1–7*, 452.
12. Montefiore, *The Synoptic Gospels*, 2:555.
13. Fuller, *The Foundations*, 142–81, 243–44.

the first focus. At his Parousia Jesus is the Messianic Judge whose judgment is according to the authoritative word he had spoken during his earthly career. This is the second focus. The soteriology presupposed in the Sermon fits the christology. What God's messenger demands is repentance (cf. Matt 4:17). What the Sermon delineates is the content of the repentance demanded (the higher righteousness). What the Matthean Jesus says is that one's status at the Last Judgment depends on his or her embodying this repentance. Why, then, were no christological titles employed in Matthew 5–7?

Aristotle, *Poetics* 1452a, 1454b–55a, contends that the best recognition of who one is is based on "that which arises from the actions alone." In the Sermon, Jesus' teachings and actions by themselves offer the auditors a knowledge of who he is. He is the one who speaks God's authoritative word in the here and now and will function as the eschatological judge on the Last Day. Readers of Matthew 1–4 would have been conditioned already by that narrative to see Jesus in terms of multiple titles and descriptive labels. In the Sermon, his activity alone speaks loudly about his identity.

Part Two (7:28–8:1) functions as the conclusion of the Sermon on the Mount. The conclusion forms an inclusion with 4:32–5:2.

4:23–5:2	*7:28–8:1*
great crowds followed (4:25)	great crowds followed him (8:1)
the crowds are present (5:1)	the crowds are present (7:28)
the mountain (5:1)	the mountain (8:1)
Jesus goes up (5:1)	Jesus goes down (8:1)
Jesus teaches (5:2)	Jesus' teaching (7:29)
opening his mouth (5:2)	when Jesus had finished these words (7:28)

Similarly, the opening (9:35–10:5a) and closing (11:1) of the discourse in Matthew 10 frame it, just as the beginning (13:1–3a) and ending (13:53) of the speech in Matthew 13 frame it.[14]

The conclusion indicates that Matthew regards the Sermon on the Mount as teaching (7:28; cf. 5:1–2) and that Jesus' teaching was perceived by the crowds as different in style from that of the scribes (7:29). Key to this closing point is 7:29— "He taught them as one having authority, and not as their scribes." How would an ancient auditor have heard this statement? It would have been heard as a contrast between two different styles of teaching. In the scribal world, authority resided in the past, in one's teacher and his teacher and his teacher. One appealed to those who had come before. A rabbinic text illustrates the issue. In *b. Baba Mezia* 58b–59b, set in the period of the second generation of Tannaim (90–130 C.E.), there was a debate

---

14. Davies and Allison, *Matthew 1–7*, 725.

between R. Eliezer and R. Joshua that was resolved against Eliezer. This was done in spite of miracles supporting R. Eliezer's position (the uprooting of a carob tree and its relocation; water flowing up hill; and a *bath qol* [heavenly voice]) because the Torah had already been given on Sinai. That is, authority did not reside in spiritual power made manifest in the present but in the established tradition from the past. In *j. Pesah* 6.1.33a, a similar tradition is found. The great teacher Hillel had discoursed on a matter all day, but the other rabbis did not receive his teaching until he said: "Thus I heard from Shemaiah and Abtalion." Again, it is the succession of tradition from the past that settles an issue. By contrast, the Matthean Jesus is said to have taught with authority ("out of himself"), with no appeal to a chain of tradition. The difference in style was striking to the auditors. The difference in style, we have seen, functioned as a catalyst for the formation of the character of the disciples.

The Contribution of Matthew 7:13–8:1 to Decision Making

How should this material be used in normative Christian teaching? Two questions need attention. How can Jesus' disciples recognize legitimate teachers and leaders? Does a disciple's ultimate destiny depend on his/her response to Jesus' teachings? These questions must be considered in light of three contexts.

Reading Matthew 7:13–8:1 in the context of Matthew as a whole yields assistance on both scores. How can legitimate teachers and leaders be recognized? Matthew 24:11–12, 26–27 states that false prophets are lawless and teach wrongly. Does a disciple's destiny depend on a response to Jesus? Matthew 10:32–33 calls for one to acknowledge Jesus before others; Matthew 11:2–6 calls for a believing response to Jesus' deeds (cf. 11:23); Matthew 12:36–37 says one is justified on the last day on the basis of his or her words that reveal the heart; Matthew 19:27–29 calls upon disciples to leave houses, brothers, sisters, father, mother, children, and fields for Jesus' name's sake; Matthew 24:44, 45–51; 25:1–13, 14–30 all expect disciples to remain ready and faithful till the End; Matthew 25:31–46 contends judgment is on the basis of one's treating the "little ones" right; Matthew 28:19–20 assumes disciples will be baptized in name of the Father, Son, and Holy Spirit and will obey all that Jesus commanded.

Reading in the context of the New Testament as a whole adds another dimension to one's understanding. How can legitimate teachers be recognized? 1 Corinthians 12:3 says false prophets do not confess Jesus as Lord; 1 John 4:2 says false prophets deny the incarnation; 2 Peter 2 says false prophets teach a false christology and are libertines; Revelation 19:20 (16:13; 20:10) says a false prophet works miracles to deceive and to lead people into idolatry. Does one's ultimate destiny depend on a response to Jesus? John 3:16 says that one must believe in God's son (3:36—obey God's son); John 6:54 has Jesus say that one must "eat my flesh and drink my blood"; Acts 2:38 exhorts people to repent and be baptized in the name of Jesus Christ; Acts

16:31 has Paul and Silas demand that the jailer believe in the Lord Jesus Christ; Romans 10:9 speaks about confessing with your lips that Jesus is Lord and believing in your heart that God has raised him from the dead; Galatians 2:16 speaks about believing in Christ Jesus.

Reading in the context of the Bible as a whole has its contribution to make on the first question. How can Jesus' disciples recognize legitimate teachers and leaders? Deuteronomy 18:20 says false prophets speak in the name of other gods; Jeremiah 8:10 indicates that false prophets are greedy; Jeremiah 28:9 claims the false prophet's words do not come true; Jeremiah 2:8 says false prophets prophesy by Baal (cf. 23:13); Jeremiah 23:14 indicates that they commit adultery and strengthen the hands of the evildoer; Micah 3:11 says false prophets prophesy for money.

False prophets are known both by what they say and by what they do. One's ultimate destiny depends on one's response to Jesus in the totality of his being and doing.

At this point Matthew 7:13–8:1 can be used in Christian decision making.

TWELVE

A Précis

Matthew 4:18–8:1

Having finished our reading of the various sections of the Sermon on the Mount, it may very well be a help to the reader to look back to gain an overview and a summary of what has been covered.

Prologue (Matt 4:18–5:2)
> Disciples are called; crowds are attracted; Jesus is in the posture of a teacher.

1. Matthew 5:3–12
> Congratulations to those whose vertical and horizontal relations are right for they will receive eschatological blessings.

2. Matthew 5:13–16
> Be who you are for the glory of God.

3. Matthew 5:17–20
> Since Jesus came to realize the intent of the Law, following him yields true righteousness.

4. Matthew 5:21–48
> a) vv. 21–26
>> Be a person who neither breaks relationships nor fails to restore broken ones.
>
> b) vv. 27–30
>> Be a person who does not violate another's marriage partner, either by act or by thought.
>
> c) vv. 31–32
>> Be a person who does not violate the indissoluble marriage bond.
>
> d) vv. 33–37
>> Be a person who is not deceitful but is truthful in all relations.

e) vv. 38–42

Be a person who does not retaliate but who returns good for evil.

f) vv. 43–48

Be a person who does not exclude your enemies from the love shown to your friends.

5. Matthew 6:1–18

a) vv. 1–6, 16–18

Be a person who avoids ostentatious displays of piety, because they are directed to the wrong audience.

b) vv. 7–15

Be a person who avoids babbling in prayer, because it assumes an incorrect view of God.

6. Matthew 6:19–24

Be a person for whom wealth is not a functional deity but one who lets God be God.

7. Matthew 6:25–34

Be a person who does not suffer from debilitating anxiety but who trusts in God's providential care.

8. Matthew 7:1–5

Be a person who does not condemn others for their flaws until having first corrected one's own.

9. Matthew 7:6–12

Be a person who does not fail to discern the difference between good and bad, using the wisdom given by God, and does not fail to act appropriately.

10. Matthew 7:13–27

Be a person whose life is in line with God's will and Jesus' words, who will not be led astray by spiritual leaders who fail to do God's will, even if they have a proper christological confession and do mighty works in Jesus' name.

11. Matthew 7:28–8:1

The crowds recognize the teaching of the Sermon on the Mount as different in style from that of the scribes, and they continue to follow Jesus.

SOURCES

Quotations from Jewish sources

Charlesworth, James H., ed. *The Old Testament Pseudepigrapha.* Garden City, N.Y.: Doubleday, 1983.

Danby, Herbert. *The Mishnah.* London: Oxford University Press, 1933.

Epstein, I., ed. *The Babylonian Talmud.* London: Soncino Press, 1935–60.

Freedman, H., and Maurice Simon. *Midrash Rabbah.* London: Soncino Press, 1961.

Goldin, Judah. *The Fathers according to Rabbi Nathan.* New Haven, Conn.: Yale University Press, 1955.

Hammer, Ruven. *Sifre: A Tannaitic Commentary on the Book of Deuteronomy.* New Haven, Conn.: Yale University Press, 1986.

Martinez, Florentino Garcia. *The Dead Sea Scrolls Translated.* 2nd ed. Leiden: Brill, 1996.

Neusner, Jacob. *Mekhilta according to Rabbi Ishmael: An Analytical Translation.* Atlanta: Scholars Press, 1988.

———. *Sifre to Deuteronomy: An Analytical Translation.* Atlanta: Scholars Press, 1987.

———. *The Talmud of the Land of Israel.* Atlanta: Scholars Press, 1998.

———. *The Tosefta.* New York: KTAV, 1977–81.

Quotations from Greek and Roman sources

Copenhaver, Brian P. *Hermetica.* Cambridge: Cambridge University Press, 1992.

The Loeb Classical Library. Cambridge, Mass.: Harvard University Press.

Malherbe, Abraham J. *The Cynic Epistles.* Missoula, Mont.: Scholars Press, 1977.

Quotations from the Bible

New Revised Standard Version Bible. Copyright 1989 by the Division of Christian Education of the National Council of Churches of Christ in the United States of America. Nashville, Tenn: Thomas Nelson, 1990.

Sources cited in text

Allison, Dale C., Jr. "Divorce, Celibacy, and Joseph (Matt 1:18–25 and 19:1–2)." *Journal for the Study of the New Testament* 49 (1993): 3–10.

———. "The Eye Is the Lamp of the Body (Matt 6:22–23 = Lk 11:34–36)." *New Testament Studies* 33 (1987): 61–83.

———. "A New Approach to the Sermon on the Mount." *Ephemerides theologicae lovanienses* 64 (1988): 405–14.

———. *The New Moses: A Matthean Typology.* Minneapolis: Fortress, 1993.

———. *The Sermon on the Mount.* New York: Crossroad, 1999.

———. "The Structure of the Sermon on the Mount." *Journal of Biblical Literature* 106 (1987): 423–45.

Arndt, William F., and F. Wilbur Gingrich. *A Greek-English Lexicon of the New Testament and Other Early Christian Literature.* 2nd ed., rev. and augmented by F. Wilbur Gingrich and Frederick W. Danker. Chicago: University of Chicago Press, 1979.

Augustine. *The Lord's Sermon on the Mount.* Translated by J. J. Jepson. Ancient Christian Writers 5. London: Longmans, Green, 1948.

Austin, J. L. *How to Do Things with Words.* Cambridge, Mass.: Harvard University Press, 1962.

Bacon, B. W. "The 'Five Books' of Matthew against the Jews." *Expositor* 15 (1918): 56–66.

———. *Studies in Matthew.* New York: Holt, 1930.

Barr, David L. "The Drama of Matthew's Gospel: A Reconsideration of Its Structure and Purpose." *Theology Digest* 24 (1976): 349–59.

Barth, G. "Matthew's Understanding of the Law." In *Tradition and Interpretation in Matthew,* 58–164. Philadelphia: Westminster, 1963.

Bauer, David R. *The Structure of Matthew's Gospel.* Sheffield: Almond, 1988.

Bauman, Clarence. *The Sermon on the Mount: The Modern Quest for Its Meaning.* Macon, Ga.: Mercer University Press, 1985.

Beardslee, W. A. "Parable Interpretation and the World Disclosed by the Parable." *Perspectives in Religious Studies* 3 (1976): 123–39.

———. "Uses of the Proverb in the Synoptic Gospels." *Interpretation* 24 (1970): 61–73.

Beare, F. W. *The Gospel according to Matthew.* Oxford: Basil Blackwell, 1981.

Becker, Adam H., and Annette Y. Reed, eds. *The Ways That Never Parted: Jews and Christians in Late Antiquity and the Early Middle Ages.* Texte und Studien zum antiken Judentum. Tübingen: Mohr Siebeck, 2003.

Berner, Ursula. *Die Bergpredigt: Rezeption und Auslegung im 20. Jahrhundert.* 3 Aufl. Göttingen: Vandenhoeck & Ruprecht, 1985.

Betz, Hans Dieter. *Essays on the Sermon on the Mount.* Philadelphia: Fortress, 1985.

———. *Nachfolge und Nachahmung Jesu Christi im Neuen Testament.* Beiträge zur historischen Theologie 37. Tübingen: Mohr, 1967.

———. "The Problem of Christology in the Sermon on the Mount." In *Text and Logos: The Humanistic Interpretation of the New Testament: Essays in Honor of Hendrikus W. Boers,* edited by T. W. Jennings Jr., 191–209. Atlanta: Scholars, 1990.

———. *The Sermon on the Mount.* Hermeneia. Minneapolis: Fortress, 1995.

———. "The Sermon on the Mount: In Defense of a Hypothesis." *Biblical Research* 36 (1991): 74–80.

Bietenhard, H. "*onoma.*" In *Theological Dictionary of the New Testament,* edited by G. Kittel and G. Friedrich, translated by G. W. Bromiley, 5:242–83. 10 vols. Grand Rapids, Mich.: Eerdmans, 1964–1976.

Birch, Bruce C., and Larry L. Rasmussen. *Bible and Ethics in the Christian Life.* Minneapolis: Augsburg, 1976.

Blass, F., A. Debrunner, and R. W. Funk. *A Greek Grammar of the New Testament.* Chicago: University of Chicago Press, 1961.

Blundell, Mary Whitlock. *Helping Friends and Harming Enemies: A Study in Sophocles and Greek Ethics.* Cambridge: Cambridge University Press, 1989.

Boccaccini, Gabriele. *Middle Judaism: Jewish Thought, 300 B.C.E. to 200 C.E.* Minneapolis: Fortress, 1991.

Bockmuehl, M. N. A. "Matthew 5:32; 19:9 in the Light of Pre-rabbinic Halakha." *New Testament Studies* 35 (1989): 291–95.

Boring, Eugene. "Matthew." In *New Interpreter's Bible,* 8:87–105. Nashville, Tenn.: Abingdon, 1995.

Bornkamm, Günther. "Der Aufbau der Bergpredigt." *New Testament Studies* 24 (1978): 419–32.

———. "Das Doppelgebot der Liebe." In *Neutestamentliche Studien für Rudolf Bultmann,* 85–93. 2nd ed. Berlin: Alfred Töpelmann, 1957.

———. "End-Expectation and Church in Matthew." In *Tradition and Interpretation in Matthew,* 15–51. Philadelphia: Westminster, 1963.

Bousset, W. *Die Religion des Judentums im neutestamentlichen Zeitalter.* Berlin: Reuther & Reichard, 1903.

Boyarin, Daniel. *Dying for God: Martyrdom and the Making of Christianity and Judaism.* Stanford, Calif.: Stanford University Press, 1999.

Brant, Jo-Ann. "The Place of *mimesis* in Paul's Thought." *Studies in Religion* 22 (1993): 285–300.

Brewer, D. J. "Jewish Women Divorcing Their Husbands in Early Judaism: The Background to Papyrus Se'elim 13." *Harvard Theological Review* 92 (1999): 349–57.

Brown, Raymond E. *An Introduction to New Testament Christology.* New York: Paulist, 1994.

Brueggemann, Walter. *Praying the Psalms.* Winona, Minn.: St. Mary's Press, 1982.

Bruner, Frederick Dale. *Matthew 1–12.* Dallas: Word, 1987.

Bultmann, Rudolf. *Jesus and the Word.* New York: Charles Scribner's Sons, 1958.

———. *Primitive Christianity in Its Contemporary Setting.* New York: Meridian Books, 1956.

Burchard, Christoph. "The Theme of the Sermon on the Mount." In *Essays on the Love Commandment,* edited by R. H. Fuller, 57–91. Philadelphia: Fortress, 1978.

Byrskog, Samuel. *Jesus the Only Teacher: Didactic Authority and Transmission in Ancient Israel, Ancient Judaism and the Matthean Community.* Coniectanea biblica: New Testament Series 24. Stockholm: Almqvist & Wiksell, 1994.

Carlston, Charles E. "Betz on the Sermon on the Mount: A Critique." *Catholic Biblical Quarterly* 50 (1988): 47–57.

Carter, Warren. *What Are They Saying about Matthew's Sermon on the Mount?* New York: Paulist, 1994.

Charlesworth, James. "Jewish Prayers in the Time of Jesus." In *The Lord's Prayer,* edited by Daniel L. Migliore, 36–55. Grand Rapids. Mich.: Eerdmans, 1993.

Cohen, Shaye J. D. "The Significance of Yavneh: Pharisees, Rabbis, and the End of Jewish Sectarianism." *Hebrew Union College Annual* 55 (1984): 27–53.

Combrink, H. J. B. "The Structure of the Gospel of Matthew as Narrative." *Tyndale Bulletin* 34 (1983): 61–90.

Corbett, P. *The Roman Law of Marriage.* Oxford: Clarendon, 1930.

Cothenet, E. "Les prophètes chrétiennes dans l'Evangile selon saint Matthieu." In *Evangile selon Matthieu: Rédaction et théologie,* edited by M. Didier, 281–308. Bibliotheca ephemeridum theologicarum lovaniensium 29. Gembloux: Duculot, 1972.

Cousland, J. R. C. *The Crowds in the Gospel of Matthew.* Supplements to Novum Testamentum 102. Leiden: Brill, 2002.

Crossan, John D. "Jesus and Pacifism." In *No Famine in the Land,* edited by James W. Flanagan and Anita Weisbrod Robinson, 195–208. Missoula, Mont.: Scholars Press, 1975.

Danby, Herbert. *The Mishnah.* London: Oxford University Press, 1933.

Daniel, C. "Faux prophètes: Surnom des Esseniens dans le sermon sur la montagne." *Revue de Qumran* 7 (1969): 45–79.

Daube, David. *Civil Disobedience in Antiquity.* Edinburgh: Edinburgh University Press, 1972.

———. *The New Testament and Rabbinic Judaism.* London: Athlone Press, 1956.

Davies, W. D. *The Setting of the Sermon on the Mount.* Cambridge: Cambridge University Press, 1966.

Davies, W. D., and Dale C. Allison Jr. *A Critical and Exegetical Commentary on the Gospel according to Saint Matthew.* Vol. 1, *Introduction and Commentary on Matthew I–VII.* International Critical Commentary. Edinburgh: T. & T. Clark, 1988.

Deidun, Tom. "The Bible and Christian Ethics." In *Christian Ethics: An Introduction,* edited by Bernard Hoose, 3–46. Collegeville, Minn.: Liturgical Press, 1998.

Dibelius, Martin. *The Sermon on the Mount.* New York: Charles Scribner's Sons, 1940.

Donaldson, Terence L. "The Law That Hangs (Matthew 22:40): Rabbinic Formulations and Matthean Social World." *Catholic Biblical Quarterly* 57 (1995): 689–709.

Douglas, R. C. "On the Way Out: Matthew's Anti-Pharisaic Polemic." *Studia Biblica et Theologica* 11 (1981): 151–76.

Droge, Arthur J. "Call Stories in Greek Biography and the Gospels." In *Society of Biblical Literature 1983 Seminar Papers,* edited by Kent H. Richards, 245–57. Chico, Calif.: Scholars Press, 1983.

Dumais, Marcel. *Le sermon sur la montagne: Etat de la recherche, interprétation, bibliographie.* Sainte-Foy, Québec: Letouzey et Ané, 1995.

Ellis, Peter F. *Matthew: His Mind and His Message.* Collegeville, Minn.: Liturgical Press, 1974.

Eskola, Timo. "Paul, Predestination and Covenantal Nomism—Reassessing Paul and Palestinian Judaism." *Journal for the Study of Judaism in the Persian, Hellenistic, and Roman Periods* 28 (1997): 390–412.

————. *Theodicy and Predestination in Pauline Soteriology.* Wissenschaftliche Untersuchungen zum Neuen Testament 2.100. Tübingen: Mohr Siebeck, 1998.

Farrer, Austin. *St. Matthew and St. Mark.* Westminster: Dacre, 1954.

Fascher, E. "Bergpredigt II: Auslegungsgeschichte." In *Religion in Geschichte und Gegenwart,* edited by K. Galling, 1:1050–53. 7 vols. 3d ed. Tübingen: Mohr, 1957–1965.

Fenton, J. C. "Inclusio and Chiasmus in 'Matthew.'" *Studia Evangelica* 1 (= TU 73) (1959): 174–79.

Finkel, Asher. *The Pharisees and the Teacher of Nazareth.* Arbeiten zur Geschichte des Spätjudentums und Urchristentums 4. Leiden: Brill, 1974

Fiorenza, Elizabeth Schüssler. *In Memory of Her.* New York: Crossroad, 1984.

Fitzmyer, J. A. "The Matthean Divorce Texts and Some New Palestinian Evidence." *Theological Studies* 37 (1976): 197–226.

Foster, Robert. "Why on Earth Use 'Kingdom of Heaven'? Matthew's Terminology Revisited." *New Testament Studies* 48 (2002): 487–99.

Frankemölle, Hubert. *Matthäus.* Dusseldorf: Patmos Verlag, 1997.

————. *Yahwebund und Kirche Christi.* Neutestamentliche Abhandlungen 10. Münster: Verlag Aschendorff, 1974.

Franklin, Eric. *Luke: Interpreter of Paul, Critic of Matthew.* Journal for the Study of the New Testament: Supplement Series 92. Sheffield: Sheffield Academic Press, 1994.

Froehlich, Karlfried. "The Lord's Prayer in Patristic Literature." In *The Lord's Prayer,* edited by Daniel L. Migliore, 71–87. Grand Rapids, Mich.: Eerdmans, 1993.

Fuller, Reginald H. *The Foundations of New Testament Christology.* New York: Scribners, 1965.

Gaechter, Paul. *Das Matthäus Evangelium.* Innsbruck: Tyrolia Verlag, 1963.

Garland, David. *Reading Matthew.* Macon, Ga.: Smyth & Helwys, 1993.

Garrison, Roman. *Redemptive Almsgiving in Early Christianity.* Journal for the Study of the New Testament: Supplement Series 77. Sheffield: JSOT, 1993.

Gerhardsson, Birger. *The Ethos of the Bible.* Philadelphia: Fortress, 1981.

————. "Hermeneutic Program in Matthew 22:37–40." In *Jews, Greeks, Christians,* edited by R. Hamerton-Kelly and R. Scroggs, 129–50. Leiden: Brill, 1976.

————. "The Matthean Version of the Lord's Prayer (Matt 6:9b–13): Some Observations." In *The New Testament Age: Essays in Honor of Bo Reicke,* edited by W. C. Weinrich, 1:207–20. 2 vols. Macon, Ga.: Mercer University Press, 1984.

————. *The Shema in the New Testament.* Lund: Nova Press, 1996.

————. *The Testing of God's Son.* Cultura Biblica. NT 2/1. Lund: Gleerup, 1966.

Glasson, T. F. "Anti-Pharisaism in St. Matthew." *Jewish Quarterly Review* 51 (1961): 316–20.

Goldsmith, Dale. "'Ask and It Will Be Given' . . . toward Writing the History of a Logion." *New Testament Studies* 35 (1989): 254–65.

Goodenough, Erwin R. "The Political Philosophy of Hellenistic Kingship." *Yale Classical Studies* 1 (1928): 55–102.

Goulder, Michael D. *Midrash and Lection in Matthew.* London: SPCK, 1974.

————. Review of *Matthew: Structure, Christology, Kingdom*, by J. D. Kingsbury. *Journal of Theological Studies* 28 (1977): 145.

Grant, Robert M. "The Sermon on the Mount in Early Christianity." *Semeia* 12 (1978): 215–31.

Grawert, Friedrich. *Die Bergpredigt nach Matthäus*. Marburg: Elwert, 1900.

Grayston, Kenneth. "The Decline of Temptation—and the Lord's Prayer." *Scottish Journal of Theology* 46 (1993): 279–95.

Grundmann, Walter. *Das Evangelium nach Matthäus*. Theologischer Handkommentar zum Neuen Testament 1. Berlin: Evangelische Verlagsanstalt, 1968.

Guelich, Robert. "The Matthean Beatitudes: Entrance Requirements or Eschatological Blessings?" *Journal of Biblical Literature* 95 (1976): 415–34.

————. *The Sermon on the Mount*. Dallas: Word, 1982.

Gundry, Robert H. *Matthew: A Commentary on His Literary and Theological Art*. Grand Rapids, Mich.: Eerdmans, 1982.

Hagner, Donald A. "Ethics and the Sermon on the Mount." *Studia Theologica* 51 (1997): 44–59.

————. "Matthew: Apostate, Reformer, Revolutionary?" *New Testament Studies* 49 (2003): 193–209.

————. *Matthew 1–13: Word Biblical Commentary*. Dallas: Word, 1993.

Hamm, Dennis. *The Beatitudes in Context*. Zacchaeus Studies. Wilmington, Del.: Michael Glazier, 1990.

Hanssen, Olav. "Zum Verständnis des Bergpredigt." In *Der Ruf Jesu und die Antwort der Gemeinde*, edited by E. Lohse, 94–111. Göttingen: Vandenhoeck & Ruprecht, 1970.

Hare, D. R. A. *The Theme of Jewish Persecution of Christians in the Gospel according to St. Matthew*. Society for New Testament Studies Monograph Series 6. Cambridge: Cambridge University Press, 1967.

Harrington, Daniel J. *Gospel of Matthew*. Sacra Pagina. Collegeville, Minn.: Liturgical Press, 1983.

Harrington, Daniel J., and James F. Keenan. *Jesus and Virtue Ethics*. Lanham, Md.: Sheed & Ward, 2002.

Harris, William V. *Restraining Rage: The Ideology of Anger Control in Classical Antiquity*. Cambridge, Mass.: Harvard University Press, 2002.

Hartman, Lars. *Into the Name of the Lord Jesus: Baptism in the Early Church*. Studies in the NT and Its World. Edinburgh: T. & T. Clark, 1997.

Hays, Richard B. *The Moral Vision of the New Testament*. San Francisco: Harper, 1996.

Hendrickx, Herman. *Sermon on the Mount*. Manila: East Asian Pastoral Institute, 1979.

Hock, Ronald F., and Edward N. O'Neil, *The Chreia in Ancient Rhetoric: The Progymnasmata*. Society of Biblical Literature Texts and Translations 27. Graeco-Roman Religion Series 9. Atlanta: Scholars, 1986.

Hummel, Reinhart. *Die Auseinandersetzung zwischen Kirche und Judentum im Matthäusevangelium*. Munich: Kaiser, 1966.

Hunter, A. M. *A Pattern for Life*. Philadelphia: Westminster Press, 1953.

Ilan, Tal. "On a Newly Published Divorce Bill from the Judean Desert." *Harvard Theological Review* 89 (1996): 195–202.

Ingelaere, J. C. "Structure de matthieu et histoire du salut: Etat de la question." *Foi et vie* 78 (1979): 10–33.

Jackson, Bernard S. "Liability for Mere Intention in Early Jewish Law." *Hebrew Union College Annual* 42 (1971): 192–255.

Janzen, David. "The Meaning of PORNEIA in Matthew 5:32 and 19:9: An Approach from the Study of Ancient Near Eastern Culture." *Journal for the Study of the New Testament* 80 (2000): 66–80.

Jeremias, Joachim. *New Testament Theology: The Proclamation of Jesus*. New York: Charles Scribner's Sons, 1971.

St. John of Damascus. *On the Divine Images: Three Apologies against Those Who Attack the Divine Images*. Translated by David Anderson. Crestwood, N.J.: St. Vladimir's Seminary Press, 1980.

Johnson, R. M. "The Least of the Commandments: Deuteronomy 22:6–7 in Rabbinic Judaism and Early Christianity." *Andrews University Seminary Studies* 20 (1982): 205–15.

Juel, Donald. "The Lord's Prayer in the Gospels of Matthew and Luke." In *The Lord's Prayer*, edited by Daniel L. Migliore, 56–70. Grand Rapids, Mich.: Eerdmans, 1993.

Käsemann, Ernst. "The Beginnings of Christian Theology." In *New Testament Questions of Today*, 82–107. Philadelphia: Fortress, 1969.

Keck, Leander. "Ethics in the Gospel according to Matthew." *Iliff Review* 40 (1984): 39–56.

Keegan, T. J. "Introductory Formulae for Matthean Discourses." *Catholic Biblical Quarterly* 44 (1982): 415–30.

Keener, Craig. *And Marries Another: Divorce and Remarriage in the Teaching of the New Testament*. Peabody, Mass.: Hendrickson, 1991.

———. *A Commentary on the Gospel of Matthew*. Grand Rapids, Mich.: Eerdmans, 1999.

Kennedy, George A. *New Testament Interpretation through Rhetorical Criticism*. Chapel Hill: University of North Carolina Press, 1984.

Kingsbury, Jack Dean. *Matthew: Structure, Christology, Kingdom*. 2nd ed. Minneapolis: Fortress, 1989.

———. "Observations on the Miracle Chapters of Matthew 8–9." *Catholic Biblical Quarterly* 40 (1978): 556–67.

———. "The Place, Structure, and Meaning of the Sermon on the Mount within Matthew." *Interpretation* 41 (1987): 131–43.

———. "The Verb *akolouthein* ('to follow') as an Index of Matthew's View of His Community." *Journal of Biblical Literature* 97 (1978): 56–73.

Kirschner, Robert. "Imitatio Rabbini." *Journal for the Study of Judaism in the Persian, Hellenistic, and Roman Periods* 17 (1986): 70–79.

Kissinger, Warren S. *The Sermon on the Mount*. Metuchen, N.J.: Scarecrow Press, 1975.

Klauck, Hans-Josef. *The Religious Context of Early Christianity*. Studies of the NT and Its World. Edinburgh: T. & T. Clark, 2000.

Kotva, Joseph. *The Christian Case for Virtue Ethics*. Washington, D.C.: Georgetown University Press, 1996.

Krentz, Edgar. "The Extent of Matthew's Prologue." *Journal of Biblical Literature* 83 (1964): 409–15.

Kupp, David. *Matthew's Emmanuel: Divine Presence and God's People in the First Gospel*. Society for New Testament Studies Monograph Series 90. Cambridge: Cambridge University Press, 1996.

Laato, Timo. *Paul and Judaism: An Anthropological Approach*. South Florida Studies in the History of Judaism 115. Atlanta: Scholars, 1995.

Lambrecht, Jan. *The Sermon on the Mount*. Good News Studies 14. Wilmington, Del.: Michael Glazier, 1985.

Lawrence, Louise Joy. "'For truly, I tell you, they have received their reward' (Matt 6:2): Investigating Honor Precedence and Honor Virtue." *Catholic Biblical Quarterly* 64 (2002): 687–702.

Levison, Jack. "A Better Righteousness: The Character and Purpose of Matthew 5:21–48." *Studia Biblica et Theologica* 12 (1982): 171–94.

Liddell, Henry George, and Robert Scott, comps. *A Greek-English Lexicon*. Rev. and augmented edition by Henry Stuart Jones. 2 vols. Oxford: Clarendon Press, 1951.

Ligon, Ernest. *The Psychology of Christian Personality*. New York: Macmillan, 1953.

Lischer, Richard. "The Sermon on the Mount as Radical Pastoral Care." *Interpretation* 41 (1987): 157–69.

Lohr, C. H. "Oral Techniques in the Gospel of Matthew." *Catholic Biblical Quarterly* 23 (1961): 403–35.

Luz, U. *Matthew 1–7: A Commentary*. Continental Commentaries. Minneapolis: Augsburg, 1989.

Malina, Bruce J. *The New Testament World: Insights from Cultural Anthropology*. Atlanta: John Knox, 1981.

Martin, Brice L. "Matthew on Christ and the Law." *Theological Studies* 44 (1983): 53–70.

Marxsen, Willi. *New Testament Foundations for Christian Ethics*. Philadelphia: Fortress, 1993.

Matera, Frank. "The Plot of Matthew's Gospel." *Catholic Biblical Quarterly* 49 (1987): 233–53.

McArthur, Harvey K. *Understanding the Sermon on the Mount*. New York: Harper & Brothers, 1960.

McEleney, Neil J. "The Principles of the Sermon on the Mount." *Catholic Biblical Quarterly* 41 (1979): 552–70.

———. "The Unity and Theme of Matthew 7:1–12." *Catholic Biblical Quarterly* 56 (1994): 490–500.

Meier, John P. *Law and History in Matthew's Gospel: A Redactional Study of Mt. 5: 17–48.* Analecta biblica 71. Rome: Biblical Institute Press, 1976.

————. *The Vision of Matthew: Christ, Church, and Morality in the First Gospel.* New York: Paulist Press, 1979.

Meyer, Ben F. *Five Speeches That Changed the World.* Collegeville, Minn.: Liturgical Press, 1994.

Mohrlang, Roger. *Matthew and Paul: A Comparison of Ethical Perspectives.* Society for New Testament Studies Monograph Series 48. Cambridge: Cambridge University Press, 1984.

Montefiore, C. G. *The Synoptic Gospels.* 2 vols. London: Macmillan, 1909.

Moore, George Foote. *Judaism in the First Centuries of the Christian Era: The Age of the Tannaim.* 3 vols. Cambridge, Mass.: Harvard University Press, 1927–30.

Moule, C. F. D. "'As We Forgive . . .': A Note on the Distinction between Deserts and Capacity in the Understanding of Forgiveness." In *Donum Gentilicium: New Testament Studies in Honour of David Daube,* edited by E. Bammel, C. K. Barrett, and W. D. Davies, 68–77. Oxford: Clarendon, 1978.

Neirynck, Frans. "*Apo Tote Erxsato* and the Structure of Matthew." *Ephemerides theologicae lovanienses* 64 (1988): 21–59.

Neusner, Jacob. *From Politics to Piety.* Englewood Cliffs, N.J.: Prentice-Hall, 1973.

Ogletree, Thomas W. *The Use of the Bible in Christian Ethics.* Philadelphia: Fortress, 1983.

Ouspensky, Leonide. *Theology of the Icon.* Crestwood, N.J.: St. Vladimir's Seminary Press, 1978.

Overman, J. Andrew. *Church and Community in Crisis: The Gospel according to Matthew.* Valley Forge, Penn.: Trinity Press International, 1996.

————. *Matthew's Gospel and Formative Judaism.* Minneapolis: Fortress, 1990.

Pammet, Margaret. "The Kingdom of Heaven according to the First Gospel." *New Testament Studies* 27 (1981): 211–32.

Parkes, J. W. *The Foundations of Judaism and Christianity.* London: Vallentine, Mitchell, 1960.

Patte, Daniel. *The Gospel according to Matthew.* Philadelphia: Fortress, 1987.

Pedersen, Johannes. *Israel: Its Life and Culture.* London: Cumberlege, 1946–47.

Perkins, Pheme. *Jesus as Teacher.* Understanding Jesus Today. Cambridge: Cambridge University Press, 1990.

Pink, Arthur W. *An Exposition of the Sermon on the Mount.* Reprint, Grand Rapids: Baker, 1992.

Pitt-Rivers, Julian. "Honor." In *International Encyclopedia of the Social Sciences,* edited by D. Sills, 6:503–11. 18 vols. New York: Free Press, 1968–1979.

Porten, B., and A. Yardeni. *Textbook of Aramaic Documents from Ancient Egypt.* Vol. 2, *Contracts.* Jerusalem: Akademon, 1989.

Powell, Mark A. *God with Us: A Pastoral Theology of Matthew's Gospel.* Minneapolis: Fortress, 1995.

Prsybylski, Benno. *Righteousness in Matthew and His World of Thought.* Society for New Testament Studies Monograph Series 41. Cambridge: Cambridge University Press, 1980.

Rabinowitz, Peter J. *Before Reading: Narrative Conventions and the Poetics of Interpretation.* Ithaca, N.Y.: Cornell University Press, 1987.

———. "Truth in Fiction: A Reexamination of Audiences." *Critical Inquiry* 4 (1977): 121–41.

Reiser, Marius. "Love of Enemies in the Context of Antiquity." *New Testament Studies* 47 (2001): 411–27.

Reumann, John. *Righteousness in the New Testament.* Philadelphia: Fortress, 1982.

Riches, John. *Matthew.* NT Guides. Sheffield: Sheffield Academic Press, 1996.

Rivkin, E. *The Hidden Revolution.* Nashville, Tenn.: Abingdon, 1978.

———. "Pharisees." In the supplementary vol. of *Interpreters Dictionary of the Bible,* edited by Keith Crim, 657–63. Nashville, Tenn.: Abingdon, 1976.

Robbins, Vernon K. *Jesus the Teacher: A Socio-Rhetorical Interpretation of Mark.* Philadelphia: Fortress, 1984.

Robinson, Paul W. "Luther's Explanation of *Daily Bread* in Light of Medieval Preaching." *Lutheran Quarterly* 13 (1999): 435–47.

Rutenber, Culbert G. *The Doctrine of the Imitation of God in Plato.* Morningside Heights, N.Y.: King's Crown Press, 1946.

Saldarini, Anthony J. "Delegitimation of Leaders in Matthew 23." *Catholic Biblical Quarterly* 54 (1992): 659–80.

———. "Johanan ben Zakkai's Escape from Jerusalem: Origin and Development of a Rabbinic Story." *Journal for the Study of Judaism in the Persian, Hellenistic, and Roman Periods* 6 (1975): 189–204.

———. *Matthew's Christian-Jewish Community.* Chicago: University of Chicago Press, 1994.

Sanders, E. P. "Defending the Indefensible." *Journal of Biblical Literature* 110 (1991): 466–67.

———. *Jesus and Judaism.* Philadelphia: Fortress, 1985.

———. *Paul and Palestinian Judaism.* Philadelphia: Fortress, 1983.

———. *Paul, the Law, and the Jewish People.* Philadelphia: Fortress, 1985.

Saunders, Ernest W. "A Response to H. D. Betz on the Sermon on the Mount." *Biblical Research* 36 (1991): 81–87.

Schnackenburg, Rudolf. *The Moral Teaching of the New Testament.* New York: Seabury Press, 1979.

Schweizer, Eduard. *The Good News according to Matthew.* Atlanta: John Knox, 1975.

Segal, Alan. "Matthew's Jewish Voice." In *Social History of the Matthean Community,* edited by David L. Balch, 3–37. Minneapolis: Fortress, 1991.

———. *Paul the Convert.* New Haven, Conn.: Yale University Press, 1990.

———. *Rebecca's Children: Judaism and Christianity in the Roman World.* Cambridge, Mass.: Harvard University Press, 1986.

Segal, Phillip. *The Halakah of Jesus of Nazareth according to the Gospel of Matthew.* Lanham, Md.: University Press of America, 1986.

Sim, D. C. *The Gospel of Matthew and Christian Judaism.* Edinburgh: T. & T. Clark, 1998.

Smith, Morton. "Palestinian Judaism in the First Century." In *Israel: Its Role in Civilization,* edited by Moshe David, 67–81. New York: Harper & Brothers, 1956.

Snodgrass, Klyne. "Matthew and the Law." In *Treasures Old and New: Recent Contributions to Matthean Studies,* edited by David Bauer and Mark A. Powell, 99–127. Society of Biblical Literature Symposium Series 1. Atlanta: Scholars Press, 1996.

Spohn, William C. *What Are They Saying about Scripture and Ethics?* Rev. ed. New York: Paulist Press, 1995.

Stanton, Graham N. *A Gospel for a New People: Studies in Matthew.* Edinburgh: T. & T. Clark, 1992.

———. "The Gospel of Matthew and Judaism." *Bulletin of the John Rylands University Library of Manchester* 66 (1984): 264–84.

———. "The Origin and Purpose of Matthew's Sermon on the Mount." In *Tradition and Interpretation in the New Testament,* edited by G. F. Hawthorne and O. Betz, 181–94. Grand Rapids, Mich.: Eerdmans, 1987.

Stendahl, Krister. "Matthew." In *Peake's Commentary on the Bible,* edited by Matthew Black and H. H. Rowley, 769–98. Rev. ed. New York: Thomas Nelson & Sons, 1962.

Sternberg, Meir. *The Poetics of Biblical Narrative.* Bloomington: Indiana University Press, 1985.

Stott, John R. W. *The Message of the Sermon on the Mount.* Leicester, U.K.: InterVarsity, 1978.

Strecker, Georg. "Die Makarismen der Bergpredigt." *New Testament Studies* 17 (1970–71): 255–75.

———. *The Sermon on the Mount: An Exegetical Commentary.* Translated by O. C. Dean Jr. Nashville, Tenn.: Abingdon, 1988.

———. *Der Weg der Gerechtigkeit: Untersuchung zur Theologie des Matthäus.* Forschungen zur Religion und Literatur des Alten und Neuen Testaments 82. Göttingen: Vandenhoeck & Ruprecht, 1962.

Suggs, Jack. *Wisdom, Christology, and Law in Matthew's Gospel.* Cambridge, Mass.: Harvard University Press, 1970.

Syreeni, Kari. *The Making of the Sermon on the Mount: A Procedural Analysis of Matthew's Redactoral Activity.* Helsinki: Suomalainen Tiedeakatemia, 1987.

Talbert, Charles H. "The Church and Inclusive Language for God?" *Perspectives in Religious Studies* 19 (1992): 421–39.

———. *Romans.* Smyth & Helwys Bible Commentary. Macon, Ga.: Smyth & Helwys, 2002.

Talbert, Charles H., and J. H. Hayes. "A Theology of Sea Storms in Luke-Acts." In *Society of Biblical Literature 1995 Seminar Papers,* edited by E. H. Lovering Jr., 321–36. Atlanta: Scholars, 1995.

Talbert, Charles H., and Edgar V. McKnight. "Can the Griesbach Hypothesis Be Falsified?" *Journal of Biblical Literature* 91 (1972): 346–47.

Tannehill, Robert. *The Narrative Unity of Luke-Acts.* Foundations and Facets. Minneapolis: Fortress, 1990.

———. *The Sword of His Mouth.* Semeia Studies 1. Philadelphia: Fortress, 1975.

———. "Tension in Synoptic Sayings and Stories." *Interpretation* 34 (1980): 138–50.

Tappert, T. H. *The Book of Concord.* Philadelphia: Fortress, 1959.

Theodore the Studite. *On the Holy Icons.* Translated by Catharine P. Roth. Crestwood, N.J.: St. Vladimir's Seminary Press, 1981.

Thom, Johan C. "'Don't Walk on the Highways': The Pythagorean *Akousmata* and Early Christian Literature." *Journal of Biblical Literature* 113 (1994): 93–112.

Thomas, John C. "The Kingdom of God in the Gospel according to Matthew." *New Testament Studies* 39 (1993): 136–46.

Thornton, Martin. *English Spirituality.* Cambridge, Mass.: Cowley, 1985.

Tombs, L. E. *The Threshold of Christianity: Between the Testaments.* Philadelphia: Westminster, 1960.

Topel, John. Review of *The Sermon on the Mount,* by H. D. Betz. *Catholic Biblical Quarterly* 59 (1997): 370–72.

Unnik, W. C. van "Dominus Vobiscum: The Background of a Liturgical Formula." In *New Testament Essays: Festschrift for T. W. Manson,* edited by A. J. B. Higgins, 270–305. London: Manchester University Press, 1959.

Vetter, Dieter. *Jahwes Mit-Sein: Ein Ausdruck des Segens.* Arbeiten zur Theologie 1/45. Stuttgart: Calwer Verlag, 1971.

Via, Dan O., Jr. "Structure, Christology, and Ethics in Matthew." In *Orientation by Disorientation,* edited by R. A. Spencer, 199–215. Pittsburgh Theological Monograph Series 35. Pittsburgh: Pickwick, 1980.

Warren, William F., Jr. "Focuses on Spirituality in the Sermon on the Mount." *Theological Educator* 46 (1992): 115–24.

Weber, F. W. *System der altsynagogalen palästinischen Theologie aus Targum, Midrash und Talmud dargestellt.* Edited by F. J. Delitzsch and G. Schnedermann. Leipzig: Dürffling & Franke, 1880.

Widdicombe, Peter. *The Fatherhood of God from Origen to Athanasius.* Oxford: Clarendon, 1994.

Wilkins, Michael J. *The Concept of Disciple in Matthew's Gospel.* Supplements to Novum Testamentum 59. Leiden: Brill, 1988.

Windisch, Hans. *The Meaning of the Sermon on the Mount.* Philadelphia: Westminster, 1951.

Wink, Walter. "Beyond Just War and Pacifism: Jesus' Nonviolent Way." *Review and Expositor* 89 (1992): 197–214.

———. "We Have Met the Enemy." *Sojourners* 15/11 (1986): 15–18.

Witherington, Ben. "Matthew 5:32 and 19:9—Exception or Exceptional Situation." *New Testament Studies* 31 (1985): 571–76.

INDEX OF SCRIPTURE
AND OTHER ANCIENT SOURCES

INDEX OF MODERN AUTHORS